COMMUNION OF SAINTS:

A PASTOR'S POT-POURRI OF PARISHIONERS

JOHN M. MILLER

To Bev & Bob
with thanks for your
friendship and support
John N. Miller
Feb. 26, 2014

ISBN 978-1-63525-906-3 (Paperback)
ISBN 978-1-63525-907-0 (Digital)

Christian Faith Publishing, Inc.
296 Chestnut Street
Meadville, PA 16335
www.christianfaithpublishing.com

Printed in the United States of America

This book is dedicated to
the many thousands of saints
still living on earth or living eternally
it has been my privilege
to serve as a pastor
for the past fifty plus years

and

to Katy and Jan VerHagen,
whose extraordinary kindness made possible
the publication of this book.

CONTENTS

AN INTRODUCTION
TO THE COMMUNION OF SAINTS

THERE IS NO accounting for the diversity of human personality and behavior. As a species, we are terrific, terrifying, majestic, mysterious, exhilarating, exasperating, wonderful and woeful. We are a tad unpredictable as well.

Most people spend much or most of their lives in the company of other people. We live together in families and/or in marriages, most of us spend a good part of every day in our occupations with other people, and we join groups or organizations which consist of other people. Undeniably we are, as Spinoza said, social animals.

John Donne declared that no man is an island. We are all connected to one another, he said. Throughout history, there have been some intentional or accidental Robinson Crusoes. But as a percentage of the human populace, they are very few and far between. Even the people who choose to live as hermits in the midst of the madding crowd have interaction of a sort with the rest of us simply by their refusal to interact with the rest of us. We know who they are by not knowing who they are. We touch their lives by not touching their lives, just as they touch us by avoiding touching us. They become the people they are by deliberately averting social contact with us. They are the "un-us. " They define themselves by saying they are not as we are. Best of luck to them in trying to pull that off.

Every personality inevitably influences every other personality to one degree or another. All of us have people who have had a profound effect on our lives. Our parents and siblings and teachers were instrumental in helping to determine who we turned out to be in our early stages. Later, in our teenage years and our twenties and thirties, mentors, friends, and co-workers helped to shape who we have become. And so the process continues to the end of our lives. Each personality is a patchwork quilt consisting of bits and pieces of multitudes of other personalities. Even when we are totally unaware of it, we share our humanity with one another, and some of each of us rubs off on all of us.

In its last paragraph, the Apostles' Creed says this: "I believe in the Holy Ghost; the holy Catholic Church; *the communion of saints*; the forgiveness of sins; the resurrection of the body; and the life everlasting." It is to the third in that string of six credal statements, "the communion of saints," that this book is dedicated.

I have been immensely blessed by the communion of saints. Having been an active member of the clergy for more than half a century, I have known a marvelous mélange of church folk. They have spanned the entire spectrum of human attributes—from conservative to liberal, from very laid back to very uptight, from highly opinionated to completely un-pin-down-able. They have been kind, stingy, gracious, hard headed, loving, self-centered, altruistic, self-serving, ever-faithful, and ever-fearful. But for whatever reason or reasons, they affiliated with a church, and it was in that capacity I got to know them. Perhaps God has often wondered how they made the decision to become part of a religious community as did many of the rest of us, but decide they did. And a congregation became an integral part of their existence. And thus, they became part of my existence.

In the common understanding, the term "communion of saints" refers to the notion that all Christians throughout all time are not only connected to one another, but also to all believers of all time. Thus, each of us purportedly has communion with Abraham, Isaac, Jacob, Moses, Joshua, David, *et al.* We also have communion with Jesus and the twelve disciples and the apostle Paul and with Charlemagne and Thomas Aquinas and Martin Luther and John Calvin as well as with everyone else through all of Christian history and everyone associated with whatever congregation with which we are currently connected, if any. It also includes everyone from every congregation everywhere with which we have ever been affiliated, whether all those folks are living or have died.

It is also possible, and I personally believe it is probable, that the communion of saints includes such historical figures as Lao Tzu, Zarathustra, Siddhartha Gautma (the Buddha), Muhammad, and Joseph Smith. I well realize that many would disagree with that, and I may be completely wrong in my supposition. I suspect that the breadth of the communion of saints will astound us in eternity when we are in the necessary state of being to be able to comprehend more completely what it really is.

To return to the Christian concept of the communion of saints, it is well to note that there are two common descriptors regarding the Church, meaning the whole Christian enterprise from the year 30 of the Common Era or so to the present. There is the Church Militant, and then there is the Church Triumphant. (Why it is specifically called "the Church Militant" is beyond me although at times it has been far too militant. The very term is one of those mysteries about the Church that endures.)

The Church Militant consists of those of us who are still inhaling air on a frequent and quite necessary basis. As we do that, many of us militantly are trying to convince everyone else in the Church or the world that we are right about most things and that they need clearly to understand that. Of all institutions which have survived for many centuries, nothing is more theologically and doctrinally militant than the Church. Christians are probably the most dedicated humanoid squabblers ever to have inhabited the planet.

The Church Triumphant on the other hand, according to usually understood thinking, consists of all those saints who have died and are now in heaven. (Where or what heaven is will scarcely be addressed in these pages.) But the term "communion of saints" has always suggested that all Christians through all time are united by God into one enormous fellowship that is, at once, both temporal and eternal.

The word, "saint," however, is a problematic one, especially for anyone of the Protestant Persuasion in any of its ever-multi-

9

plying and mind-numbing varieties. Roman Catholics and Eastern Orthodox are much more prone regularly to utilize this word because they have been recognizing official "saints" for many centuries. Each of the twelve apostles, with the exception of Judas Iscariot, has been declared a saint. (Did you ever hear of St. Judas? I thought not.) Then, there is St. Irenaeus, St. John of the Cross, St. Anselm, the aforementioned St. Thomas Aquinas, and so on and so on. Each of the many hundreds or thousands of these sorts of saints went through a thorough and rigorous ecclesiastical vetting process to be admitted into the Catholic or Eastern Orthodox Sainthood Hall of Fame. Don't Google it by that nomenclature, however, because you won't find it. But you know what I mean.

Roman Catholic saints are nearly always considered to have been Roman Catholics. The Second Vatican Council referred to the Eastern Orthodox and Protestants as "separated brethren." Regarding sainthood, however, *separation* prevents any of us *brethren* from being named Catholic saints. So there is no St. Martin Luther, no St. Henry VIII, no St. John Calvin, or St. Alexander I of Russia.

However, those are not the kinds of saints I will be writing about anyway. Nor shall I be describing the other common usage of the word, "saint," meaning someone of extraordinary virtue and godliness. "She is a saint," we often say, and we usually say it because she has put up with *him* or *them* for so long. However was she able to survive all that, we wonder. When we declare, "He is a saint," it means that someone displays unusual, even unique, holiness in how he lives his life. Singular moral goodness is what this concept of sainthood connotes.

If the truth is told, there is something both inspiring and dispiriting in that particular concept of sainthood. We like to admire people whose virtue exceeds that of most of the rest of us. But if we dig sufficiently deeply into their life stories, all such folks also have a few bones, and perhaps even entire skeletons, hidden in their closets. No one can be both human and faultless; it isn't possible. It is imperative that all of us recognize that.

St. Peter, for example, was a liar, an occasionally inept buffoon, a frequent sufferer of foot-in-mouth disease, a theological klutz, and someone who couldn't be counted on in the absolute fell clutch of circumstance. But no one would deny that the Prince of Apostles was, and by rights most certainly ought to be, a saint.

Furthermore, the Bible calls people saints whose behavior was clearly anything but saintly in the goody-two-shoes sense. Abraham, Sarah, Isaac, Rebekah, Jacob, Rachel, Moses, Aaron, Joshua, David, Bathsheba, Amos, Hosea, Isaiah, and Jeremiah, among others, come to mind. In holy writ, fidelity and commitment almost always trump excellent behavior and nobility of character in the Department of Sacred Sainthood.

I am not saying there aren't people who are more virtuous than most of us because there are. But they are not the sorts of saints I shall be reviewing here.

The people about whom I shall be writing are neither properly beatified Roman Catholic historical personages nor necessarily singularly exemplary contemporary personages. *In my understanding, everybody who is a believer in God and Jesus Christ is a saint. You don't need to be recognized by an official ecclesiastical apparatus as a saint or be a paragon of high merit to be a saint; everyone in every church everywhere is a saint. That's what I learned before, during, and after seminary, and I have no reason to doubt its veracity. It's my story, and I'm sticking to it.*

Thus whoever is reading this is a saint, even if your faith is decidedly tepid or poorly glued together and your behavior is far less saintly than you would like it to be. Nonetheless, by my reckoning and that of many other saints whom I have respected, you are a saint, whether you like it or not or agree with it or not.

Might all other believers also be saints: Jews, Muslims, Hindus, Buddhists, Sikhs, Taoists, Rosicrucians, Wiccans, and also the Church of Jesus Christ of the Latter-Day Saints, the Mormons, either Regular or Reorganized? Only God knows the definitive answer to that, but as far as I am concerned, they too are saints. I would be happy to add all believers of all religions of all time or all believers who could never quite stomach any religion to be among the entire panoply of the saints of God. I guess it would be too heretical to imply that everyone ever born is a saint because many people never had faith of any variety (so far as we know), and many never attempted to live saintly lives (which has seemed evident to believers as long as there have been believers.)

In my book, though, the folks whom I shall be telling you about unquestionably are all saints. Their faith varied enormously among themselves as you shall see. They viewed themselves as Christians and church members in a whole host of ways. Many of them would strongly disagree that they were saints at all. Some doubted that they were proper Christians, much less saints; and they also had serious reservations that anyone, least of all God, should consider them orthodox church members. Many of them might also strongly disagree that most of the others I shall tell you about were saints. But since it is my book, and I am declaring that all believers of all sorts are saints, then everybody you shall encounter here is a participant in God's inspiring, ambiguous, dismaying, outstanding, disarming, alarming, charming, and colossal communion of saints.

I shall be telling you about a few members from each of the five churches I served as a called minister and about a few others from the four congregations I served as an interim pastor. Three of these congregations had less than two hundred members each. Six of them had from twelve hundred to three thousand members. Prior to that, however, I will describe two saints who have been the most influential in my adult years, four saints from my family of origin, and some seminary saints from my years at McCormick Theological Seminary in Chicago and Trinity College of Glasgow University in Scotland.

As I calculate it, these numbers translate into a total of roughly sixteen thousand official parishioners with whom I have been associated to varying degrees in my five decades of ministry. In addition, there were probably at least four thousand others who were technically not members at all, but who were affiliated in some way with these particular churches: children who were not yet confirmed members in the years I was at these churches; spouses of members who were members of other congregations but who attended these nine

THE COMMUNION OF SAINTS
churches from time to time with their spouses; people who wouldn't be caught dead having their names on any church roll anywhere but who attended with greater regularity than many official members; people who thought they were on the church roll but who had been removed long before and nobody had the courage or honesty to tell them that they were actually no longer members; a handful who were never connected to any church anywhere and didn't believe in God at all but nevertheless were admired and highly valued friends; and finally, people who wandered into church one Sunday, stayed for a few or many Sundays but never joined, and then disappeared as quietly as when they first arrived without ever telling anyone why they came or why they left. This latter bunch may actually number an additional five thousand all by themselves. I had a marvelous knack for sending people packing before they even had time to unpack.

It would be the epitome of self-delusion for me to suggest that I was closely acquainted with up to twenty thousand or more church people over my adult lifetime. I, like every other member of the clergy, have known relatively few parishioners on a truly close basis. Very likely, most of these folks felt they "knew" me far better than I "knew" them because they heard me preaching to them on many if not most Sundays throughout the year, and thus they believed they knew me. To use a highly elasticized analogy, we may claim that we know George W. Bush or Barack Obama, but do Presidents Bush or Obama know us? The *knowledge* gained by mere acquaintanceship may be fleeting indeed.

Further, the clergy rarely, if ever, get to know the inner core of existence of their parishioners as those parishioners really are. Instead, the clergy see only a sea of masks, cleverly molded, carefully worn, seldom relinquished. Clergy usually encounter only the personas our people want us to encounter, and the Real McCoy is too coy to allow himself or herself to appear before parson or priest as he or she truly is.

To some extent, all people wear masks most if not all the time. After all, isn't that what the Greek *persona* (person) originally meant—mask? Most of us like to appear to be better or more moral

13

or upright or righteous than we really are, and therefore, we keep our masks tightly fixed to our carefully concealed faces.

The clergy themselves, of course, might claim that they never wear masks. Heaven forbid! They all let it all hang out all the time. What you see is what you get. Oh, sure. Naturally. No masks for the men and women of the cloth. Personal or psychological duplicity would never occur to those upon whose heads ecclesiastically authorized hands were once placed. Why ever would the clergy want to prevent anyone from seeing them as they really are? It is unthinkable!

But of course that is precisely what the clergy also do; they wear their carefully crafted masks. And like everyone else, they do it most of the time. As Rabbie Burns said, "O wad some Power the giftie gie us/ To see oursels as ithers see us!" Or as Shakespeare said, "What fools these mortals be!" We work very hard to maintain our "front," little realizing that in time, most people manage to see through it. Thank heaven they do. It is far better to be known as we truly are than as we want ourselves to be known. And that is true both for us and for those who truly know us.

Although I did not know most of the twenty thousand parishioners well, I was quite well acquainted with several hundred of them. If you wonder why I chose to include the particular saints described here rather than others, I can only say I wanted to cover as wide a variety of people as possible who would interest readers and to suggest by so doing that saints come in all shapes, sizes, personalities, and behaviors. None of these people shall be perfect, but none shall be hopelessly outside the love and care of God. They were all in God's Church, as divergent and disarming as they may seem to be as they truly were.

Having addressed the disparity issue, it is imperative for you to understanding something very important at the outset. The portraits I shall attempt to paint for you inevitably are colored by the masks these folks wore, the mask or masks I wore, and the level of maturity they or I had at the time the snapshots of memory were taken. I shall try to be as objective as possible, admitting that complete objectivity is a human impossibility. So bear that in mind as you read on.

Here is the list of congregations I have served and the years I served them:

- Bayfield Presbyterian Church, Bayfield, Wisconsin (1965–1968)—Pastor
- Fourth Presbyterian Church, Chicago, Illinois (1968–1973)—Assistant Pastor
- The Presbyterian Church in Morristown, Morristown, New Jersey (1973–1979)— Pastor
- First Presbyterian Church, Hilton Head Island, South Carolina (1979–1996)—Pastor
- First Presbyterian Church, Lynchburg, Virginia (1997)—Interim Pastor
- House of Hope Presbyterian Church, St. Paul, Minnesota (1998)—Interim Pastor
- Fairmount Presbyterian Church, Cleveland Heights, Ohio (1999)—Interim Pastor
- Second Christian Church, Warren, Ohio (2000)—Interim Pastor
- The Chapel Without Walls, Hilton Head Island, South Carolina (2004 to the present)—Pastor

I shall introduce you to few saints from each of the churches in which I was the pastor, a few in the one church where I was an assistant pastor, and a few collectively from the four churches I served as interim pastor. Even if I could offer a portrait that is accurate in every detail, I would not try to do so. There are far too many details that would not be of general appeal, and far too many of them would be of little if any literary interest. Further, I am utterly ignorant of many aspects of the lives of my selected saints. I knew them only as they intersected with my life in a certain place at a certain time.

Now for a very important explanation followed by an unvarnished admission. All the saints in this narrative are actual parishioners or other people I shall identify by their actual names. But all of them also are deceased. You need to remember that. In some instances, I shall refer to spouses or other family members who are still living, but the focus will be on deceased saints, not living ones.

But why, you may ask, would I deliberately write only about people who have died? Here is where the unvarnished admission comes in.

It is a long-established principle in legal case law that a writer cannot defame the reputation of someone who is deceased. Defamation can be suffered only by the living, according to the law. The dead, simply because they are no longer living, cannot be legally slandered. Nor can the relatives of deceased people bring suit against writers who paint what the potential litigators believe is a false or unfair portrait of the deceased.

Please understand this: I do not intend to impugn anyone in these pages, living or dead. After all, they are all saints, for heaven's sake! Why would I defame saints? Besides, I am only telling it like it was. I trust that nothing I shall say is either inaccurate or misleading.

Nevertheless, as I have discovered countless times as a minister, people's feelings can easily be hurt, even when it was certainly not my intention to hurt them. Someone who is as outspoken as I have chosen to be is almost bound to tread heavily on some dainty toes, without ever having intended to do so.

I admit, however, that I shall be utilizing a firmly established principle behind numerous instances of case law which shall protect me from lawsuits over what I shall be saying about some folks who genuinely are the dearly departed. I am not going to write about any-one I don't admire; I shall write only about those I do admire. This is, after all, the communion of saints.

Nonetheless, I take comfort in knowing no one can come storming up out of the grave to take me to court in Bayfield County, Wisconsin; Cook County, Illinois; Morris County, New Jersey; or in Beaufort County, South Carolina. As for relatives of the deceased about whom I shall be writing and who might peruse these pages, I hope you shall agree that I did not mean to besmirch your loved one. Further, I sincerely hope that in fact, I did not do so.

Each saint shall be a particular individual. However, the older I get, the more sieve-like my memory becomes; and in some instances, it may be a literary necessity for me to homogenize several characteristics from several people into one person. At my advanced age, I am astonished at how few actual and irrefutable conversations my gray matter can summon up that I had with any of these folks. I simply do not recall conversations from past years with very much clarity at all. There will be a glaring shortage of dialogue in this monologue. I wish that I *could* recollect actual conversations with these saints, but I cannot. And I'm not going to make up things which might have been said but probably were not. It does not seem fair or proper to me to do so.

Some of the readers of this book may have known or known about a few of the saints to whom I shall be referring. If so, you may wonder why I wrote about each of the particular people from each of the churches I served as a minister, and why not other people. It is both an excellent and an eminently understandable question.

The first answer is that if I wrote about everyone who deserves to be included in this litany of noble souls, I would never finish this book. There are many other parishioners who were equally worthy or perhaps more worthy of being included, but obviously, I cannot include everyone I ever knew.

To repeat something I said earlier, however, the second answer is that I wanted to incorporate a wide variety of personalities in order to suggest that saints don't come in only one unique "saintly" personality but in an infinite variety of personalities. Not everyone you are going to read about was like everyone else you are going to read about. As similar as we may be to one another, each of us is unique unto herself or himself. Saints may be discovered in every corner and crease of the ecclesiastical or anthropological map.

Without question, I could have written about scores or hundreds of other folks I have known very well during my years as a minister. Some who read this tome will assume I really should have chosen others to highlight, people quite different or perhaps more colorful or intriguing than those I shall consider. But I chose these flesh-and-blood folks because to me, they represent particular examples of the huge plethora of types who comprise the temporal and eternal communion of saints.

Finally, before we begin, you may properly want to ask: Are these portraits fiction, or are they fact? Yes, I answer; without question, yes. The characters you shall encounter here are all actual people whom I have actually known. Holy saints, are they ever! These are real people.

Shall I employ literary license to embellish them? Of course. Shall I take snippets of events from one person's life and insert them into another person's life for the sake of maintaining intrigue and interest? Very likely. Shall I burnish the image of someone to make him appear more saintly than he really was, or shall I perhaps slightly pierce the image of someone to make her seem more ordinarily human than otherwise she would have wished to be seen? You bet.

But all these saints were or are flesh-and-blood people, actual parishioners from the four congregations I served as pastor, the four congregations I served as interim pastor, and the one congregation I served as an assistant pastor. In these pages, I hope you shall come to know, appreciate, and love them as I did. They were God's grace in human flesh to me, and for each of them and all the thousands of others, I shall be forever grateful to God for enabling them to shower their blessings upon me. The clergy derive far greater benefit from their flock than the flock derives benefit from the clergy. It has been ever thus.

I believe in the communion of saints. With every ounce of my being, I truly do.

FOUR FAMILY SAINTS

IT IS IMPOSSIBLE for me to quantify how much of who I am currently is the result of family influences from my formative years. However, a very substantial percentage of who John Miller is was determined by who Warren, Margaret, Bob, and Ray Miller were. I was very fortunate to have been born into a strong, intelligent, industrious, honest, forthright, and also opinionated family. I have unquestionably inherited the "opinionated" part, and perhaps some of the other characteristics as well.

There were four sons in our family, of whom I was the fourth. Now, two-thirds of our original family are in the Church Triumphant, and only two of us, my brother Al (or Stuart) and I, are in the Church Militant. Well, actually, Al is barely in the Church at all as he would readily admit. He is not militant in matters ecclesiastical, but he retains militancy in nearly every other factor of life, especially after having served a career as a Regular Army officer. In any case, only he and I are left of the original Millers Six.

St. Warren Harris Miller

As Dad frequently reminded us through the years (as though he would ever let us forget it), he was born on a farm near Mt. Elgin, Ontario. In the winter, he said he used to walk barefoot to Mt. Elgin to school. He said the snow was so deep that he could hop from fencepost to fencepost. A little kid hopping barefoot fifteen or twenty feet from one fencepost to the next: it was astonishing. But a couple

19

of miles—amazing! He said many other similar things through the years, many of which we learned to swallow with a grain or two of salty gullibility. Often, sitting around the dining room table, he would start to regale us with tales of when he was a boy on the farm in Mt. Elgin, and we five would groan and object in an utterly pitiless fashion. (I doubt that anyone would describe any of the six of us as being gentle above all else. Other things for certain; gentle, no.)

Mom was born in Ingersoll, Ontario, a few miles north of Mt. Elgin and about thirty miles east of London, Ontario. My parents met there when Dad's family moved from exurban Mt. Elgin into metropolitan Ingersoll when he was a teenager. After graduating from high school, Dad went to work for the Borden Company in Ingersoll. It was the only corporation for which he worked in his entire career. He and Mom were married in 1928. A year later, Dad was transferred to North Lawrence, New York, which is ultimately how the four Miller sons all ended up as native-born Americans. Two of us were born in Fort Scott, Kansas, and two in Dixon, Illinois, as a result of further moves on behalf of the Borden Company.

Dad was raised in the Methodist Church. When he married Mom, he defected to the Presbyterians. They remained Presbyterians for the entire sixty years of their marriage.

Dad was an elder in every church of which our family were members, at least during my lifetime. Whether he was an elder prior to my entry onto the scene, I don't know. By the time I was in fifth grade, I had decided I wanted to be a minister. A major factor in that decision, probably the major factor, was my parents' involvement in the church. They (and thus, we boys) were active in many programs of the four congregations we attended during my childhood and youth. If the church doors were open, the Millers were likely to pass through them for whatever was happening.

Even though Dad was on the session (the governing board) of those churches, I don't ever remember him telling about what went on in session meetings. Had he done so, my ardor for the ministry might possibly have cooled. Being an elder is a privilege, an honor, and a responsibility, but it can also occasionally be a major threat to the proper exercise of one's religion. However, I was to learn that only after becoming an elder myself at the University Presbyterian Church in Madison, Wisconsin, and especially after becoming an ordained parson. Maybe that's why Dad never talked about session meetings; he didn't want to sully our innocent outlook.

Looking back on it, I can readily see why my father was elected an elder in those churches. He was a committed church member and attended every Sunday. Financially, he contributed liberally (He gave 10 percent of his income to the church for most of his adult years). He had excellent judgment, and he could be counted on by the pastors of those churches to do whatever he said he would do that he was asked to do. Serving annually as a minister on church officer nominating committees through the years, we always sought people like my father to accept nomination; they are the human bedrock of the church. Without such people, every church would swiftly crumble to dust.

Dad didn't wear his religion on his sleeve. He sometimes talked about what he believed, but he didn't proclaim it on a daily basis to everyone with whom he came into contact. My father would prefer to chew broken glass rather than ask friends or strangers if they were saved. In other words, he was like most Mainline Protestants: committed, convicted, and quiet. He would say what he believed if asked, but in our circles, almost no one asked. It wasn't considered couth to do so.

I am certain my father never read a book on how to become a good parent, nor did my mother. We four sons were raised in the '30s and '40s, and back then, there were not many "how-to" books, which may have been one of the blessings of those simpler, more do-it-yourself-as-best-you-can times.

Dad and Mom intuitively realized that they could not attempt to rear the four of us on the basis of a single, one-size-fits-all cookie cutter mold. Instead, they readily perceived that each of their sons was his own person and that therefore, they needed to exercise their parental authority and responsibility by utilizing that important discovery.

Two of us were relatively hard to raise and two relatively easy. However, you need to understand this is my subjective conclusion, and I have made it by looking back sixty-five or seventy years. It may not have seemed that way at all to our parents, but I can't see how it couldn't. (I was one of the two easy sons, don't you see?) Anyway, they treated each of us as individual humanoids and not as four peas in one pod. Thus, they didn't have One Inflexible Set of Parental Principles. Instead, they had four. In retrospect, they are to be commended for their great wisdom in concluding that was the best way to rear two pairs of two sons: the first two born within thirty months of one another and the second pair born eighteen months apart, starting six years later.

Parenting came naturally to our parents, and probably, that was because it apparently came naturally to their parents. Three of my grandparents died before I was born, so I knew only my maternal grandmother, who died when I was in college. But from what I know of these four forebears, they too were well suited to parenthood. Those of us who have been so very fortunate as to have outstanding parents and grandparents are fortunate far beyond what we deserve, although we could not properly appreciate that when we were children and teenagers. Perhaps we cannot fully comprehend such a genetic blessing even now, when we are the age our parents or grandparents were when they died.

In contemporary America (or Canada as well), many fathers conscientiously spend many hours each week and month with their children. That does not reflect the pattern of our particular paternal parent. Dad was not a throw-the-ball-with-the-boys dad. Perhaps we spent more time together as a complete family than many other families although I don't recall that being especially apparent. I have no recollection of Dad ever assiduously devoting time to each son individually as an illustration of his carefully chosen paternal duty. Instead, all six of us did things together. We went on picnics to the park or on Sunday drives around the countryside or to visit family friends on summer evenings, sitting on the porch to observe the world of the late `40s slowly passing by. As the years went on, the older two brothers did less of this because they had their own teenage fish to fry, but Al and I were happily conscripted into these familial expeditions. If any of the four of us boys obviously required some individual attention, Dad would administer it, especially in matters of serious oral or corporate discipline. Otherwise, all four of us were "us;" we were rarely "me." And yet——we were "me," each of us, in how Mom and Dad treated us. It was a marvel of family mathematics.

There was one father-and-sons activity in which Dad did participate with all four of us, however, and that was hunting. I don't know how much he hunted when he was "a boy on the farm," but he did take us hunting with him,—both when we lived in Dixon, Illinois, and in Fort Scott, Kansas. I never received the impression that Dad personally was wildly enthusiastic about traversing hill and dale in search of creatures with feathers or fur, but he always seemed to enjoy the comradeship of the five of us being together. From the time I was perhaps ten until I was almost thirty, I never hunted with Dad. However, when I was a minister in northern Wisconsin in my first parish, he joined my oldest brother, Bob, some of Bob's friends, and me on a pheasant-hunting trip to South Dakota. Although at that late date he didn't have much wind because of his growing problems with emphysema, and he couldn't walk long distances, he had a wonderful time just being there.

In adulthood, three of the brothers became avid hunters: Bob, Ray, and I. Bob and Ray both were excellent marksmen. I, on the other hand, was a mere enthusiast but hardly a modern-day Nimrod or Natty Bumppo. Nonetheless, the biographical fact of the matter is that probably none of us would have the lifelong interest we had in hunting were it not for Dad taking us out into the fields and woods to begin with. For that, all three of us were forever grateful.

Previously, I mentioned that Dad went to work for the Borden Company in Ingersoll, Ontario, almost directly out of high school. My mother's father was the superintendent of the Borden factory there, and it was he who hired Dad. This may sound like blatant nepotism, but it wasn't, because it was a few years before Dad and Mom were married. They may not yet have even been "an item" for all I know. However, that providential first job evolved into a forty-five year career with Borden's. Eventually, Dad ended up as the divisional manger of the Midwest Food Products Division of the company. He got along very well with fellow employees, whether they were above or below him in the corporate pecking order or at the same level. He always worked hard and spent far more hours doing his work than would be expected by his superiors. For that reason, he worked his way up the Borden ladder as far as he could likely go.

Dad had some innate engineering skills he acquired and utilized on the job. He invented some devices that were used in processing milk and other food products. He never was associated with fluid milk, the kind you buy at the grocery store to drink. His stock in trade was processed milk: evaporated or condensed or powdered.

When I was born, Dad was the assistant superintendent at the Borden plant in Dixon, Illinois, which was the largest such operation in the entire company. Then, when I was eight years old, Dad was transferred to Fort Scott, Kansas, to become the superintendent of the condensery there. After three years, he was sent to western New York State, there to learn the details of the powdered milk business. This was in preparation for him to become the assistant district manager of the Midwest Division in Madison, Wisconsin, and eventually, the manager of the division.

If it sounds like our family moved around a fair amount, we did—both before and after my entrance into this vale of tears. We didn't know it, but all of us were corporate gypsies before the term had been invented. However, Borden's was a different kind of corporation. It was an excellent company to work for, particularly during the Depression. Because everyone had to continue to eat, there never was a serious possibility that Dad might lose his job. And in the Depression, people especially used the kinds of inexpensive milk products from which he made his living.

In my introductory sociology course at the University of Wisconsin, we were told that there were nine classes in three class-clumps in America: lower-lower class, middle-lower, and upper-lower; lower-middle class, middle-middle, and upper-middle; and lower-upper class, middle-upper, and upper-upper. I cannot recall ever having wondered what socio-economic class our family belonged to when I was growing up until I got to that sociology course. But if someone now put a gun to my head and said I had to decide immediately, I would think we were probably always in the middle-middle class—not lower-middle or upper-middle, but middle-middle. Even though Dad had a very responsible vocational position, he never made a big income. Within eight years of graduating from seminary, my income as a minister was what his was in his best year. Food companies in those days—and perhaps in these days as well—did not pay well, but they always needed a certain number of employees. And as I said, people have always made it their business to eat three square meals each day if at all possible. Food corporations are happy to oblige their gustatory indulgence.

I don't know this for a fact, but I can easily imagine that even in Dixon, Illinois, in the late `30s and early `40s, Dad and Mom were thinking forward to living in Madison, Wisconsin, which happened providentially for our family in 1951. Dad was quietly but purposefully ambitious, and he may have perceived himself as the division manager twenty years before he received that promotion. He imbued his sons with ambition as well but without ever directly instructing, "Be ambitious!" He led by example more than by words although sometimes, he did lead with words as well.

But why would my parents envision the Millers living in Madison? It was because Madison, Wisconsin, was and is a superb community. It is the seat of the state government. It is the home of one of the greatest state universities in the nation. And its people are some of the brightest, most interested and interesting, and highly talented people to be found in any city anywhere in the country. Without ever telling us this, that is what our parents wanted for us. They wanted to give us all the possible advantages people in their status can offer to their sons. And these, incidentally, were advantages they themselves did not have in their teens and early twenties.

Growing up from seventh grade on in Madison was surely one of the happiest of happenstances in my whole life. It wasn't Shangri La, but it was as close to it as any family in our circumstances could get. People with more assets or pedigree might end up on Lakeshore Drive in Chicago or in suburban Winnetka or River Forest, Illinois, or on the Upper East or West Sides in New York City or in Larchmont, New York, or Greenwich, Connecticut, but for folks such as ourselves, Madison became Valhalla, courtesy largely of St. Warren.

I feel compelled to reiterate that my parents were always heavily involved in whatever Presbyterian congregation with which we were affiliated in those early years. Dad was active in the men's organization and Mom in various women's organizations. In high school and college, I went with Dad a few times to the National Presbyterian Men's Convention, which was always held at the Palmer House Hotel in Chicago. Though I had long since decided to become a minister, attending those meetings with their collection of outstanding speakers and preachers of national note was always an inspiring experience. It authenticated my intention to become a minister. No doubt Dad knew that, but he never said much about it, if anything. He was an Example Dad, not a Talker Dad. About other things, he talked: politics, work, sports, and so on; but about the deepest things, he said little. Since that pattern was all I knew, it was all right with me. I suspect my own children would observe the same tendency in their father.

When our parents moved back to Dixon, Illinois, in 1960, after having lived in Madison, Wisconsin, for the previous nine years (years which were particularly pivotal for Ray, Al, and me), Dad became especially involved in the First Presbyterian Church of Dixon in his retirement years. He greatly admired the longtime pastor of the Dixon church, Dr. Malcolm Ludy, and Dad became a volunteer office manager of sorts and pastoral assistant. He spent many happy hundreds of hours over several years as a latter-day specialized church saint. Malcolm, the church secretary, Ann Clausen, and Dad became a wonderful team on behalf of all the First Presbyterian saints.

Dad was always a reader. He read books on many subjects, and there were always many books on our bookshelves. He particularly enjoyed humorous books. He would be silently reading away, and then, suddenly, uncontrolled laughter would loudly emit from his tickled being. In later years, because of his emphysema, it would sound as though he was about to wheeze his last breath when he chortled at his humorists. It never happened, but if it had, he would have died happily with a final highly amused and unfulfilled gasp for breath.

There were several magazine and newspaper subscriptions in our house as well: *Time, Life, The Saturday Evening Post, National Geographic, Field and Stream,* and one or two different newspapers. Mom read the *Ladies Home Journal* and other such magazines, but in our mainly male household, she did not have to wait in line to peruse those periodicals.

If either parent ever urged us to "take up and read," as St. Augustine famously noted in his autobiography, I don't recall it. But the books and magazines and newspapers were there, and to varying degrees, depending upon the particular son, we took up and read. It served all of us well in our adult lives. Those lives were immeasurably enriched with all those words pored over in all those written works during our youth.

What I am attempting to suggest here is that our parents *showed* us how to live much more than they *told* us how to live. They were example saints, not spoken saints. It isn't that they were essentially quiet in personality because neither of them was. They talked about countless things to themselves and to us. But about the deepest things they tended to encourage us, without ever actually verbalizing it, that we needed to sort those things out for ourselves. They didn't say what we should believe; they showed what we might believe.

Were they shy about such matters or uncertain or tentative? I don't think so, not at all. But they didn't preach to us—about behavior and values, yes, but about beliefs, no.

On the other hand, Sunday dinner was frequently a free-for-all regarding the sermon we had all just heard less than an hour earlier. Everyone felt free to put in his (or her) oar. As in most things in the Miller family, unanimity was hard to come by. Sunday dinner was the most memorable of weekly meals, and at it, we all did our best to solve all the world's problems, especially those of a political bent. Dad was a Robert Taft Republican, and his thinking influenced our thinking for decades to come. Mom was probably a tepid and fairly apolitical Republican. Bob and Al always remained rock-ribbed conservative Republicans, but I became a bleeding-heart liberal by my mid-thirties. I can't truly evaluate Ray's politics because he was in the

Army and out of the country for many of the years prior to his death in late 1965, and I simply don't know the nature of his politics.

In our extended family, all the males were handshakers; they were not huggers. That was true way back when, and it is also true now—when other grown men, especially of a younger sort, are consummate huggers. Dad was certainly not a hugger. He didn't openly express many feelings, except happiness and occasionally anger or, more properly, displeasure.

Therefore, I was astounded by an action of my father's on the day I was ordained. Immediately after the service, there was a receiving line for my wife and me. Mom and Dad were two of the first people to come through the line. Mom hugged me; that I expected. But so did Dad. Not only that, he had tears in his eyes, and he kissed me on the cheek. I was nearly undone; my father was displaying a level of emotion I have never observed in him before! Typically, however, neither of them had ever said they were proud of me; instead, on that occasion, they showed it. It was their way.

From the time I announced my intention to become a parson when I was eleven years old, my parents always expressed support for my decision. They didn't gush about it because they weren't gushers, but they quietly affirmed it. Only in the immediate aftermath of the ordination service did I realize how pleased they were, and because it was so uncharacteristic of him, that was particularly apparent in Dad.

But then, they were Old-School Parents. In those days, Old School Parents did not excessively praise their children; they hardly praised them at all. They were like the parents of President George H. W. Bush, who said his parents carefully refused to praise their children for fear it would give them big heads. Enlarged crania in offspring were to be avoided at all costs seventy-five or a hundred or a hundred and fifty years ago. Whether that was wise or unwise, the child psychologists and the rest of the populace who argue about the findings of the child psychologists will decide; but that's the way it was. Thus was I astonished by my parents' display of pride on the occasion of my becoming a proper Presbyterian parson. I shall forget multitudes of things before I forget that singular thing. Dad and

Mom were in the receiving line immediately after the service with my wife, Nancy, and me. Before anyone got there, Dad hugged me with tears in his eyes, and he kissed me on the cheek. My dad! Amazing!

Dad was one of the most highly and genuinely respected people I have ever known. He was fair, he was compassionate, he listened well to opposing points of view, he was an excellent thinker, and he was a devoted member of Christ's Church. When he died at age eighty-six, the church was nearly full for his funeral. For an eighty-six-year-old ordinary man, that is extraordinary. Most contemporaries by that age have previously died, so it was mainly younger people and family members who gathered to give thanks to God for the life of Warren H. Miller. That speaks volumes of his person and personality. He wasn't in *Who's Who*, but he was in the *Who's Who* of everyone who knew him.

St. Margaret Hutt Miller

Mom's family of origin was very similar to the nuclear family she established with our father. Her own father also spent his entire working career with the Borden Company, albeit it the Canadian subsidiary of the American Borden Company. Milk is in all our veins; what can I say?

Mom was raised in St. Paul's Presbyterian Church in Ingersoll, Ontario. Her grandfather, Erastus Hutt, was pastor of that congregation for many years. (Imagine being named Erastus! Even back then, there were hardly any Erastuses; now, perhaps thankfully, the name has become almost illegal.)

There were four children in her family, two boys and two girls. Mom and her two brothers were clumped together in one batch, quickly delivered. And then, a dozen years passed before the fourth child, a daughter, made her appearance. That was likely a shock to my grandparents and maybe a disappointment to our mother and her two brothers. The birth of Irma changed the family dynamic enormously.

Because Irma came so much later than the first three, and because she was so much younger than our other aunts and uncles on both sides of the family, Irma was always just "Irma" to all of the cousins; she was never "Aunt Irma."

Mom and Irma were to sisterhood what Jean Valjean and Javaert were to the legal system. They were oil and water. They were an open can of gasoline and a match. They were cat and dog in the dryer. As long as I can remember, they engaged in frequent and volatile disputes.

Every summer, we drove to Canada for Dad's two weeks of vacation, and every time we got close to Ingersoll, Dad would say, "Now Margaret, you and Irma are going to behave yourselves, and if you don't, we're going to get in the car and go right back home." And every year, within a few hours of our arrival, Mom and Irma would engage in their inevitable sisterly disagreements; and we never got in the car to go right back home.

I begin with this dubious chapter in my mother's life because it was the only such negative chapter she had. And the amazing thing is that both she and Irma were outstanding human beings. Furthermore, each of them was a "church lady" in absolutely the best sense of that term. In matters ecclesiastical, they were dependable, diligent, helpful, encouraging, considerate, and kind. Perhaps, more importantly, they were *there*; they always were there. Many people counted on them, and they always came through. Yet for one another, they had a flawed, even a somewhat tortured, relationship. It was one of the mysteries of their lives and the lives of the rest of us.

No one who knew them well could be unaware of the tension which existed between them. And yet, everyone who knew them got along with each of them. Why not? They were both exemplary women.

I tell you this to suggest that sainthood does not and cannot connote perfection. The communion of saints is not restricted to goody-two-shoes types. In fact, among genuine saints there are no goody-two-shoes because all saints are sinners. It can't be otherwise. St. Margaret Miller and St. Irma Hutt truly were saints, but their sanctity was a tad tarnished with respect to one another. And so it is with all God's saints. All of us are damaged goods. We have much in us that is good, but it is inevitably damaged in some perhaps ultimately inexplicable manner.

Other than her frayed connection to her younger sister, our mother was the epitome of all that is noble in the human race and in motherhood. Mom became so used to raising a small herd of boys that she became, probably unwittingly, the quintessential Boys' Mom. How she would have raised girls is impossible to say—even for her, I suspect. But she certainly knew how to be a mother to four sons.

In the '30s and '40s, most moms were stay-at-home moms, except for those mothers who became Rosy the Riveters during the War. When the war was over, most of them once again took up the position American society expected of them—to become fulltime wives and mothers. And so it was with our mom, who had always been a stay-at-home mom.

She was always there when we came home from school for lunch, which all of us did in our earliest years. She was there most of the time when we got home from school, and if she wasn't there, she was soon there. She spent a few hours each day cooking, baking, and preparing meals and a few other hours each week "doing the wash" as she described it. She was so old-fashioned that up until a few years after Dad died and she moved into an apartment (her first such domicile) which had an automatic washer and dryer (her first), she used a ringer washing machine, running the clothes through the wringer and then hanging them out to dry on a retractable clothesline by the back door. Never mind that no one in the entire U.S. of A did that anymore; she did it, and she continued to do it until she could no longer do it. And then, she reluctantly capitulated to modernity. A devotee of the latest in technology she wasn't. It is a trait which she possibly handed down genetically to her fourth-born son.

Mom was more mercurial than Dad. When Dad's dander got up, which happened very infrequently, he could become unusually irate. Then, we were in serious trouble. Mom, on the other hand, got exasperated quite easily. With four boys messing up the house and her life, that is not surprising.

Our mother never uttered a profanity in her life, but she kept a collection of Sayings for All Occasions to cover any situation which might emerge around her. When she had more than enough of male-issued misbehavior, she might say, "I'm going to give you your head and your hands and your ears to play with!" We didn't know exactly how she would do that or what precise physiological dismemberment it would entail, but it sounded serious. On other occasions, she would exclaim, "I'll put a tin ear on you!" Tin ears did not seem like something we would choose to have if given a choice, so we thoughtfully considered refraining from whatever behavior elicited the threat of a tin ear. Other times, she would thunder, "I'll skin you alive!" Such threats always elicited our attention but rarely our mortal terror. When she did not think our misdeeds warranted having our heads or hands or ears to play with, the imposition of tin ears, or being skinned alive, she would simply exclaim, "By the holy pink-toed prophet!" Most people never encounter a holy pink-toed prophet, I suspect, and thus wouldn't know one if they fell over him, but the expression gave one pause—even if only momentarily.

Did she ever smite us for our sins of omission or commission? Never. There were countless threats of what sounded vaguely like extraordinary examples of corporal punishment, but she only lacerated us with colorful sayings, not calculated clouts. Did we therefore ignore her amusing imprecations? By no means. She was our mother, and we listened, often in sheer linguistic awe.

Almost always, she was over the top in her dire-sounding threats. She never intended any of the excruciating wrath she so cavalierly threatened, but without fail she always managed to get our attention. The punishment threatened was nearly always far in excess of the nature of the crime committed, and perhaps that was the essence of it; if she captured our attention and our imagination, maybe we would not repeat the infraction. Well, maybe.

"Great Caesar's ghost!" she would say when astounded or aghast at something. "Wow!" wouldn't cut it for Mom; "Great Caesar's ghost!" seemed ever so much more fitting. I didn't know Caesar actually had a ghost, but it seemed a worthy observation to make on certain worthy occasions.

And rather than using the prosaic "from A to Z" or "from Alpha to Omega" or "from start to finish" to express the wide limits of any matter in under the sun, Mom would say, "That's it, from stem to gudgeon." Anyone can say from A to Z or Alpha to Omega or start to finish, but Margaret Miller is the only person I ever knew who expressed that concept as "from stem to gudgeon." In order to verify exactly what a gudgeon is, I looked it up in my trusty *Webster's Collegiate Dictionary*. None of the definitions helped explain whatever might have been the circumstances under which she first heard that expression. You can check it out for yourself. But the meaning of "stem to gudgeon" is always self-explanatory from the context, it seems to me, and I use the expression on a fairly regular basis in honor of my sainted mother.

"You have more nerve than a canal horse!" she would say when we did something we should not have done. That saying I later understood in its full unveiling. Back in the days when there were barge canals throughout Canada and the United States, horses pulled the barges. A long rope was attached to the barge, and then, a loop was slipped over the horse's neck. Knowing that it would be hard to get the barge moving again if the horse had to stop for anything, the plodding beast would just keep walking, no matter what was in its way. "You have more nerve than a canal horse" at least came from an arcane aspect of fairly recent North American history, but where the tin ears and the pink-toed prophets and the other expressions came from, only heaven knows.

If we were still sleeping in the morning when we should be awake, she would never say, "Boys, it's time to get up!" Instead, she would shout up the stairs, "Arise, and put your armor on!" From whence cameth that injunction? I don't know. I doubt that she knew. But it became the unique wake-up call of the Miller boys for years. In fact, I told my wife, Lois, about it, and there are times when morning slumber still holds me in its pleasant grip. And I will hear from afar, "Arise, and put your armor on!"

Mom had a great palette full of these sayings, and she painted them frequently at the appropriate moments. Often, they defused potentially tense situations when we boys were prepared to do some sort of battle with one another. But whatever the circumstance which prompted their usage, they produce indelible memories of a remarkably gifted woman who utilized the English language in her own particular ways.

Our mother also had a memory bank of humorous little poems that she would recite from time to time. Examples are the following: "How much wood would a woodchuck chuck/ If a woodchuck would chuck wood?/Well a woodchuck would chuck lots of wood/ If a woodchuck could chuck wood." Or "Fuzzy Wuzzy was a bear/ Fuzzy Wuzzy had no hair/ Fuzzy Wuzzy wasn't very fuzzy/ Was he?" They weren't quite up there with *Ode: Intimations of Immortality from Recollections of Early Childhood* or *How do I love thee?/ Let me count the ways*, but they were Mom-poems. And in my mind, they are a part of her unique maternal sainthood.

Another thing is this: No large male of our species was ever merely a big man to Mom; he was always a big galoot. On the other hand, she never referred to any small or medium-sized galoots, only big galoots. It was just the way it was.

Our dog, Butch, wandered into the tent where Bob and Ray were sleeping on summer nights when we lived in the Swissville section of Dixon, Illinois. Butch was the dog who came to dinner and stayed ever after. Later, when we moved to Kansas, brother Bob found a strange item made of paper mache in a novelty store somewhere. This item was meant to look like a canine's excretory offering, and it had an uncanny and revolting resemblance to the real thing, even with the proper recently deposited sheen.

All of us liked to tease Mom. She enjoyed being teased. One day, we four boys were all sitting in the living room. Bob had placed the putative poop in the dining room. Mom came walking through the dining room on the way to the living room and saw the disgusting small heap on the floor. "Oh Butch, what have you done!" she shrieked. Butch instantly went into his copyrighted Great Guilt Mode. He had no idea what he had done, but he knew it must have been unusually odious. We four hooted with mirth. Mom did not understand instantly why we were hooting, but a moment later, she realized she had "been had." "Oh, you boys!" she huffed. "You'll be the death of me yet."

It was a delicious "Get Mom" episode, and it was repeated a couple more times successfully, but only after a few months of Bob waiting for the right time to spring the trap. The last time he tried his subterfuge, she calmly reached down, picked up the revolting representation, and crushed it into oblivion over the gaping maw of the wastebasket. It was the laconic ending to a thrice-successful trick. We all were greatly amused. Secretly, I think no one was more amused than Mom—once she recovered from her initial shock at our dog's purported alimentary accident.

Mom had a deep and natural understanding of human psychology even though she never took a psychology course, or any other college course, in her life. She had a natural knack for befriending anyone, even those whom most other people would avoid if at all possible.

There was a lady who was related to one of Mom's best friends at church. The lady's name was Joy, but her name did not suit her at all. Joyful she wasn't, and joy she did not exude. She was cloyingly religious, and she wrote sickening-sweet religious poetry. Mom insisted that I read it, perhaps hoping I might be able to find something of recognizable value, which had thus far managed to escape her. Furthermore, Joy was as self-absorbed as humanly possible, and if conversations with Joy did not revolve around Joy, Joy was utterly uninterested in the conversations. Nevertheless, Mom was unfailingly kind to Joy, who experienced little kindness from anyone else simply because she was so tragically and constantly "into herself." Mom would talk to Joy on the phone regularly. Well, actually, Joy talked; Mom listened. But she did it because she knew Joy needed whatever friends she could find anywhere she could find them. Joy was her own worst enemy, and Mom wanted to offer her a needed ally in her subconscious war against herself.

Mom was the kind of homemaker who would regularly take food to sick friends or neighbors or visit them in their times of need. After World War II, when many returned soldiers came home from the war, they couldn't find work. Those were the days of hoboes and hobo colonies along the railroad tracks of America. The informal hobo network declared that there was a lady at 331 Lincoln Way in Dixon or at 401 S. Main Street in Fort Scott who would always provide a meal when anyone was really up against it. She never invited any of these homeless men into the house for their dinner; even in those relatively safe days, she was not that trusting. They ate their meal on the porch. But she never turned anyone away unless he came so often it shriveled her natural generosity.

In the late `50s, the market for powdered and condensed milk had dried up, and Borden's decided to close the Midwest Food Products Division. So what to do with Dad? Fortunately, the superintendent's position at the Borden plant in Dixon, Illinois, happened to be open; so Dad and Mom moved back to the town in which Al and I had been born and Bob and Ray had spent ten of their elementary and high school years.

The first time the Millers lived in Dixon, Mom was a very active member of a group at church called the Candlelighters. There were a handful of women who were in their thirties who were Candlelighters, but most were in their sixties and above. When Mom and Dad moved back to Dixon from Madison in 1960, Mom immediately became active again in the Candlelighters. By this time, however, she was in her late fifties, and the old gals in the group were in their eighties and nineties. So she and a couple of her young cohorts from the old days became the "youthful" glue which held the Candlelighters together until the organization finally collapsed from exhaustion, debilitation, and widespread death.

In the years from 1960 until her death in 1997, Mom became the unofficial pastor to a group of elderly ladies who needed someone younger and slightly more able to care for them in their many and varied needs. Mom was always there for them. They loved her, and she loved them. Through many years during Dixon I and Dixon II, she spent thousands of hours ministering to these women in their particular situations: driving them to the grocery store, taking them food, phoning them to see how their day was going, literally or figuratively holding their hands when troubles engulfed them. Most of them were widows. A few were single ladies and in the earlier years.

Some still had husbands. Mom lived to age ninety-three, and it is sad but very understandable that there were almost no Candlelighters left to give her a proper sisterly send-off at her memorial service. But I have no doubt that all those dearly departed women were waiting for her on The Other Side because she had been a major part of their lives for decades.

As with Dad, Mom's faith was very deep but infrequently verbalized. She displayed it in deep emotion but not with words. She read devotional booklets every day, and I assume, though I do not know for a fact, that she also prayed every day.

Mom had strong opinions on many subjects. In fact, there was hardly anything Mom did not have an opinion about. In that respect, three of her four sons were very much like her. (Ray might also have acquired the excessive opinionated behavior of Mom and her sons, but if so, so many years have passed since his death that I simply do not recall it. But about that, more later.) If Mom disagreed with someone, she would rarely express her disagreement to that person. Ordinarily, she would simply remain silent. However, if she felt deeply about something, and someone had quite different thoughts on a particular matter, she would debate it. She never got angry with anyone (except her sister Irma and occasionally, her husband or sons); she would express her opinion, but she would also refuse to allow the disagreement to become disagreeable.

This isn't to say she was perpetually silent about her differences with others. Often, she would mercilessly dismantle their arguments in our hearing, though never in theirs. It was her way of dealing with disputes in a nondisputatious manner with the people with whom she had disputes. She felt it was not worth it to go at it hammer and tongs with someone and potentially destroy a friendship and probably create an enemy. She was fundamentally a peace lover, and she would do anything to avoid serious conflict with anyone, except Irma and the above-mentioned other familial exceptions.

Mom and Dad never had very serious arguments. Constant small arguments, yes, but serious large arguments, never. When she would get especially exasperated with him, she would say—and this was a constant refrain throughout their sixty years of marriage—

"Warren, do you want a divorce?"And he would always give the same response: "Only if you can make it worth my while, Margaret." Margaret never made it worth his while, and they made it through ten thousand minor differences with one another and at least a thousand "Warren(s), do you want a divorce?" This repartee became legendary in our extended family. I have cousins who to this day will ask their spouses in exasperation, "(Name), do you want a divorce?"And the spouse, male or female, responds, "(Name), only if you can make it worth my while."

I think I can claim with a fair degree of confidence that Mom had more of an effect on the four of us than Dad, simply because we were in her presence much more than we were with Dad. Prior to Madison, he was always at the milk factory from before we got up until he came home for dinner at six o'clock or so.

That having been said, the influence of both of them on our lives has been both profound and incalculable. They were not flawless parents, nor were they bigger than life. Instead, they were the best Warren and Margaret Miller they could be with respect to their sons and everyone else.

They were major illustrations in sermons I preached over the decades. Before they died, I even preached a sermon specifically about them called *In Praise of My Parents*. In the early days, I sent them carbon copies of all my sermons in my less-than-perfect typing. Then, when I began to use a word processor in the late `80s, I would send them a hard copy of the finished product. But I wanted them to know that publicly I homiletically applauded them. They may not have been the best parents in the history of humanity, but if there were ever any better, I challenge anyone objectively to prove it beyond the shadow of a doubt, especially my own doubt. That's my opinion, and you cannot possibly dislodge it.

St. Raymond Hutt Miller

My brother, Raymond, was the first of the original six Millers to die. He died almost twenty-four years before Dad and almost thirty-three years before Mom. I have learned professionally as a minister that it is uniquely difficult for a parent to lose a child—even an adult child—and I learned it personally by observing my parents over the decades following Ray's death. But I shall say more about that when it comes time to describe the circumstances for how Ray happened to die.

It is not surprising that my recollections of Ray are the sketchiest of all three of my brothers because I saw a lot of him only during my first twelve years. Furthermore, because he was six and a half years older than I, I wasn't very much in his world anyway. I was a little kid, and he was a big teenager. When we moved to Wisconsin, Ray was already a sophomore in college. He graduated from the University of Wisconsin as did Al and I. But because he was in college, even though he lived at home, he often left the house before I left for school, and he often got home late in the evening. Then, soon after he graduated, he was married. He immediately became a Regular Army officer, and he was away at Army posts in this country and in Korea and Germany. And we did not see much of him in those years.

My early impressions of Ray are inextricably connected to Bob. When I was little, they were always Very Big, and I was always Very Little. With the exception of going hunting with them, which began when I was nine or ten, I didn't spend much time with either of them. I have no doubt that biographical factor did not cause either of their hearts to break. Who wants a little brother hanging around all the time? It was hard enough for Al that he was stuck with me far more than he ever desired, but I just did not do much with my older two brothers during my childhood. We spent time together as an entire family but not much as four or three brothers together. It isn't as though Bob and Ray were always together because they weren't, but neither of them wanted a very young brother hung like an ailing albatross around their necks. For the most part, they went their way, and I went mine. Their way was much more expansive than mine as chronologically it should have been.

Perhaps some boys in some families never quarrel, squabble, or fight. That does not at all characterize the sons of Warren and Margaret Miller. The older pair had their disputes and differences with one another as did the younger pair. These oral or physical altercations were by no means constant and rarely violent, but they were also not infrequent either. None of the six Millers was ever a shrinking violet, and that reality manifested itself in various ways among the four male offspring.

I well recall a fight between Ray and Bob when we lived in Kansas. I have no idea what prompted it, but it went on for some time in the living room and the vestibule, as I recollect. All this time, Mom was beside herself with concern, anxiety, and not a little anger, but she was unable, by dire threats, to stop them from their impromptu wrestling and boxing match. Finally, in desperation, she took a pail of water and poured it on them—right on the floor, even. It was instantaneously effective. Sputtering, they released their grip on one another, and it was over. But none of the five of us who were witnesses to this fraternal fracas ever forgot it. Fortunately, Dad wasn't there, or the ceasefire might have been of quite a different sort. His warnings sank much more deeply into our youthful psyches than did those of our longsuffering, frazzled mother.

Why do I insist on telling you about the dustups of the Miller boys? Wouldn't it be better to leave those episodes out of this litany of purported saints?

I do so because I am at pains to make the point that the sainthood that is implied by "the communion of saints" is not primarily about unusually good behavior. Rather, it is about personality, personhood, and how each of us and all of us live within our own skins as individuals and unique personalities along with the individuality and personality of everyone else. Are we true to ourselves? And of far greater importance, are we true to God? That is what determines genuine sainthood. And to my way of thinking, all God's chillun have the capacity to exhibit their natural sanctity, despite the personal imperfections woven into the fabric of being of each of us. God does not expect perfection of anyone, but He does command integrity and continuous moral effort from everyone.

My impression of Ray as a student at the university is that he was serious, intentional, and hardworking. He also was one of the most gung-ho ROTC students ever to walk up Bascom Hill on the University campus.

How Ray became so devoted to the U.S. Army is unknown to me. Dad was never in the military. He was too young for World War I and too old for World War II. Bob enlisted in the Navy and served his required short stint. Al also became an Army officer via ROTC and served for over twenty years in the Regular Army. He no doubt was influenced by Ray's career path.

We lived in western New York State for a year when Ray started college at St. Bonaventure University, and they may have had an ROTC program although I am not sure. By the time Ray got to the University of Wisconsin, where they had mandatory ROTC for all male students for the first two years (it originated as a land grant college), Ray became Mr. Military. He was named the outstanding Army ROTC cadet and became commandant of the entire corps of ROTC cadets. He was president of several student military organizations. When he graduated, he received a Regular Army commission as a second lieutenant, which was fairly rare for ROTC students.

Ray was already an outstanding marksman before he got into ROTC or the Army. That was due to his avid interest in hunting. Some of my happiest memories of him when I was in junior high and high school are when he took Al and me hunting with him. We went duck hunting occasionally, but more frequently, we went pheasant and rabbit hunting. Usually we would take our dog, Butch, with us until Butch got too old to hunt. There is an advantage in having at least three hunters and an eager, if somewhat unruly, dog trying to flush pheasants from a cornfield, and Al and I were happy to comply as was Butch. Ray had made friends with several farmers around Madison, and we would go out on their land in the game of searching for game. They were golden times.

When Ray and his wife, Ruth, lived in El Paso, Texas, where he was stationed at Fort Bliss, he went antelope hunting for the first time in New Mexico just across the state border. He saw a small group of antelope out in the mesquite of the desert and crawled on his stomach a quarter of a mile to get close enough to take a shot. Knowing almost nothing about pronghorns, he shot the largest one. Its horns turned out to be the second-largest set of pronghorn headgear ever taken in the state of New Mexico up to that time. Ray discovered the magnitude of his feat only after he turned in the antelope at the hunters' check-in station. Beginner's luck is sometimes the best luck of all.

While at the university, Ray met and married Ruth Pickett, who also lived in Madison. Her father was a brilliant professor in the civil engineering department of the Engineering School. Ruth was a year younger than Ray. They married in the summer after Ray graduated, and they left immediately for his first Army assignment.

From then on, we saw relatively little of Ray and his family. When he was in Korea, Ruth came back to Madison and lived with her parents during his Korean sojourn, so we often saw her and the oldest of their children. Otherwise, they were hither and yon in the USA or in Germany.

Ruth and Ray were very well suited to one another. Each was very intelligent and independent, and that served them well, whether they were together or separated by his various deployments. Ruth was an ideal Army wife. She loved military life, and she adjusted quickly to wherever they were stationed. That is an invaluable characteristic in someone who was frequently transplanted. She also helped the children rapidly to settle in wherever they were sent. In addition, Ruth was happy to fulfill the social obligations expected of Army wives without resenting the customary expectations.

As far I could observe from my distant and necessarily limited vantage point, Ray seemed like an outstanding husband. That is especially true considering the fact that he was gone long hours every day when the family were all together or gone for many months at a time when he was separated from them. For the far-too-brief ten years of their marriage, Ray and Ruth had a mutually very supportive relationship. He handled his responsibilities admirably, as did she hers.

Ray also was an excellent father. They had their six children over a span of eight years: five girls, the last two of whom were identical twins, and then a boy. I recall Ray reading bedtime stories to the girls, playing games with them, and singing songs to them on the rare occasions they were in Madison. When he was home, he was home almost exclusively for Ruth and the children and never just for himself. He seemed like a natural father, if such a trait is truly possible.

Because Ray, like all four of the Miller boys, went to church each Sunday growing up, he and Ruth continued to attend church regularly with their family in their marriage. When they lived on an Army base, they attended the post chapel; and when they lived in civilian housing, they attended a neighborhood church. I presume it was for his children like it was for Dad and Mom's four sons: No one was offered the option of going to church; everyone went to church, period. End of story. That may sound too dictatorial or doctrinaire to outside observers, but those who are raised in a religious community as youngsters are much more likely to raise their own youngsters in a religious community as parents. Statistical studies have proven that many times over.

It was as an Army officer where Ray shone the most brightly to outside onlookers. From his youth, he displayed obvious leadership abilities. In Fort Scott, he was the president of the student body, co-captain of the football team, and was active in a number of extra-curricular organizations. He had a stellar record as an ROTC cadet at Wisconsin and was awarded many honors. He was promoted as rapidly as possible in the peacetime years prior to the U.S. involvement in the Vietnamese War. Had events evolved differently, it is highly likely he would have spent several years in combat during that conflict as it expanded, and he would have gone up the ranks even more rapidly.

But it was not to be. Ray had gone through airborne and Ranger training at Fort Benning, Georgia, and was serving with the 101st Airborne Division at the time of the Cuban Missile Conflict. Later on, he and the family left for Germany, where he became the commander of a company of Long Range Reconnaissance Patrol paratroopers or LRRPs—"Lerps" as they were called in Army-speak. They were training to be sent to Vietnam, where they would be dropped behind enemy lines to gather information on movements of the Viet Cong and North Vietnamese and to engage in counter-insurgency warfare. They were like Green Berets without technically being Green Berets. In today's terminology, they would be like the Army Special Ops or Navy SEALs, I suppose.

In mid-December of 1965, Ray's LRRPs were involved in a parachute exercise in southern Germany. Everyone left the airplane before Ray. The commanding officer apparently is always the last one out of the plane in such circumstances. All the other paratroopers landed safely. Everything was going well for Ray until he was about to land. He came down on his heels on a steep hillside instead of the intended flat fields and was thrown backwards onto his head. He suffered an instantaneous major brain injury, from which he never recovered. He remained in a coma for fourteen days.

A couple of days before Christmas, Ray was air-evacuated back to Walter Reed Army Hospital in Washington DC. His family also returned to the States. On Christmas Eve, a few minutes before midnight, Ray died.

Christmas seemed less like Christmas under such circumstances, and the concept of the communion of saints was thrust into an entirely different perspective because of Ray's death. Here was a thirty-three-year-old husband and father with a brilliant military record, whose career lay before him—prospects virtually unlimited. His oldest child was nine, his youngest nine months. And his life was over.

My brother, Al, had already been deployed to Vietnam at the time. He happened to be in Hong Kong for a short leave with his wife when Ray died, and he was unable to come to Washington in time for the military service at Arlington National Cemetery. Dad, Mom, Bob, and I flew to Washington to be with Ruth for the committal in Arlington. A general who had known Ray previously told Dad following the service that had Ray lived, he would certainly have become a general. But, as is sadly true of many factors in the lives of everyone, it was not to be.

Had Ray lived, I choose to believe he would have become well known in military circles, if not in a larger arena. I realize these matters are very unpredictable and also very political. But he could have become a very senior Army general, and in my fantasies perhaps even the Army Chief of Staff. Without question, he would have been the most overtly successful of the four Miller brothers.

In 1961, Ray was stationed in Korea, where he was the commander of the security force at Panmunjom on the border with North Korea. He happened to be back in Madison on leave when Nancy Christensen and I were married. Because it was such a rare occurrence when his path and mine crossed as adults, I asked him to be my best man. In retrospect, I have always been pleased about that. Although I had become much closer to Bob as an adult at that time, having been hunting deer with Bob nine days each year for the previous three years, it was providential that Ray could be my best man at a pivotal point in my life.

If I were limited to only one word to describe the character of Raymond Miller, this would be that word: commitment. Ray was as admirably committed a human being as I have ever known. He was committed to our family, he was committed to his wife, and he was committed to his own family. In the most obvious but not necessarily the deepest sense, he was committed to the United States of America and to the United States Army. He was "Airborne all the way," a Ranger all the way, a soldier all the way. Few military officers had the abilities or the potential that Ray possessed in abundance.

It was one thing for me to lose a brother at that point in my life. It was quite another for Ruth to lose her husband, for six children to lose their father, and for my parents to lose their son. Though it occurred over half a century ago, and my memory has become much more porous, I am still filled with wonder to recall how well Ruth, the children, and my parents adjusted to his death. All of them had unusual inner strength before the accident, and that gave them the ability to get through Ray's death as well as humanly possible. Fortunately, my nieces and nephew were close enough in age that they all had one another for support as they went through the adjustment process. They could help their mother, and she could help them. Mom, who was an instant weeper at emotional moments in the best of circumstances, managed to tough it out with remarkable strength. No doubt, Dad was of great assistance to her as both of them were to Ruth and the six children.

Ruth was married to Ray for ten years, she was a widow for ten years, and then she was married again to Bob Anderson of Manhattan, Kansas, for ten years. Bob was the principal of the elementary school all of the children attended in Manhattan. Ruth and her family lived in Manhattan when her father was on the faculty at Kansas State University. Then, Prof. Pickett took his position on the engineering faculty at the University of Wisconsin. Because Fort Riley, Kansas, was just outside Manhattan, Ruth decided to move back to her childhood home because she was so familiar with Manhattan, and she and the children could take advantage of the services especially available to them at an Army post. Bob's first wife had died of cancer a few years before Ruth and Bob were married, and they maintained a very happy marriage until Ruth herself died of cancer ten years later.

Ironically, the communion of saints took on far deeper meaning for me specifically because of Ray's early death than otherwise would likely be the case. From the time I was a child, every Sunday, the Apostles Creed was recited in church. It proclaims in conclusion, "I believe in the communion of saints, the forgiveness of sins, the resurrection of the body, and the life everlasting."

Though Ray was the first of our family to die, to be followed many years later by Dad, then Mom, and then Bob, I feel a spiritual kinship with the latter three because I have always felt an eternal kinship with the first. I believe I shall see Ray again. But he will not be the Ray I knew in this life, nor shall I be to him the little brother he knew in this life. In the first place, Ray was thirty-three years old when he died, and I am seventy-seven and still physically alive.

Is it even conceivable that Ray would forever be thirty-three in eternity and I seventy-seven-plus? Never. In eternity, there are no years of earthly longevity because there are no years at all. Time exists only in temporality. Maybe that's why the language inventors long ago linguistically connected the two words. I know virtually nothing about heaven, but I know enough to realize it cannot be essentially or even tangentially like life on earth. As they say, heaven is a "whole-nother" entity altogether.

Nevertheless, the communion of saints exists among those currently inhabiting this mid-sized planet, and it also exists among those of us now living here with all those living there, including my deceased parents and two brothers. They are deceased here, but they are alive there—wherever "there" is. However, heaven (or eternity) surely is not a *place*; it is an entirely different *state of being*. We will be alive there, more alive than we have ever been, but it won't be a life like this life. I cannot imagine what sort of life it will be, but it will far exceed any little glimmers any of us might imagine.

In any case, I frequently and consciously experience the communion of saints with the four saints of my family of origin who have died. They are with me in memory, and they are with me in spirit. I dream of all four of them periodically—sometimes all together, sometimes separately. I am profoundly who I am because they were (and are) who they were—and are. My life has been enormously blessed because those four people were willing to allow me into their lives. They are among my greatest blessings.

St. Robert Warren Miller

From birth, my brother, Bob, was a handful. That is, he was strong willed, not easily disciplined. In his early years, he was extraordinarily impulsive, independent to a fault, and literarily and spiritually related to Henry David Thoreau, which is to say, he marched to the beat of his own drum—always.

I, of course, neither knew Bob at all in his first nine years since I was not part of the scene during those years, nor do I really remember anything up to the time he was twelve years or so. How many three-year-olds are fully aware decades later of their big brother anyway? Many, maybe, but not this one, I can assure you.

The first major and recurring memories I have of Bob are when he was about fourteen or fifteen. He was determined to learn how to drive. He wanted to get his driver's license the first day he was old enough. I suppose Dad decided it would be a hassle and not worth the almost certain side effects if he tried completely to thwart Bob's obsession, so he reluctantly allowed Bob to drive the car back and forth in our short but straight driveway. We had a '39 Chevrolet, if memory serves me correctly; and back and forth he went, back and forth, hundreds of times, putting on many fruitless but purposeful miles. He wanted to be ready so that when he turned sixteen, he could instantly head out onto the streets of Dixon, Illinois. Citizens, beware! He turned out to be an excellent driver. In his working career in later life, he drove well over a million miles, and the couple of accidents in which he was involved were the fault of other drivers who slid into him in the snows of Wisconsin.

By the time we moved to Kansas, Bob had both his driver's license and a Cushman motor scooter. Bob was starting his senior year of high school when we moved to Fort Scott. He was an excellent athlete in several sports, but he was short. He grew four inches after he graduated from high school, which he considered a physiological and genetic travesty. Where was that extra height when he needed it? Nonetheless, he was on the high school football team (until he was invited off for missing practice the opening day of quail season); he played in a community basketball league; and he was a member of a semi-pro baseball team that traveled to towns all around Kansas, Missouri, and Oklahoma. One of his proudest athletic memories was that his team played Mickey Mantle's team in Oklahoma shortly before Mickey went to the Yankees.

Unlike Ray, Bob was not a Big Man on Campus at the Fort Scott High School. He spent many hours and days hunting and fishing, some of them perhaps school days. But *school* activities? Not so much. He also managed to get into more than his allotted share of various sorts of trouble but nothing that ever caused him seriously to lock horns with the long arm of the law. A few small brushes, maybe—just enough to keep him on the proper path.

Bob joined the Navy soon after he graduated in 1948 from Fort Scott High School. He and Marilyn Pulliam were married in 1949. He worked on several different jobs after he returned to Fort Scott from the Navy, but he ended up taking a position with the Western Insurance Company, which had its headquarters in Fort Scott. In 1958, they sent him to Wisconsin to be their auditor and inspector for businesses throughout the upper Midwest. For years, he was on the road four or five days a week. He continued with the Western until his retirement in 1992.

Bob's wife, Marilyn, loves to tell the story of how he was home on furlough from the Navy before they got married. He took our family car and said he was going to give Marilyn a ride around town. Impulsively, I said I would go along. I couldn't imagine they both wouldn't be thrilled about this arrangement. When we got to Marilyn's house to pick her up, I insisted on sitting between my brother and my future sister-in-law, so I have been told. Subconsciously, I suppose I figured I had a prior claim on him anyway. Besides, they no doubt needed a chaperone, and I was happy to serve as such. Marilyn was not pleased. Years later, however, she took great pleasure in relating this calumny to various relatives or anyone else willing to hear it. I, on the other hand, don't remember it at all. She probably made it all up.

Because Bob was such an avid hunter, he wanted to move from the small city of Wisconsin Rapids where they first lived in Wisconsin to somewhere in the countryside near there where he could hunt deer on his own property. That opportunity came in 1964 when Bob, Marilyn, and their young daughter, Susie, moved to a farm of 120 acres near Pittsville, Wisconsin, which the sign at the entrance to the village declares is the exact center of the state. Marilyn called the farm Ironquill, and they happily lived at Ironquill for the next forty-eight years.

I started deer hunting with Bob in 1958 and continued to do so almost every November until my family and I moved to New Jersey in 1973. Because he and I were together continuously for nine days each hunting season, I came to understand and appreciate Bob the most of all three of my brothers simply because those occasions were so special and so action-packed for me. After my divorce in 1997, I returned to the years of hunting with Bob each fall, and I did so until he died in 2012.

Bob's greatest hunting exploit occurred one November day in the long interim when I did not come each year to Ironquill. Bob went up to the house to get warm. He hated cold, but he willingly if painfully endured it during deer season. As he approached the house, he happened to look south across the field in the open back-forty. There, he saw a buck running full tilt from the woods east of his house west towards his own woods. He lifted his rifle and brought the buck down at two hundred yards with one shot. Then, he saw another larger buck racing the same direction. Two shots at three hundred fifty yards, and as they say, brown was down. Then, another even larger trophy was running flat out the same direction, and with two more shots at four hundred yards, it went down. Three big bucks in a matter of several seconds with five shots. He was the best marksman I ever knew, even better than Ray.

Seventeen years after Marilyn and Bob's daughter, Susan, was born, their son Robert Hutt Miller was born. Rob was, it is safe to say, a grand and glorious hugely belated surprise. Susie's husband, Mike, and their three sons and *their* sons and daughters also became hunters, along with Rob's sons. Thus, the final years of the Great Ironquill Deer Hunt were a four-generation affair—with Bob and I in the oldest generation; Mike and Rob in the second generation, even if widely separated in age by nearly eighteen years; seven of Bob's grandsons in the third generation; and assorted great-grand-sons-and-daughters in the fourth generation. What a fabulous familial fractious fracas it became!

Of the original four Miller sons, anyone familiar with us would likely agree that Bob was the most noted of the four for being a determined sower of mild wild oats. However, most of his oat-sowing fortunately took place in his teenage years. That included imbibing more beverages of an alcoholic nature than is probably either required or wise. However, when he was married, he settled down into the life of a model citizen, albeit one who was far more devoted to hunting than even most devoted hunters. Two decades later, he gave up drinking, cold turkey, which was a good thing since by then, he had consumed more than his share of Wild Turkey and Jim Beam.

For the seven years Bob and Marilyn lived in Fort Scott, they attended the First Presbyterian Church, the congregation our family attended for the three years in which we lived there when Al and I were part of the Miller tribe. This was a concession on Marilyn's part because that was not the church her family attended. Bob was a Miller-Hutt, however, and the Miller-Hutts—with the obvious exception of the one whose words you are currently reading—are nothing if not hard headed. And they like to do what they like to do.

Even at that, though, there were many Sundays during hunting season, which is very long in Kansas, when Bob Miller was not in the sacred precincts of God's holy assemblage, as God Himself would verify were you to ask Him. It is alleged that He keeps tally of such matters. Fortunately, however, they are far less influential in divine decisions regarding sainthood than most people would ever imagine. Believing in God and putting that faith into practice is what establishes true sanctity and not church attendance per se. There are many Christians, Jews, Muslims, and others who would dispute that, though. They insist sainthood necessitates much more than merely putting faith into practice, that extraordinary piety is a minimum requirement. If that is true, the communion of saints involves a much smaller body of believers than I could ever be prepared to affirm. The communion of saints is mammoth, not minuscule. There are far more people, and more kinds of people, in it than most of us would ever conceive.

In Wisconsin Rapids, Marilyn and Bob attended a United Church of Christ congregation (the Congregationalists) and also a Methodist church. When they moved to Pittsville, they became members of the UCC church there. Years later, Marilyn moved her membership to an Evangelical Free church. That denomination is much more theologically conservative, much like the church in which she had grown up in Fort Scott. Bob chose to stay in the Pittsville United Church of Christ because its theology and worship was more akin to the Presbyterianism in which Bob had grown up.

Besides being hard headed, most of the Miller-Hutts have always been very traditional. Mild, even wishy-washy incipient Calvinism is what Bob had always known; and predictable, unemotional worship is what he and the rest of us have always liked. As opinionated as we are, we don't get very far afield in issues religious—with the exception of the one, again, whose words you are currently perusing.

I was always proud of Bob that he became a deacon and elder in the Pittsville church. He served on their governing board for many years. He also was their treasurer and financial auditor and an usher for years. That congregation had a passing parade of pastors through the decades, and he always stuck with the church, whoever its parson was. Parsons can kill participation of certain church members in a congregation, but Bob refused to allow that to happen as long as he was there.

One of the primary social centers of Pittsville, Wisconsin, was Laura's Café. In latter years, I would go there with Bob and Marilyn during hunting season for a late breakfast or lunch, and it was obvious they knew virtually everyone who came in unless it was a traveler passing through town. Greater Pittsville's main business district stretches for two hundred yards along the main drag. My sister-in-law and brother seemed to know every local who ever set foot onto that hub of commerce, and they and the locals always had an encouraging word to say to one another, even though they were not quite home on the range since the range was a few hundred miles to the west and south of them.

Bob smoked for most of his teenage and adult years. As with drinking, he gave up smoking cold turkey not long before he died. Not nearly long enough as it turned out. Increasingly, he suffered from emphysema or chronic obstructive pulmonary disorder – COPD (take your pick), and it severely limited his breathing and the health of his heart.

In 2003, he was taken to the emergency room, having severe chest pain, and within three hours of his arrival, he was in surgery for a heart bypass. The next day, he went into cardiac arrest, and his cardiac surgeon saved his life. The doctor said if he had not been physically in such good shape (apart from his cardiovascular system), he surely would have died.

There was a great irony in the ethnicity of his physician. He was from Bangladesh. Because of the Gulf War, the War in Afghanistan, and the War in Iraq, the latter of which began within weeks of when Bob went into the hospital, Bob had come to the inflexible conclusion that all Muslims were quasi- if not actual terrorists. Yet here it was a nominal Muslim from Bangladesh who plucked him back from the cold clutches of the Grim Reaper. It never occurred to Bob that there was anything strange or odd about that. Dr. Rashid was his doctor and his friend; he was nothing like an Islamic terrorist. In other words, up close and personal Arabs or others of Islamic persuasion were fine to Bob, but as a group, they were implacable enemies. Go figure.

Bob was in a medically-induced coma for a couple of weeks, while he healed from his surgery and the trauma of his cardiac arrest. Afterward, he had something of a personality transformation, and decidedly not for the better. He always had a hair-trigger temper, and his language was always—how shall I put this?—*colorful*. His temper became even more pronounced, and his language acquired hues scarcely previously known to the English-speaking world.

Furthermore, his politics, which had theretofore tended toward the far right side of the spectrum, lurched even more to the right. His best friend became Rush Limbaugh, to whom he listened religiously every day. Lest you deduce I am suggesting that by telling you this, I am implying that it is only people who are not getting enough blood or oxygen to their cranial cavity who list to the far right; I have not said that. If *you* deduce it, however, I can't stop you. Would I encourage such a deduction? Only you can decide that. Perish the thought that I would nudge you in that direction.

A year and a half before he died, Bob was barely able to hunt at all, and six months before his death, he did not get out into the woods whatsoever. His life was drawing to a close, and he knew it. But thanks to the skillful ministrations of Dr. Rashid, Bob lived nine years longer than he would have had otherwise.

It is an enormous credit to the person Bob was that no one really held against him the person he became after his very serious brush with death at the time of his heart surgery. They knew the former Bob, not the latter one, was the real Bob, and they remained friends with the old Bob.

When he died, there were three hundred people at his funeral. For someone eighty-two years of age, many of whose contemporaries had preceded him in death, that was an amazing number. Almost half of metropolitan Pittsville was there plus assorted relatives and other hangers-on.

Ministers tend to pay closer attention than normal folks to the attendance at memorial services. Depending on several understandable factors which can lessen the number of people who come to such services, attendance is often *the* factor which bespeaks how well regarded the deceased was in his or her community. Three hundred people in Pittsville, Wisconsin, on a hot July day proclaims volumes about the life of the eighty-two-year-old man the people gathered to celebrate, giving thanks to God for his unique and uniquely widespread existence.

I have provided you more biographical details about my family members than I shall about anyone in the upcoming list of saints. That is because I know much more about their biographies than about any of the rest. Each of us has our own particular collection of the community of saints, and we possess a plethora of facts for only a very few of our own saintly vanguard.

It is impossible to quantify how much I have been influenced by these four Miller saints who have entered the eternal communion of saints. But it would be a great mistake for me to diminish the importance each of them had in shaping who I have become. Would they agree with everything I believe? Heavens no! They are Millers, aren't they? They believed what they believed. They were who they were. But I am who I am in large measure because of who they were, and what they were, and how they were.

If we knew more facts about everyone, would it enlarge or shrink our own communion of saints? What if we uncovered some unpleasant truths about the people we have most admired? Would that make us admire them less?

But that is just the point! True sainthood does not depend on rare moral nobility or unique behavior. It depends on how children of God enhance the lives of one another through their singular, if also less than perfect, existence. It depends on whether people live only for themselves or for others, and especially for God and His dominion. No one is sinless. No one is without moral blemish. Even

54

those people who are far above most of us in genuinely excellent behavior are still not flawless. And the worst of people can have the best of influence on other people under the proper circumstances. In the providence of God, that moral miracle occurs on a regular basis.

After all, wasn't it the escaped prisoner, Abel Magwitch, who exponentially transformed the life of Pip for the better in Charles Dickens' *Great Expectations*? And wasn't it the dissolute lawyer, Sidney Carton, who gave up his life for Charles Darney in *A Tale of Two Cities*? There is no one, no matter how misspent his life may have been, that cannot be allowed by God to say in the end, "It is a far, far better thing I do than I have ever done; it is a far, far better place I go to than I have ever known." The communion of saints is infinitely unlimited because it is God who creates us, God who sanctifies us, and God who redeems us—all of us. That is what three-quarters of a century has led me to believe. And I doubt that I will change my mind about that, as much as I have changed my mind about many other things.

SAINTS ELAM AND GRACE DAVIES

IT IS ONLY proper that I begin my litany of post-familial saints with two very special people who have had a profound impact on my entire adult life. Not to do so would be to diminish the enormous influence they have exerted on me in the last fifty years or more. Because of certain circumstances, one of them was much more influential in my early life as a minister, and the other, also by circumstances, came to exercise an increasingly gracious effect on me in later life, which befitted the Christian name given to her by her parents.

My wife, Nancy, and I were married in 1961, two months after we graduated from the University of Wisconsin. For the first two or three months after we arrived in Chicago when I had begun my studies at McCormick Theological Seminary, we attended a variety of churches. We felt we would never have a better opportunity to see what other denominations were all about since after seminary, I very likely would be involved every Sunday at some Presbyterian church or another somewhere. So we went to a fascinating variety of congregations, including Roman Catholic and Greek Orthodox. Then, one Sunday (and it was probably sometime in November of 1961), we attended the particular Presbyterian congregation I had been most eager to visit ever since arriving in Chicago, the Fourth Presbyterian Church on North Michigan Avenue.

"Fourth Church," as it is most commonly and affectionately known to its members, was then a church of three thousand people. (Now it has over five thousand members.) It was located on what is called "the Chicago Gold Coast," situated as it is just two blocks south of the place where Michigan Avenue merges into Lakeshore

Drive. In those days, tens of thousands of people lived in high-rise apartment buildings within easy walking distance of the church. Now, half a century later, there are additional tens of thousands who live in newer buildings between the church and the Chicago River to the south, west, and east.

The English Gothic sanctuary and church complex were designed in 1914 by Ralph Adams Cram. At the time, he was the premier American architect of Gothic churches all over the country. Structurally, Fourth Church is a visible testimony to the transcendent God who created the universe and everything in it. It is man-made magnificence proclaiming God-created munificence.

Fourth Church had the reputation of being a congregation of wealthy people, and without question, many of the movers and shakers of the Windy City were affiliated with it. But most of the members were what sociologists or demographers would classify as middle class—whether upper-middle, middle-middle, or lower-middle. In addition, eighteen hundred of the three thousand members were single adults. Through its single-adult groups, Fourth had been a noted marriage mill for decades. However, many of the Fourth Church singles simply were what were known back then as confirmed bachelors or spinsters. Surely, not a few were not widely recognized then (because their true status was not known) as homosexuals or lesbians, or in modern parlance, gays.

It happened that a new pastor came to Fourth Church at the same time we came to McCormick Seminary. His name was Elam Davies. *St. Elam Davies* was originally from Wales, and he was very proud of his Welsh heritage. He had served two congregations in Wales prior coming to the United States, where, for ten years, he served the First Presbyterian Church of Bethlehem, Pennsylvania, before coming to Chicago.

Until I heard Elam Davies in the pulpit, I had never heard a preacher quite like him anywhere in any setting, nor have I since then. He grew up in a fundamentalist home and the Presbyterian Church in South Wales, but he was anything but a fundamentalist. Nevertheless, he preached with great evangelical fervor, although he also could not truthfully be described as either a 1960s evangelical or

57

a twenty-teens evangelical. He was the most theologically and psychologically astute parish preacher I ever heard, and my admiration
for his preaching prowess only increased as the years went on.

Dr. Davies was named one of America's greatest preachers by
Time magazine. Most, but not all, who ever heard him expound biblical truths would enthusiastically agree with that assessment. His
sermons were always eloquent and educational as well as insightful
and inspiring. I readily confess to a strong bias, but for me, he was
simply the most powerful and influential preacher I ever heard. It
was an additional wonderful privilege to get to know him well over
a forty-year period.

The Fourth Church pulpit is elevated high above the main floor
of the sanctuary. Above it was a kind of octagonal roof which shel-
tered the pulpit itself. It is claimed this covering in large European
or British churches was intended to prevent pigeons from making
their deposits on unprotected clergy. As to the veracity of this claim,
I can offer no certitude. I will say this, however: In the eight years
I watched others preach from that pulpit or when I was preaching
in it myself, I never observed a single pigeon make a single deposit.
But then, I never observed a pigeon inside either, except one nestled
inside the sport coat of a young Hungarian with an eye patch from
the abortive Revolution of 1956, who was part of the colorful collage
of characters who frequented that singular city church.

If the preacher was very tall (which Dr. Davies wasn't; he was
about 5'7"), he could almost reach up and shake hands with parishioners in the north balcony. Still, Elam Davies filled that pulpit to
a splendiferous oratorical degree. He grandly moved around in the
small space like an energetic jack-in-the-box. He would lean out over
the lectern, thrusting his outstretched hand high or his upturned
index finger in gestures that seemed like those of a giant, which he
was, and not like the movements of a smaller-than-average man,
which he also was.

Much of what I learned about preaching I learned from observing Elam Davies for the aforementioned eight years—first for three
years during seminary and then from 1968 to 1973, when I later
served on the Fourth Church staff. Going to church there during

seminary was a uniquely spiritually uplifting weekly experience not only because of Dr. Davies' always-outstanding sermons, but also because of the magnificent choir (which, as far as I am concerned, were surely the match of the celestial chorus); the Aeolian Skinner pipe organ, which at full capacity could rumble the very fillings in one's vibrating jaw or raise one ever so slightly from the floor; and the fourteen hundred ready, eager, and expectant people who jammed into the pews every Sunday—winter (they provided much of the necessary heat) and summer (alas without air conditioning), rain or shine. Were I ever able to preach one-tenth as well as that wee Welshman, I would feel completely fulfilled.

During our third year in seminary, everyone was required to take a preaching class. Elam Davies was a visiting professor for that class, so I had the dreaded opportunity to be subjected to his critiques of my homiletic efforts. For him to judge my fledgling sermons would be like Stephen Strasburg having to observe a newcomer pitcher on the Mudville Little League team. I doubt that Elam Davies knew Nancy and I attended Fourth Church every Sunday. However, even if he did, I am certain it would not have influenced his assessment one iota of my potential as a preacher.

Elam Davies heard the last sermon I preached in homiletics class in that final year of seminary. The text was from the story of the woman at the well in John 4. It pains me beyond adequate description, even now, to admit that I had failed to read the commentaries about this famous passage. What a disastrous mistake! Had I done so, it would have been a very different sermon from the one that I actually preached. I was utterly unaware of the complex and fascinating background of this infamous (whom I was too ignorant to know was a famously infamous) lady. When I finished the sermon, the master of Welsh woe innocently asked if I had read any commentaries at all about the biblical passage. I readily, if also warily, admitted I had not. He enumerated, in excruciating detail, some of the factors that I had ignored in my youthful oblivion. Had I noted these factors, he said, I would have had preached a very different and far more accurate kind of sermon.

However, his final summation shall live in my skull as long as my skull continues to function properly. "Nevertheless," he concluded, "I believe that if you really work at it, you could one day become a preacher, Mr. Miller. "

I was overwhelmed. I had survived! He even gave me a sort-of compliment, a slender encouragement for my homiletic future! To paraphrase and then expand on Kipling, though he belted me and flayed me, by the living God who made me, Elam Davies gave me hope for what I most wanted to be as a minister—which is to say, a *preacher*! I knew I could never preach like him, but if I could even preach acceptably for him, I would be forever satisfied!

For the next three years after I graduated from seminary, I did not encounter Dr. Davies at all. I was busily occupied as the pastor of the Presbyterian Church in Bayfield, Wisconsin. But then, as much as Nancy and I loved the people of Bayfield and the beauty of northern Wisconsin, even in winter when it tended to become a tad snowy and chilly, we longed to return to the Chicago area, which we had also greatly enjoyed.

After being a solo pastor, I felt it would be a good experience to become an assistant or associate minister on a large-church staff. It happened that three Chicago area churches were looking for such a minister—two in the suburbs and one in the city. I applied at all three. The one to which by far I most hoped to receive a call, however, was Fourth Presbyterian.

In 1968, the office of assistant minister was still permissible by the Presbyterian Book of Order. An associate minister was officially called by the congregation, but an assistant minister was called only by the governing board, the session, and the pastor. Technically, an associate could not be fired, but an assistant could. The other two suburban positions were as associates, but the Fourth Church position was as an assistant. The other churches were offering a higher salary. When Elam Davies found out what I was paid in Bayfield, he offered a hundred dollars less than that. He wanted to make certain any ministers who came to Fourth were truly committed to being there. If we had had to live in a tent pitched in the parking lot and subsist on Cheerios and Campbell's soup, we would have done it.

60

Well, to be realistic, *I* would have done it. Fortunately, at the beginning of the next year, I got a very sizable raise—as I did every year after that—and thus, financially, it all worked out very well.

Ecclesiastically and personally, it could not possibly have worked out any better. I have often said that I could not have received as much valuable experience in most other churches over a fifty-year period than I was privileged to observe in Fourth Church in just five years. The church itself is unique in so many ways that the lessons learned there could be productively duplicated in almost no other Presbyterian congregation anywhere in the USA. But the primary factor in my preparation for the future was due to St. Elam Davies. Apart from the influence of my parents in my youthful formative years, Elam Davies was by far the most significant influence in my adult formative years. Whatever in me is unhelpful and disruptive he strove mightily to eradicate. Whatever is useful or effective in me has his imprints all over it.

When I came to Fourth Church, there were two other assistant ministers, Gerry Hazelrigg and Andy Tempelman, who had each been there for a few years. Gerry and Andy regularly referred to Dr. Davies as "The Boss," and so did I. A couple of years later, Gerry and Andy both received calls to be the pastors of large Presbyterian congregations, Gerry in Omaha and Andy in Springfield, Illinois. Their places were filled by two other young ministers. Dave Robertson had been a classmate of mine at McCormick Seminary, and Jim Fleming had grown up in Delaware and had attended Princeton Theological Seminary in New Jersey.

Elam Davis has decide that one particular thing he hoped to contribute to the Presbyterian denomination was to see to it that pastoral calls would be extended to assistant ministers he considered to be good candidates to serve as pastors of large congregations. Over the twenty-three year period he was at Fourth, he managed to turn nearly ten of his assistants directly into parsons who were called to churches which averaged from one to two thousand members. Thus, his continuing influence was extended to many tens of thousands of people from then until now. Elam felt a specialized calling to train young ministers for large-church pastorates. It would be impossible to serve with Elam Davies and not have many of his many pedagogical pearls of wisdom to become inculcated into the pastoral *raison d'etre* of his pastoral protégés.

In the Hebrew language, there are several words that translate as "fear." Some of these words specifically connote terror, dread, fright, or sorrow. But one of them, *yirah*, can mean either "fear" or "reverence." Bob Kincheloe was a semi-retired minister on the staff of First Presbyterian Church on Hilton Head Island, South Carolina, for over ten years when I was the pastor there. Whenever he came to the phrase, "the fear of the Lord," when reading a biblical passage in worship, he automatically changed it to "the reverence of the Lord." Bob did not think it was proper to suggest anyone should ever be fearful of God as the word "fear" is commonly understood.

I say all this as background to tell you that for the first two years I was at Fourth Church, I never referred to Dr. Davies, publicly or privately, as anything other than "Dr. Davies." The reason for this was a virtually equal combination of fear *and* reverence, with a pinch of terror thrown in. I lived in dread of doing anything of which he might disapprove, so I was constantly watching my p's and q's. But I also revered him so completely as a pastor and as a person and mentor that it seemed unthinkable to refer to him by his first name. Fairly soon, I came to call him "The Boss" either in or out of his presence because it would occur to no one on the church staff that he was not the boss. Besides, the other clergy always called him "The Boss." Nevertheless, for almost half my tenure at Fourth Church, he was usually the feared and revered "Dr. Davies."

I am a dreamer; by which, I simply mean that in sleep, I frequently dream. Even now, Elam Davies appears in these nighttime visitations fifty times more often than all other ministers I have known combined. In fact, there is scarcely anyone else who has penetrated my subconscious mind with greater persistence than he. What can I say? It is *yirah* all over again—and again, and again, and again. Is it fear or reverence? *Yes.*

Individually, Elam Davies influenced the greatest total number of people more by his preaching than by any other factor in his ministry. On most Sundays, we had from one to two or even three hundred visitors in attendance. Many were local Chicagoans who wanted to hear the preacher they had heard so much about, and many of those visitors eventually became members of Fourth Church. Other periodic visitors came to the church whenever they happened to be in the city for any reason. Still, others attended regularly but refused officially to join the church and for a whole host of reasons. Dr. Davies's style of preaching did not appeal to everyone, but it wonderfully served the needs of many thousands through the years. And in my opinion, he certainly was the most consistent and effective proponent of the Christian Gospel I ever heard.

Perhaps because he was Welsh, Elam was a born raconteur. He told stories in his sermons. He told them in church staff meetings and other meetings, and he told them in informal settings. He was even more adept as an embellisher than as a mere storyteller. Why should someone simply be walking down the street when a rabid pit bull terrier might leap out of the bushes or an out-of-control Buick might come careening along or a double rainbow might be observed towering over tall buildings?

He stored many jokes in his cranial hardware, and as with other stories, he told them well and with great relish. In the unlikely event he might forget an important point, he could instantly manufacture an alternate of his own, equally salient and with humorous equivalence. He never laughed uproariously at his jokes, but he did visibly enjoy them.

I don't know what his IQ was, but whatever it was, it was close to being off the charts. He also was a master at perceiving the inner workings of other people's minds. Some of that talent was no doubt a God-given gift, but he perfected it through the years by becoming an extremely adept pastoral counselor. Each week, he spent many hours meeting with stressed or troubled people. Many of them came to him because of insights they gained from his sermons, and they wanted to probe further. He was a masterful mass psychologist as well as one-on-one psychologist. His preaching reached into the very depths of human experience, and it enabled people disturbed by many factors to be able to leave the Sunday service calmer and more refreshed. I suspect that over his forty-plus years of ministry, he helped hundreds or thousands of people through countless personal crises, enabling them to find faith and courage to withstand whatever onslaughts might come their way.

During his tenure at Fourth Presbyterian, Dr. Davies established a center at the church called The Door. Its primary purpose was to provide mental health assistance and other forms of help to people who could otherwise not afford it, particularly homeless people. At the time of his retirement from Fourth, the name of the center was changed to The Elam Davies Social Service Center. On a per capita basis, I don't know whether there are more mentally and emotionally troubled people in cities than in other less crowded locations, but I was always struck by the number of troubled souls who came to Fourth Church, hoping that there, at last, they would find something or someone who could help them cope with their demons. It was very fitting that eventually, Grace and Elam Davies' daughter, Judith Davies Schneider, became one of the professional counselors at the center named in honor of her father.

The Boss often used an alliterated phrase to describe those to whom Christ's Church was always obligated to reach out. They were, he said, "the least, the last, and the lost." Whether he was the first to utilize that phrase, I cannot say, but he said it with sufficient frequency that all of us who had a very positive association with Fourth Church came to believe that it was our collective duty to reach to such folk as well. A tutoring program had been in operation for years prior to the time Elam came to Fourth Church. He inspired many more people to become volunteers to reach out to children from low-income families who attended nearby Chicago public elementary schools. He also established The Culture Center, a means whereby adults met each week with a particular child on a one-to-one basis, trying to expand their horizons for what the Windy City offered to its citizens. Many Culture Center volunteers established long-term relationships with their charges, and each side of each duo offered insights into the world of the person on the other side. It was a fruitful symbiosis which enabled people from two quite different worlds to better understand the people inhabiting the other world.

Without question, many youngsters who attended the Tutoring Center and the Culture Center were motivated to go on to college or graduate school because of the mentoring assistance they received from their volunteers. Without that form of Christian outreach, some of those young people might never have escaped the invisible but powerful bonds that sought to keep them imprisoned in the low-income neighborhoods a few blocks to the west of North Michigan Avenue.

As I mentioned earlier, the church building designed by Ralph Adams Cram was finished in 1914. From that time on, perhaps because of its very architecture, it became a "traditional" city congregation. When Nancy and I first attended Fourth Church in 1961, we instantly observed that formality was strongly but silently proclaimed in every facet of the service of worship. The ushers, all of them males, wore striped trousers and morning coats. After the offering had been received, they walked with it from the back of the nave to the front, marching in locked step, the heels of their highly polished black shoes clicking in tandem on the hard tiles of the center aisle.

The first few pews at the front of the church were rented. No one was allowed to sit in those pews until five minutes before the service began, in case the people who rented the pew came to claim their perch. Some of the pew renters were scandalized that anyone could ever sit there, even if they themselves did not show up.

Quietly, but quickly and effectively, Dr. Davies rounded up enough votes among the elders and trustees to eliminate what he rightly believed was a tradition which time should previously have passed. Elam was not a confrontational politician like a Rand Paul or a Ted Cruz. Rather, he was a behind-the-scenes man like a Lyndon Johnson or a Tip O'Neill. He used the telephone and private conversations to great and good gain.

Another of the ancient traditions of Fourth Church is that it had never had any female elders or trustees despite the fact that almost two-thirds of its members were women. The Welshman, who knew what it felt like to be part of an oppressed group, decided that pattern must be overturned. Again, quietly but with great Celtic determination, he saw to it that two very able women were nominated in the same year to become elders, and later (horror of horrors!), some female trustees also were elected. If this does not seem especially noteworthy in the Twenty-Teens, one must remember that this was in the 1960s, and this was Fourth Church. Later, female ushers were also instituted. Saints preserve us. And now, Fourth Church has an excellent female pastor. Will wonders never cease?

No pastor of any sized church can avoid being an administrator of some sort. Elam Davies had a very clear and compelling managerial style. With the church staff, he sought to convince everyone of what her or his job and job description was; and then, he gently but firmly oversaw what we were doing. He never looked over anyone's shoulder, but the Tuesday morning staff meeting, which was almost as sacrosanct a time as Sunday morning, was the place where we talked about what we were involved with during any given week. If we did not say enough, The Boss would probe. If we said too much, he would cut us off at the knees, or, if need be, the neck. He was direct but not at all dictatorial, incisive but not intrusive.

Elam set the meeting time of the elders at four o'clock on a Friday afternoon, if my memory is correct. The trustees also met in the late afternoon, but on a different day. (The assistant ministers attended trustees meetings only when asked, which was next to never.) Without question, the scheduled late afternoon time was intentional. It almost always guaranteed short meetings because the elders wanted to get home for or to go out for dinner. The committees of the two governing boards met at their own discretion. They did most of the discussion regarding their committee's assignment, and then, the chairman gave brief reports at the general meetings of the boards. Almost always, committee recommendations were approved with little discussion.

This may sound heavy-handed, but there were eighteen trustees, thirty elders, and fifty-one deacons. In order for anything at all to happen, there had to be a mechanism for effectively turning discussions and recommendations into fairly quickly democratically agreed-on decisions. A few people grumbled that things were too often shoved through, but most of the officers came from business organizations that operated under the same sort of rubric.

Democracy is an excellent form of government, whether for nations or churches—if it is wisely directed. Otherwise, it can be an exercise in voluble futility. Elam Davies believed implicitly in the principle of directed democracy, and he safely captained the ecclesiastical ship through every conceivable obstacle in its course.

My first assignment at Fourth Church was to be the minister of pastoral care. I tried to visit every member who was in any hospital anywhere in the Chicago metropolitan area, and I also periodically went to see people who were no longer able to get of their homes because of physical disabilities. Each Tuesday morning, I would report on the calls I had made. The Boss was a tad squeamish when hearing about surgeries. He often told me not to engage in what he called "organ recitals." I tried my best to keep my reports brief, even though it appeared to me one cannot fully appreciate what someone has gone through in a surgical operation without a detailed reference to the particulars of a ruptured gizzard or whatever.

A few months after we arrived at Fourth Church, I was talking to Elam in his office, although I was leaning against the door jam in what I assumed would be a very brief conversation. He casually asked me how I thought things were going for me in my new position. Foolishly, I said I was very happy with everything I was involved in but that there didn't seem to be enough to do. Instantly, a dark frown came over his face, like a huge thunderhead about to shed its heavy burden of rain. "Close that door and sit down," he said coldly. I didn't know exactly what was coming, but I did know that whatever it was, it was not going to be good.

In chapter and verse, he led me to believe that for everyone on the Fourth Church staff, there were always more tasks to be accomplished than even the most talented and energetic of us could succeed in accomplishing. Besides calling on more people, which he pointedly urged me to do, I could spend more time visiting the members of the single adult group to which I had been assigned. I also could work harder on the sermons I preached at the Sunday evening services. There were three single adult groups, and on the average Sunday, there were two or three hundred who came to the church, most of whom attended the Sunday evening service along with others from the congregation or community. I could look for new things to do, he said, and to suggest new forms of ministry to the passing parade of people who passed through the doors of the Fourth Presbyterian Church every week.

By the time he was finished (and it felt like my dressing-down lasted for two full days), I felt fortunate indeed to have my hide still loosely attached to my frame. I was led to believe with no ambiguity that if I put my mind to the challenge, I could find a sufficient list of things to do that I would never again be deluded into supposing there was not enough for me to do. I have always been something of a workaholic, but Elam Davies on that never-to-be-forgotten day turned me into a workaholic of a higher order than otherwise I might have been. From then on, it did not occur to me that either my work for a day or for a lifetime was ever finished.

Probably because of that pain-wracked chat, I never called Elam anything except "Dr. Davies" for the next couple of years. Only half way through my five-year stint at Fourth did I begin to call him Elam. (Elam, by the way, is a biblical name—not a major one, but it's there. I suspect he often ruefully wondered why his parents chose that moniker for him.) But I asked his permission to do so before I altered my appellation for him. Apparently, he hadn't realized I had been addressing him so formally—perhaps because most of the people at Fourth Church also called him Dr. Davies. But I am very gratified that until he died nearly thirty-five years later, we were on a first-name basis.

One of the many pieces of advice Elam gave me was to read a lot and to read widely. Because of my peculiar personality, by which I mean "odd" not "unique," I had always been a fairly avid reader. It is important, said, Elam, for preachers constantly to be reading. Probably, I never read enough books to suit him and read more magazines and periodicals than he would approve, but at least he induced me to read many authors and writers who displayed a wide variety of opinions on a wide variety of subjects.

Some time, after Elam Davies became "Elam" to me, *St. Grace Davies* also became "Grace." But that process took longer because I did not frequently have very in-depth conversations with Grace during my five years on the Fourth Church staff. Certainly, we encountered one another often enough, but not for hours at a time.

As an interested outside observer, however, I perceived Grace Davies to be the best possible minister's wife for anyone who might be the pastor of a congregation like Fourth Presbyterian Church. In those days, there were several active women's organizations, and Grace participated in most of them. She made friends very easily, and through the years, she carefully cultivated her friendships. She frequently had social gatherings, including occasional staff parties, at the manse, which was part of the large church complex and was located right on the corner of Michigan Avenue and Chestnut Street. She was always a very gracious hostess, making everyone feel like part of the family. (The family consisted of Grace and Elam; their daughter, Judith; Grace's mother, Mary [Mollie] Owen; and their Welsh terrier named Mr. Jones.) One of Mr. Jones's many quirks is that he had been trained to do both parts of his business only on newspapers spread out in the basement, and that is the only place where he would perform. Elam loved to take Jones on his long walks, but the testy terrier never figured out it was permissible to relieve himself on bushes or grass. He would wait till they got home and then go to his newspapers. (What can I say; he was Welsh.)

Grace's father was also a Welsh Presbyterian preacher. Thus, while some are to the manor born, Grace Owen Davies was to the manse born. Her mother, Mollie Owen, was a lovely old fundamentalist lady who lived to be almost a hundred. She spent her last years in the Fourth Church manse with her daughter and son-in-law. I visited Mrs. Owen fairly often, and I discovered that Grace was in some respects a chip off the old maternal block. But a fundamentalist Grace was not. Apparently, theologically she was more akin to her father. Like her husband, Grace was a committed evangelical Christian. And also like her husband, she had an excellent and inquisitive mind. Over the years, she asked multitudes of the most perceptive questions of me, hoping (fruitlessly, as it turned out) that I would be able to answer all of them.

It was years later that I came to know Grace much better. In 1979, our family moved to Hilton Head Island, South Carolina. Before Elam retired in 1988, and then every year after that, the Davies came to Hilton Head in the winter for a couple of weeks and in retirement for two or three months. In those days, Nancy and I visited them occasionally while they were on the island, and I went to see them myself fairly often.

It was by that means that I came to appreciate Grace and Elam Davies even more than I had previously. They both had a wonderful sense of humor. When they were outside the ecclesiastical spotlight, they were delightfully spontaneous and uninhibited. Each liked to tell stories from their past, and Grace especially liked self-deprecating anecdotes that depicted her in precarious positions—all of which managed somehow to work out well in the end. Elam had developed storytelling to high a art form in his sermons, but in personal conversations, they both had the ability to regale their listeners with tales that were grand, glorious, memorable, and possibly also a tad embellished.

One of the most gratifying events of my life is that Elam accepted my invitation to preach in Hilton Head Island. It is a singular honor in the history of the First Presbyterian Church that it was for our congregation that he preached the last sermon he ever delivered. He may have had an intuition that would be the case, but I certainly didn't. Through the years, I had referred to him so often in sermons I was very pleased the folks in Hilton Head had the opportunity to hear the homiletic lion in what proved to be early to mid-winter.

For any woman, being married to Elam Davies would be a major challenge. He had a high-maintenance position in a high-maintenance church, and it took every ounce of strength for both of them to serve at the highest level of effectiveness at Fourth Church. Grace was as helpful "an helpmeet" as it says in the King James Version of the creation story as Elam was likely to find anywhere in creation. They were a marvelous team.

In 1996, after thirty-six years of marriage, Nancy and I ultimately divorced. It had been a long marriage of growing personal, mental, psychological, and spiritual separation, and we never managed sufficiently to address the major distance between us. The Davieses kept in touch with both of us, but I was very grateful and even surprised that they remained particularly comforting and consoling to me. A year and a half later, I married Lois Landis, who had been one of the elders at the First Presbyterian Church in Hilton Head Island. Lois grew up in Lancaster County, Pennsylvania. We visited Pennsylvania a few times each year. Whenever we did, we always went to see Elam and Grace, who had moved back to Bethlehem, Pennsylvania, to a Presbyterian retirement home which had been built adjacent to the First Presbyterian Church there, where Elam had been pastor four decades earlier.

At the end of our first visit with them as a couple after we were married, Grace confessed something Elam had told her before we arrived at their home. "Now, Grace," he said, "no matter what, we're going to like this girl." ("This girl" was then forty-five years old, but to them, she was a girl.) They happily admitted on that occasion that they liked Lois from the instant they laid eyes on her. That statement, so typical of them both, has meant the world to Lois and me ever since that first nerve-jangling, angst-producing introduction.

On more than one instance, Elam noted the unusual depth of the elevators in Kirkland Village, their retirement home. He said several new residents had asked him why the elevators were so deep. The boss, who had no illusions of why they had come to Kirkland Village, told the new folks it was so there would be enough room for the funeral home to take the dear departed out on a gurney. Elevators in retirement homes are a living reminder of one of the primary purposes of retirement homes. It is called Ultimate Retirement. Lois and I now live in such a facility ourselves, where we see Ultimate Retirement enacted on a predictably periodic basis.

Elam Davies had always had health problems from the time he was a teenager. He was particularly subject to colds and pneumonia. It was, he said, because of all the coal dust he had inhaled in South Wales as a youngster. When the Davieses were visiting Berlin, they were in a very dark church. There was a one-inch drop in a dimly lighted hallway from one level to another, and Elam did not see it. As he traversed what he thought was a flat surface, he fell when he stepped onto the minimal depression, and he ruptured a kidney. From that small misstep, he almost died.

Nonetheless, he outlived both his parents by many years, much to his amazement. And despite various heart problems in his latter years, he made it to age eighty-six before he took his long-anticipated final descent down the elevator.

John Buchanan, the man who followed Elam as pastor of Fourth Church in Chicago had been there for fifteen years at the time of Dr. Davies's death. He conducted the memorial service there. And while Elam had been away from that pulpit for a long time, the church was packed with people who remembered him with great fondness and admiration.

I was greatly honored that Grace asked me to deliver the sermon at Elam's service in Bethlehem. He had been gone from that pulpit for over forty years, but the sanctuary of the First Presbyterian Church was pleasantly filled with old-time parishioners,—others they had met as "new" parishioners there themselves, and friends from Kirkland Village. It is a fitting tribute to a man of Elam's advanced age that almost two thousand people came to two services a thousand miles apart. He was one of the best friends I ever had and certainly the most influential mentor I could ever have hoped for.

After Elam died, Lois and I maintained a closer relationship than ever with Grace. I telephoned her frequently, and we always tried to see her whenever we were back in Pennsylvania.

Grace was never an especially tall woman, but as a result of osteoporosis, she lost seven inches in stature. By the end, she could scarcely stand up straight; but if she were able, she would rise up regally to a mere four feet, nine inches. She found that reality to be at the same time both very humorous and a grave physiological injustice. In addition, she had severe spinal stenosis, which gave her constant back pain. Toward the end of her life, she could no longer walk. She had a motorized wheelchair which she could maneuver like a ballerina on stage.

In our many conversations, we talked often about theological issues. Because Elam had always such a keen mind for theology, she had developed an interest in what theologians with a certain degree of self-congratulation call "the queen of sciences." Grace particularly enjoyed discussing some of the fundamentalist notions of her parents. She had grown up with them, but she also had grown out of them. And perhaps she wanted to be sure she wasn't headed straight for hell because of her apostasy from the old ways; although along with other later shortcomings, she had also come to possess serious reservations about the purported locale of perpetual punishment.

In addition, Grace took particular pleasure in talking about death. The clergy and their spouses are confronted by death so often that it becomes an ordinary life issue for them. I have long had my own "death thing," so I was happy to speak at length what neither of us could truly know anything about. Throughout her declining health, Grace exhibited not one scintilla of fear about dying, but rather what I would call a healthy interest in and respect for death.

When death finally paid its visit to Grace Davies, her daughter, Judith, asked me to preach the sermon at her service in Bethlehem as I had done for Elam several years earlier. Judith had grown up in Bethlehem and felt a special affinity to its First Presbyterian Church and the old-timers who were still there who remembered Elam and Grace from the old days. And as with Elam, there was also a service for Grace at Fourth Presbyterian, where she had made so many friends and left such a positive legacy.

Prior to coming to America, Elam's last parish in Wales was in the northern seaside resort community of Llandudno. Grace and Elam had told their daughter Judith they wanted their ashes to be scattered there, at the summit of an ancient volcanic plug called the Great Orme. It rises up majestically to the west side of Llandudno's natural harbor. Grace's parents were buried there in a cemetery close to the summit of the high hill. Judith had planned to carry out their wishes herself, but due to a long and debilitating illness, she felt she would be unable to do so. Because Lois and I happened to be making a visit to Britain to see various friends and tourist sites old and new, she asked if we would perform that solemn assignment. We

73

were sorry Judith did not feel up to it herself, but yet again, we felt immensely honored to have another important ceremonial responsibility for the entire Davies family.

Standing on the Great Orme above the beautiful town of Llandudno, Wales, Lois and I released to the gusty sea breeze the remains of two of the finest people ever to have graced our lives— "earth to earth, ashes to ashes, dust to dust." They were alternate parents, beloved advisors, advocates of ecclesiastical reality, and trusted friends. In life and in death, Elam and Grace Davies had a profound effect on me, and their spirits shall live in my spirit as long as I shall live. Beyond that, I shall wait to see what is to be experienced— beyond that.

SEMINARY SAINTS

AMONG PRESBYTERIANS, PRESBYTERIAN seminaries in the `50s and `60s tended to have regional attractions for prospective students. Only Princeton Seminary in Princeton, New Jersey, drew large numbers of students from all over the country, rather than just from the Northeast.

In southern Wisconsin, where I grew up, McCormick Seminary in Chicago produced the most Presbyterian parsons in our neck of the woods, so McCormick is where I decided to go. I applied nowhere else. The thought never occurred to me. Nearly every minister in Madison Presbytery whom I knew (and by the time I was twenty-two I knew many of them) had graduated from McCormick, so it was virtually unthinkable to go anyplace else. *Was* there anyplace else? Of course not. Thus, plagiarizing and paraphrasing a statement of St. Augustine with a decided geographical twist, to Chicago then I went.

A month before starting seminary, Nancy and I were married. While I was ensconced in the seminary halls of ivy, she taught kindergarten in suburban Elmhurst, Illinois, commuting west each morning when most folks were driving east and then driving east in the afternoon when most commuters were driving west. She put many thousands of miles on our old '51 flathead V-8 Mercury.

I greatly enjoyed and benefited from my years at seminary as was also true for my sojourn at the University of Wisconsin. However, by the time I graduated from McCormick, I was more than ready to move on to the parish ministry. In my youthful single-mindedness, I had already been intent for fifteen years on becoming a minister, which by the time it actually happened was 60 percent of my then lifetime. Looking at it from that standpoint, it felt like a very long wait until it finally happened.

Nonetheless, the McCormick and Glasgow (Glasgow shall be explained later) years were very happy and fruitful ones, and I look back with fondness on the array of saints I encountered during those years. Following are ten saints in particular I choose to cite from September of 1961 through December of 1964 when I became forever paroled from the sacred halls of clerically concentrated academe.

Saints George and Nancy Knight

George Angus Fulton Knight was our professor of Old Testament and Hebrew. He and his wife, Nancy, were from Glasgow, Scotland. George was a world-renowned Old Testament scholar, whose book, *A Christian Theology of the Old Testament,* was a classic for attempting a clear biblical connection between Jewish and Christian theology, and that is a most challenging intellectual assignment. I never met anyone who had a greater appreciation for both Judaism and Christianity than George Knight. His influence on me in that regard is incalculable.

George did not sound like a native Glaswegian, even if he was one. He sounded instead like a cultured Scotsman. His wife, *Nancy,* however, always sounded as though she had just stepped off the ship from Glasgow. She had what the Scots would describe as "a guid Scots tongue in huhr heed."

The Knights had many students going in and out of their seminary-provided faculty home throughout the week. They especially liked playing the part of hosts to the single students, who even in those long bygone days represented a minority of the student body. The majority of us were married, living in two dormitories for married students or commuting from student churches throughout the greater Chicago area.

I did not participate in very many of the Knight student soirees. It was through Hebrew classes and Old Testament courses that I came most fully to know and appreciate Dr. Knight. I am sorry to report that not everyone was drawn to George as much as I. He could come across to some as being imperious although he did not strike me that way at all. He had a very warm personality, but it was somehow a uniquely distant warmth, if such is possible. He certainly genuinely cared about his students, and he wanted to do all he could to prepare us for preaching and teaching biblical truths as well and winsomely as we could. As I reflect on the various saints I shall be highlighting in this summary of the sanctified, I am mystified why it is some people come across very positively to some of us, and others not nearly so much. My conclusion is that different folks emit different strokes, and no one is everything to anyone. As my mother would say, it shall ever be thus.

It was in a course on the Eighth-Century Hebrew Prophets that I began to appreciate how radically counter-cultural the Bible can be. When we studied Isaiah, Micah, Hosea, and Amos, it became evident how radical Jesus also was, who himself was so powerfully influenced by the prophets. A heightened social conscience was one of the greatest gifts George Knight gave me. Hundreds of times through half a century have I preached from the prophets about events and circumstances which are eerily similar to events from twenty-five or twenty-eight centuries ago. As the writer of Ecclesiastes said, and also my mother, there is nothing new under the sun.

During his teaching career, George and Nancy Knight lived in many places around the world. I don't know if they were motivated by a strong inner wanderlust or if he believed he could best serve God by spending a few years in as many places as possible. Nancy was always the supportive "helpmeet," to use the King James expression, and she would dutifully pack up for their next move and their new group of students. George ended up his academic career as the principal (president) of a new seminary for the South Pacific islands in Suva, the capital of the Fiji Islands. How fitting it was that the Knights should engage on such an unusual adventure in their twilight years. Adventure was deeply etched into their Christian DNA.

One cold winter afternoon, during my first year at McCormick, I happened to be studying in the seminary library. I overheard two classmates talking about the pros and cons of going to Scotland for their middler year. (With three years required for a seminary degree, the first-year students are called juniors, then they become middlers, and finally, they end up as seniors.) Six or seven years earlier, when I was about fourteen, I had given thought to doing that. One of our assistant ministers in Madison had spent his middler year at the divinity faculty of the University of Edinburgh. However, in the intervening years, I had forgotten all about it, until I overheard Karl and Brian talking about it. As it turned out, they did not go to Scotland, but Nancy and I did.

In order to prepare for our Caledonian sojourn, I naturally sought the advice of George Knight. I told him I was considering going to Edinburgh, which is where the vast majority of Americans went back then. In a typical take-charge manner, George insisted that I go to Glasgow University, his alma mater. I would be one of few Americans, he said, which would be good. (It was.) Besides, if I wanted to get a position as a student assistant minister in a local church, it would be much easier in Glasgow, since its metropolitan area was much larger than that of Edinburgh. He put me in touch with an old friend from his years at Glasgow University, who was the stated clerk of Glasgow Presbytery—which is the Presbyterian equivalent of a diocese, sort of. Andrew Herron connected me with George Cameron, the pastor of the Glenburn Parish Church in suburban Paisley. And thus began a happy friendship with that congregation which has continued to a limited degree even to the present day, more than fifty years after we were there.

When Nancy and I returned to Chicago a year later, the Knights were still in residence at the seminary. I took various courses George taught, continuing my infatuation with the pearls of wisdom this extraordinary biblical scholar provided.

At some point during their McCormick years, the Knights had purchased a vacation home in Bayfield, Wisconsin. It was on the side of a hill, and it overlooked Lake Superior and the Bayfield marina at the end of its two-block business section. It also had a beautiful view of Madeline Island, the largest of the Apostle Islands chain. How they happened to discover Bayfield I don't remember, but it was providential for me because their Bayfield association indirectly led to my first pastorate.

It may help if I now explain the system by which Presbyterian churches find new ministers. When a pastoral vacancy occurs, a pastoral nominating committee is elected by the congregation. Their task is to present a candidate to the church as their next parson. Half a century ago, the process was much more straightforward and streamlined than it is now. The committee, if so inclined, could quickly agree on someone they either knew or knew about and in short order the ecclesiastical deed was done. Now the procedure is very elongated, and it can take up to two or more years for a pastoral nominating committee to present their candidate, especially in larger congregations. In the meantime, a church can drift aimlessly unless the leadership is diligent and careful, or unless they call an able interim minister. However, I will spare you from the explanation of why the process takes so long.

Anyway, half a year before I graduated from seminary, Nancy and George Knight happened to be in Bayfield for a few months at the time the previous pastor, Dean Johnson, accepted a call to another congregation. George preached for the Bayfield congregation for a number of Sundays, and it was during that time that their search committee was formed. They asked if he knew of any students who might be interested in coming to Bayfield. Happily, he suggested my name to them.

The committee asked me to come to meet with them although they knew I would not be available to begin for six months. If Dr. George A. F. Knight said he thought I would serve them well, his endorsement was sufficient for them. Thus, I was blessed to have a call to an excellent pastorate in a beautiful town on Lake Superior in northern Wisconsin well before I was granted my walking papers from McCormick Theological Seminary. I didn't interview with anyone else, and I was delighted to be able to end my seminary career without the anguish and anxiety of having actively to seek a pastorate. One had fallen into my lap, courtesy of George Knight.

I was ordained at my home church, Christ Presbyterian, in Madison, Wisconsin, on December 19, 1964. It seemed only proper that I asked Dr. Knight if he would preach the sermon at the ordination. I was very proud and pleased when he readily accepted.

I remember one point in particular from the sermon. In the Presbyterian tradition, if the congregation owns the home in which the minister and his or her family live, it is called the "manse." For Methodists and Lutherans it is the "parsonage," and for Roman Catholics and Episcopalians it is the "rectory." I am a verbivore; that is, I love to eat and to attempt to digest words. (Perhaps you may have noticed that.) The word "manse," said George Knight, comes from a Latin word, *mansa*, which means "table." (It is like *mesa* in Spanish.) The table in the manse, he said, is not solely for the ministerial family. It is for the whole church family, and there will be people from the congregation and community regularly coming into the manse to eat from the congregational table.

Symbolically it was as fine—and sobering—a preview of what was in store for us as Nancy and I could ever have heard. George Knight wanted us to know that our lives would not be solely our own, that in some sense, we would "belong" to every member of the Bayfield Presbyterian Church or any other congregations I might serve. As I was to learn, how very true, inevitable, and understandable that is! The ministry is, we would hope, for the inspired of heart, but it certainly is not for the faint of heart. Whether the clergy like it or not, they are potentially on call 24/7 for the rest of their lives, or at least for as long as they are pastors of churches.

I kept in touch with the Knights for the rest of their lives. When they left for Fiji and the Theological College of the Pacific, we took their West Highlands terrier, Garry (named after the Scots river). Garry was not to be allowed into Fiji.

I attended a conference in Edinburgh several years later, after George had retired and he and Nancy had moved to the village of Kirriemuir north of Edinburgh in the Scottish Highlands. I drove to see them, and they were happy with their retirement although they discovered to their sorrow that they were not thrilled with Kirriemuir. Maybe it illustrated that you really can't go home again. The town, which was the birthplace of author James Barrie of *Peter Pan* fame, was too conservative and inflexible for Nancy and George. Shrinking violets about such things they weren't.

They decided to move to Dunedin, New Zealand, instead, where George had taught Old Testament at the faculty of divinity years before. They were very happy as retired Kiwis, and George was elected the moderator of the General Assembly of the Presbyterian Church of New Zealand. Nancy preceded George in death in Dunedin. Their daughter, Ann, had moved to Dunedin and had taken a position at the university. It was providential for George that she moved there. The last time I saw George was when two other couples and Nancy and I visited New Zealand in 1996. He was then in his nineties, and was mentally as sharp as ever. He took us on a tour of the city and its environs, which all six of us remember with great fondness.

George and Nancy Knight were extremely well suited to one another as a couple. He always seemed somewhat more sophisticated than her, but it may have been because he had had an outstanding university and theological education. And she had not attended any college anywhere, if memory serves me correctly.

But what Nancy Knight may have lacked in book learning, she more than made up for in the education which life alone can teach all of us. She was a shrewd judge of character, and she did not suffer fools gladly. He was perhaps more diplomatic than she with boors and bores, and she never feared to call spades *spades*. She clearly loved her husband, even if she didn't always agree with him, and she let him know it—on innumerable occasions. She was a wonderfully supportive spouse for him in his various positions as professor, pastor, and ecclesiastical official. Their *mansa* (table) was always set for any extra guests who might show up at the last minute, and they were outstanding hosts to people from all over the world for all of the many decades of their marriage.

In his heyday, George Knight was one of the most widely recognized and acclaimed Christian Old Testament scholars in the world. However, they never stayed in any one location long enough to have a profound effect on a single theological institution. It is possible because George locked horns with other faculty members. I don't know that, but I wouldn't be surprised. Perhaps his most lasting contribution to world Christianity came through his last position as the principal of the Theological College of the Pacific, which began its influence in the South Pacific under his leadership.

In any case, George and Nancy Knight had a profound effect on me, for which I shall always be grateful. They were not flawless personalities, but they both were faithful and devoted proponents of the Christian Gospel. Their strength of both personality and opinions has been incorporated into who I am and what I believe. As they say in Scotland, Lang may their lum reek! (It literally means, "Long may their chimney smoke," but it means ever so much more than that. For me, it means their memory shall live in me as long as my chimney continues to smoke.)

Saints George and Mary Cameron

George Knight was instrumental in my going to Glasgow University for my middler year of seminary, and *George Cameron* was instrumental in making that such a fruitful and memorable year. Of all the twenty years I spent in my formal education, the year in Scotland was by far the happiest and most fulfilling.

George Cameron's paternal grandfather was a minister in the Church of Scotland as was his father and his son. They all were named George Gordon Cameron. But in order to differentiate one from another, they altered their given names from one generation to the next. Thus, his grandfather was George, his father was Gordon, George was George, and his son was Don. The Camerons and ministry, at least among those particular Camerons, were inextricably bound together.

"My" George became a widely known and admired Scots pastor. He received his theological education at the University of Aberdeen and also his undergraduate education as well, I believe. He decided to go to America to get a master's degree in theology from Union Theological Seminary in New York City. While there, he met and soon after married his wife, *Mary*, who was an American. Mary was at Union to receive a master's degree in Christian education.

From my viewpoint as an outsider, I would observe that Mary and George Cameron—for their own purposes—were not at all well fitted to one another. For the purposes of the world, however, their mismatch resulted in multifold external blessings all around them. They did not appear to spend great gobs of time with another, and both seemed quite content with that spoken or unspoken arrangement.

Both Mary and George were unusually gifted in many ways. George was a natural-born technological genius. If he had been born in America sixty years after he was actually born, and if he had not become a minister, he might have been another Steve Jobs, Steve Wozniak, Larry Ellison, or Mark Zuckerberg. Before World War II, he assembled a working television set from scratch, even before there were television stations. He loved to tinker with and make improvements in the sound system of the Glenburn Church. When my wife, Lois, and I were there a few years ago, one of the elders (who had been an elder fifty years earlier when I was a student pastor) said they still were using some of the same gizmos lovingly installed by their founding parson.

George was an excellent writer and had written several books prior to coming to Glenburn. He was a very good and careful preacher, and he was a natural pastor who loved his people. And they loved him equally in return.

Mary was very intelligent. Both of them were opinionated, but no one had to guess what Mary's thoughts were. George had a way of making his ideas clearly and unmistakably known, but he did so in a gentle if also firm manner. Mary became the national presiding officer of the Church of Scotland women's organization. As such, she traveled frequently throughout Scotland, and thus she and George were circumstantially separated from one another more than merely by their very separate personalities.

I have become convinced by watching many marriages that the world may somehow be providentially enriched by the relative marital poverty of certain couples. Tolstoy began *Anna Karenina* with this opening declaration: "All happy families are happy alike; each unhappy family is unhappy in their own way." I would never say that Mary and George Cameron were unhappy because they weren't. Nor were they really unhappy with one another. But they were so different from one another in personality that they were happy to go their own ways for much of their married life. Togetherness may have been impossible for them; separateness seemed to suit them very well.

The Camerons were the Bickersons before there were Bickersons. The comedy team of Frances Langford and Don Ameche created much madcap hilarity each week on a radio show in the `40s and `50s. Blanche and John Bickerson could not agree on anything and said so in countless colorful ways. Mary and George Cameron were like that, not only in private, but also often in public. If Mary disagreed with something George said in church, she might let him and everyone else know it. She didn't challenge him when he was preaching, fortunately; but otherwise, it was Katy bar the door. He would exhibit controlled displeasure whenever she took him on, but he would never become visibly or truly angry. Miffed, maybe, but not actually angry. Everyone in the Glenburn Parish Church understood that he was George, she was Mary, and ne'er, or at least not often, might the twain meet.

The Camerons were also one of literally many scores of couples I have known through the years who remained together when to all outward observers it would appear it was a very difficult and perhaps even painful decision for them to stay together. But many years before they had stood before a minister (perhaps George's father) and had made vows to one another and before God, and they intended to remain committed to one another "as long as they both shall live." And they did.

There is something powerfully impressive about that. So many married people seem so poorly meshed that we wonder how or why they stick it out, but they do. For some, it is for financial reasons, and that is certainly understandable. For others, it is that they are terrified of being alone, and so they hang in there. For others still, they may internally realize they would be very hard for anyone else to live with, and so they may as well continue to live with the person who has put up with them for lo these many years. For yet others, the decision to stay committed, as hard as it is, is based on those vows, vows they admirably believe they must not break.

There also is something powerfully sad about that. Is it worth the pain and heartache which is inevitable if an irreparably damaged relationship continues? Or would it be better for everyone involved— their wider family, their children, their grandchildren, their friends, and themselves—if they tossed in the marital sponge and declared, "It was great fun, but it was just one of those things?" The only answers to these questions are excruciatingly hard answers. There are no easy answers about marital discord. In the case of George and Mary Cameron, they dealt with their differences in such a way that the differences greatly benefited everyone around them, even if they themselves appeared to be advantaged little, if any.

George was the pastor of a large and influential congregation in Dundee, Scotland, when he decided to accept a request from the Church of Scotland Church Extension Board to become the founding pastor of a new congregation in a new housing development in Paisley, an industrial city just outside Glasgow. Paisley was made famous by the "Paisley print," a certain kind of fabric with colorful patterns woven into it by the textile mills of Paisley.

Most people were probably unaware of the sacrifice made by George Cameron in going to Paisley. He could have stayed in Dundee for the remainder of his ministry. He was greatly admired there, he was the minister of a strong and historic church, and he could have rested on his laurels—of which there were many upon which to rest. But he wanted to make a difference in a new residential development in an old Scottish city, and so he went to Glenburn, arriving there a few years before Nancy and I came in 1962.

There were several different kinds of Presbyterian denominations in Scotland half a century ago, as there still are today. The differences are historical, theological, ecclesiastical, and cultural in nature and do not need to be explained further. Besides, it might dismay you too much. Suffice it is to say that the Church of Scotland was and is the largest denomination in the Scots Presbyterian family, and it would widely be recognized that George Cameron was a large frog in a large pond before going to Glenburn. There, he soon became a large frog in a considerably smaller and newer pond.

Scottish churches, whether large or small, were organized very differently from American churches; and again, that was true both back then as it is now. But particularly back then, ministers in smaller congregations were involved personally in almost every facet of church life. There were no fulltime secretaries, janitors, financial experts, musicians, Christian educators, outreach specialists, or the like. At best, there were a few very part-time people in some but not all of those positions.

Almost none of even the largest congregations had more than one minister. Probably the main reason for this pattern of ecclesiastical operation is that Scotland in the `60s was still a relatively poor country, and churches could not afford to pay multiple clergy. Scotland had been bombed by the Germans during the war, and it and its economy had certainly not quickly rebounded from the pounding. People did not have much money, which meant they didn't have much money to contribute to their church, which meant their church couldn't organize itself with droves of professional people on the church staff. I was aghast to learn that Warren Miller's son and his wife were among the highest five contributors to the Glenburn Parish Church. A *student* minister and his poorly paid kindergarten-teacher-wife! The Scots have always had a national reputation for being thrifty, but that sobering fact seemed incomprehensible to me.

I tell you all this to say that George Cameron had left a pastorate where he had far more perks—such as a paid staff, even if few or none were fulltime church employees—than he was ever going to have in Glenburn. Yet he did it without hesitation, because both he and Mary believed it is what God wanted them to do. Knowing this, the Glenburn folk loved them both all the more, as oddly-suited to one another as they were.

In semi-retirement, George left the Glenburn Church and went to become the associate minister of St. Columba's Pont Street Church of Scotland in the Knightsbridge section of London. There, he and his longtime friend, Fraser McLuskey, ministered to one of the wealthiest, most influential, and highly attended congregations in all of Great Britain. While there, he wrote a history of St. Columba's.

Nancy and I visited the Camerons in London, and I had the high honor of preaching from that historic pulpit.

Even then, it was evident that some sort of dementia was beginning to affect Mary. She forgot things she should have remembered, and she repeated herself frequently. Perhaps she had Alzheimer's disease before it was widely recognized as such. George survived her, but not for very many years.

They were an extraordinarily able, talented, devoted couple; both of whom in their own unique ways were deeply committed to the mission of the Church of Jesus Christ. Pure gold they both were in multitudes of manners, but a perfectly matched set they weren't. You don't see many couples like that anymore because many simply give up in sorrow or anger. The world is poorer because of it.

St. Ian Henderson and St. William Barclay

In the early 1960s, there were only four universities in Scotland. They were St. Andrews (the oldest Scots university, made famous for Americans because it is where William and Kate met and from which they graduated), Glasgow, Edinburgh, and Aberdeen. Each of the four also had a faculty of divinity, who trained clergy either for the Church of Scotland or for other denominations in Britain or elsewhere in the world.

Up until the '60s, most of the professors in these divinity schools did not have PhDs or ThDs. Instead, they were parish ministers who had spent years studying a particular subject and had become expert in it. Because their scholarship was widely recognized, they were invited to join the faculties of divinity at the four universities to become professors there. In the present day, I presume almost all Scottish faculty members in the four faculties of divinity now have doctorates as is true nearly everywhere else in the world.

Technically, the divinity graduates of Glasgow University received their divinity degrees from Trinity College. Trinity College had originally been a Church of Scotland divinity school which officially became part of the university, even though it was located in its own building about a mile across Kelvin Park from the main campus of the university. Apparently, it had been the pattern for years or even generations that the divinity students had their systematic theology classes early in the morning at the university, and then they would schlep over to Trinity College for church history, Greek and Hebrew, Old and New Testament courses, and practical theology, finishing up there late in the afternoon.

Ian Henderson taught systematic theology. Systematic theology has always been to me what pole vaulting would be to Danny DeVito, which is to say, almost impossibly difficult. I understand why theologians attempt to systematize their thinking and why one thing is supposed to lead into another thing and that into another and that one to yet another—to the last syllable of recorded time. Unfortunately, my mind is shamefully unsystematized, and it has always been very hard for me to slog through the slough of systematic theological despond.

Professor Henderson probably did not use the teaching methods of most other systematic theologians, or so I would suspect. Instead of giving us reams of rigorous readings from some of the then contemporary giants of theology or the great historical theological gurus, he would assign short readings from certain scholars, and then, he would pass out a few mimeographed pages about certain people or subjects and ask us to come to class prepared to discuss these readings. He could miraculously exalt every valley by what he told us and also make the very rough places a plain. He was a regular pedagogical marvel, at least as far as I was concerned.

Ian Henderson seemed to be an unusually reserved man, even a shy man. I discovered within a short time of arriving in Glasgow why that may have been so, if indeed it was so. Years before, a student at Trinity College had been accused of an impropriety. Whether it was academic, personal, or moral I never learned, and no two stories about this incident were the same, nor did they seem to be hard evidence of anything.

The faculty wanted to expel the student for whatever was the alleged infraction. Professor Henderson had come to the defense of the young man. His support created a major rift among the faculty, apparently, and when the student was expelled, it created a rift between my hero, Ian, and nearly everyone else. From that time on, he kept to himself. But all this I learned only second- and third-hand.

Could it be that a man who had experienced deep personal pain because he stood up for one of his students in a very dicey situation was able to explain the confusing conundrums of "the queen of the sciences," which certain folks—mainly theologians I would guess—call theology? Does someone who graduates from the School of Hard Knocks, both in the parish and then in a faculty of divinity, have a leg up on others for describing what the Creator of the world is doing among us? Did the life experience of Ian Henderson better suit him for making theology real to a group of young men (in those days we were all *men*) sitting in the raised rows of seats rising up from the platform from which he spoke in the ubiquitous black academic gown which he and all the other faculty wore when they taught?

Professor Henderson died a very few years after I returned to Chicago from Glasgow. He was smoker, and that may have contributed to his demise. However, anyone who breathed the coal-induced pollution of the air of the Scottish Lowlands during those bygone years was flirting with diseases hideous and unimaginable anyway. Were not the Scots such a hardy race, none would have lived past the mid-twentieth century. The thick and gooey atmosphere would have killed them all.

I wish I had had the chance to know Ian Henderson better. I wish I knew what that faculty brouhaha was really about. I wish he had not died when he seemed to be in his prime, not at all like the prime of Miss Jean Brodie, but the prime of Professor Ian Henderson. But it was not to be.

All of us have people with whom our minds have meshed in an uncanny fashion. It was that way for me with Ian Henderson. I thought him to be quintessentially what the Scots would call "a lovely man," and I loved him for being who he was. Was he a great scholar? Perhaps not in the estimation of many of his fellow theologians, but in my mind, he was a giant. He was *my* giant, and that was more than enough.

And then there was *William Barclay*. In the 1960s, Willie Barclay was probably the best-known New Testament scholar among Christian laity in the Mainline Protestant English-speaking world. By then, he had published an entire set of very thorough commentaries on each of the books of the New Testament. I have used these commentaries for fifty years of preaching, and they are immensely helpful.

He had a weekly program on BBC television, he was in great vogue as a preacher and lecturer all over Scotland and Great Britain, and he evoked a warm reverence among ordinary church folk everywhere he went. Many professional New Testament authorities considered Willie to be nothing more than a popularizer, as though popularity and serious scholarship are and by right always ought to be bitter enemies to one another. But no one opened the New Testament to the depths of the Greek scriptures more effectively than William Barclay of Trinity College of Glasgow University, where he was universally known to all the students merely as "Willie."

It is one of the great regrets of my life that I was not able to take any of his classes in New Testament. In order to do so, one had to have attained a certain level of knowledge of biblical Greek. Most of the Trinity men had taken Greek as undergraduates. I had not, nor had I taken it during my freshman year at McCormick. In retrospect, I should have lobbied to sit in on his classes as an unlearned auditor, but alas, the thought never even occurred to me at the time. In fact, I only thought about it when I was writing this sub-chapter of this chapter. I was so crushed by being excluded from his sacred subject that I didn't think to try to wangle my way in over whatever objections kept folks like me out.

I *did* take a noncredit course in Greek at Trinity, however. It was taught by a retired Church of Scotland pastor, who, like nearly everyone at the time, had become proficient in his chosen subject through his own lengthy study. He was a sweet little old guy (and "sweet" is not a word I would normally use for anyone of the male persuasion, but he really was sweet). Nevertheless, he also suffered from what universally was described in those times as "senility," and as often as not, he forgot to come to class. We crowd of Greek nincompoop neophytes would wait for fifteen minutes or so, and then we trail off to the library, to engage in other academic pursuits.

Nevertheless, on the basis of that thinnest introduction to the Greek used in the New Testament, which would be utterly incomprehensible to anyone now living in Greece, I wrote an exegesis of the first eleven verses of the fourth chapter of Matthew, the so-called temptation of Jesus. Broadly speaking, a biblical exegesis is a kind of academic summary of the linguistic ins and outs of a biblical passage, with some conclusions as to what the verses really mean, and why.

I gave my exegesis to Willie Barclay to be graded. If it passed muster with him, the dean at McCormick Seminary told me I would be excused from taking Greek when I returned to Chicago. If I ever had been overcome by enthusiasm for the privilege of studying yet another foreign language (by then, I had already studied four others), it was obliterated by that cheerful news. Willie gave me an "Alpha-minus," over which I did many cartwheels and emitted several spontaneous exclamations. The powers-that-be at McCormick apparently thought that as a result of my paper, I must know Greek. They were wrong. I don't. It's still Greek to me. Nevertheless, via the largesse of Willie Barclay and that splendid little senile Scotsman whose name I don't recall, I was relieved of the unique pleasure of studying Koine Greek in exquisite detail. Well, not everyone gets everything he deserves in life, and I have never regretted the McCormick administration's decision. Besides, I did use Willie's commentaries religiously ever after.

Although I missed out on the rare opportunity of studying the intricacies of the Greek scriptures with Willie, I did have the great pleasure of singing in the Trinity College Choir under his direction. Thereby hangs a tale in itself. Dr. Barclay was almost as deaf as a proverbial post. Furthermore, whenever he lectured, I was told he would take out his hearing aids, turn them off, and then rip into his lecture, going rapid-fire through chapter and verse, allowing for no interruptions. When he was finished with what he wanted to say, he would put his hearing aids back into his outsized ears and allow his students to holler questions at him. This I know, not because I saw it happen, because I was alas prevented from seeing it happen, but because his students loved to regale the rest of us what it was like in Willie's lectures.

As the director of the Trinity College Choir, Willie had to be able to hear us, and that he managed to do, I guess. He had a voice as gravelly as a cement mixer which had only moments before had its prescribed load of gravel, lime, and whatever else thrust into its open mouth. He could sing, passably, but he was vocally destined never to make it to the Met or La Scala.

What he lacked in pure musical talent or knowledge, however, he more than made up for in enthusiasm. He loved music, and his choices of pieces for us to sing were wonderful. Willie mixed in old standard anthems, Scots folk music, songs made famous by the immortal Robert Burns, and familiar English-language songs from around the world, including the USA. We had performances in church halls and municipal facilities throughout the West of Scotland. It was a distinct honor to sing under the guidance of St. Willie Barclay.

Dr. Barclay apparently had an addiction to Scotland's most famous liquid export. I never observed that, nor, I think, did I ever hear it from anyone. But in a lengthy and excellent biography of the great man, I read that it was a factor which plagued him throughout much of his adult life. If it is true, it certainly did not hamper either his scholarship or the unparalleled level of his rich humanity. He was a magnificent scholar, minister, expositor of scripture, and human being. He had a way, both in speaking and writing, of saying things that from other people might evoke enormous controversies; but in him, it came across as reasoned and reasonable Christian observation. And almost no one ever challenged him to his face.

As with Ian Henderson, I wish I could have known Willie Barclay better or seen more of him or had the opportunity to be more exposed to his wit and wisdom. But I consider myself exceedingly blessed to have had even that brief and relatively distant relationship to a great and good soul in whom the light of God shown with uniquely bright and beneficial radiance.

Saints Al and Ruth Kalkbrenner

My best friend in seminary was eighteen years older than I. I don't know whether that says something about me, or something about *Al Kalkbrenner*, or something about both of us, but it was a fact.

We were best of buds. That may have been because we figured we were the only two people in the entire McCormick Seminary faculty and student body who voted for Barry Goldwater in 1964. Certainly, there must have been others, but if so, we never discovered who they were; and they insisted on keeping their affiliation a secret, which, given the tenor of the times, probably was wise. Over half a century later, I have evolved into anything but a conservative Republican. Coke would be rolling over in his grave over how I turned out. But then, I prefer to think he would be very uneasy over that into which the Grand Old Party has evolved. Politics, thy name is woe, man!

Al Kalkbrenner had the nickname of Coke, and he was known as Coke to practically everyone, except perhaps some of the professors. Coke and his wife, *Ruth*—who was called Shep by Coke because her maiden name was Shepherd, and therefore, I also called her Shep—were from Cincinnati, where they both had grown up. Coke had fought in combat in World War II in the infantry. He and Ruth were married either during or after the war. They remained in Cincinnati, where Coke established a very successful and lucrative general insurance agency.

The Kalkbrenners were members of a vibrant Presbyterian church in Cincinnati with an outstanding pastor. Somehow, he inspired Coke to go into the ministry. It was a wise, if also a very challenging, inspiration, as it turned out.

Nowadays, it is not at all uncommon to have students in their forties or even fifties enroll in seminary. In those days, it was fairly rare. Furthermore, for Coke it represented a huge sacrifice. He and Shep gave up a very comfortable lifestyle to live with their two teenage daughters in a relatively cramped apartment on a seminary campus in a busy commercial-residential urban neighborhood in Chicago. All four of the Kalkbrenners engendered a kind of life they had never envisioned for themselves. But they all gave it the old college try, and somehow, with God's grace, it worked out for them. But they all deserved special praise for their fortitude in sticking it through to graduation.

Coke had every conceivable gift necessary to be an outstanding pastor, save two. The first deficiency was that preparing and preaching sermons was absolutely torture for him. In our homiletics (preaching) class, he was in agony trying to collect his thoughts to go before his classmates and the professor, and he was always on the verge of great gastrointestinal eruptions over the thought of having to preach the Word of God before people whom he considered much more able than himself in the pulpit. It was painful for me to observe his torture, but my unease was child's play compared to his.

The second deficiency, however, was of much more consequence. Coke received a degree in business administration from Miami University of Ohio. He spoke like a businessman, he thought like a businessman, and he reasoned like a businessman. He could easily manage what a business degree required of him. But when he became a seminarian, his mind turned into academic sludge. Learning Hebrew from George Knight and Ted Campbell nearly killed the poor guy. It was bad enough that the ancient Hebrews were sufficiently uncaring that they did not speak English, but it was an added severe cruelty that they did not have a proper Roman-type alphabet like every reasonable earthly humanoid should employ. As for systematic theology, church history, and the rest of the seminary curriculum, nearly all of it was Greek to Coke.

Ruth and I became the two-on-one team who ganged up on Coke within the first week of starting classes until he graduated. Whenever he became depressed or morose, which was very often, we would do our best to remind him that his sole goal in seminary was to get to the finish line. He should put the trials of the moment out of his mind. The closer he got to the finish line, however, the harder it became for him. Perhaps it was the accumulation of academic accretion which weighed him down. The academic part of seminary was excruciating, but the interpersonal relationships, with either students or faculty, were his stock-in-trade. The old bit of doggerel declares that no one has endurance like a man who sells insurance. Well, Coke had enormous endurance, and he luxuriated in being with everyone in the seminary community. But he was sorely lacking in academic aptitude. In short, he loved the people; he detested the books.

Normally, I would say that such a person probably should not contemplate the ministry. One need not be a mental giant or a walking theological encyclopedia to be an effective minister, but a certain level of academic acumen would seem to be a necessity. Al Kalkbrenner is the one exception I have known to that general rule. I knew he would be a great success in the pastorate if he were just able to get the required number of credits to graduate with an ecclesiastically required bachelor of divinity degree.

Every now and then, Shep would call me and say, "John, the old boy needs your help. I've done all I can do." So I would go to their apartment, he and I would have coffee, and I would buck him up as best as I could. Both Shep and I never doubted that Coke would be an excellent pastor once he passed the ordination examination of his presbytery. They knew him and loved him, and they also believed in his ability to fulfill his pastoral obligations, despite his limitations in the classroom.

While we were in seminary, a book was published by Joseph Fletcher called *Situation Ethics*. There is much more to the book than this, but here, as I recall, was its essence: The ethic of love demands that various situations by their unique circumstances determine what Christians ethically ought to do. Although the Bible provides guidelines through the commandments and the teachings of Jesus, said Joseph Fletcher, it is each situation in and of itself which propels us to do what we ought to do.

On the basis of the Fletcherian ethic, which gained much currency when *Situation Ethics* was first published, I violated what most people, especially most Christians, would consider a serious ethical principle. One late winter afternoon in our senior year, I happened to see Coke outside the library on my way home. He was utterly distraught, and he was again threatening to leave the seminary and go back to Cincinnati with his family. But this time it seemed a dead certainty. I asked what the particular problem was. He said that he had to write a paper for one of his courses, and he resolutely declared he was simply incapable of doing it. And it had to be submitted in a couple of days.

I asked Coke what the assigned topic was and how long the paper was supposed to be. He told me the answers to both questions. Fortunately, I knew something about his topic, and I even liked it. So I told him I would write his paper for him, but only on one condition: He had to promise me he would stick it out till the end of the year, come hell or high water. Very reluctantly, he agreed, but I didn't know if he would be able to maintain his resolution. He didn't display relief, nor could he at that moment feel either gratitude or relief. He looked instead like a man who had put his finger into an empty light bulb socket with the switch turned on, and he was so overcome by the trauma he didn't know how to pull his finger out. Coke being Coke, there was considerable hell and high water yet to engulf him in his final semester, but somehow he managed to endure it to the bitter end. When he graduated, he did not feel elated. Rather, he felt like a man who had been paroled after forty years in prison.

If I had it to do all over again, would I write every word of a paper for Al Kalkbrenner, trying to guess how he rather than I would write it, let him sign it, submit it, and get his required C in the course? In a heartbeat I would. I believed in Coke. He was a stellar human being who, with his family, had sacrificed nearly everything near and dear to him in order to become "a Minister of Word and Sacrament."

It wasn't difficult for me to write the paper. In fact, I felt a certain sense of situational satisfaction in doing it. I'm not proud of it, but I confess I'm not ashamed either. As the old spiritual says, "If I can help somebody along the way, then my living will not be in vain." One day I will stand before the Supreme Judge of such actions, and I will discover whether Fletcher or Miller will pass muster in the great day of reckoning, whenever and wherever it occurs.

It surely felt to Al Kalkbrenner that he had spent a thousand years in hell to graduate in four years from seminary, whereas it took most students three years to do it. But when he finally matriculated into the life of ministry in Christ's Church, Coke, despite his anemic academic record and his debilitating terrors of the pulpit, was called to the largest congregation of all the graduates in the Class of 1965. The people on the pastoral nominating committee which recommended him to the membership of the Petoskey Presbyterian Church in northern Michigan knew that he had both the qualities and the qualifications they were looking for in their new pastor. Petoskey is a beautiful resort town on Little Traverse Bay on the east side of Lake Michigan in the northwestern corner of the Lower Peninsula.

The Petoskey Presbyterians loved their forty-four-year-old brand new seminary graduate. He became the pastor extraordinaire I was certain he would be, and he had all the administrative skills necessary from his years in the insurance business to guide a vibrant congregation in a delightful community. Nancy and I went to visit the Kalkbrenners a couple of times during Coke's years there as pastor. Ruth became a wonderful pastor's wife, as we knew she would, and the girls, Debbie and Jane, adjusted readily to being PKs (preacher's kids) even if they started the process much later in life than most other PKs.

Coke still labored mightily over his preaching. He burned the midnight oil countless times on Saturday nights when he had been unable to come up with any sermonic thoughts earlier in the week which met with his satisfaction. But because Coke was Coke, whatever he said satisfied his congregation. There is an ancient story which I suspect has been told in homiletics classes since Martin Luther was in knee pants. There was a congregation which had had a beloved pastor for over thirty years. His name, we shall decree, was John Smith. To outsiders, John Smith was a dreadful preacher, but to his people he was Henry Ward Beecher or Harry Emerson Fosdick. Because they admired him so much, they were blissfully unaware of his homiletic shortcomings. One Sunday, when he was going to be away, he asked a pulpit luminary of national renown to fill in for him. The visiting preacher was so famous that many folks from other congregations came to hear him that morning. Afterward, as they filed out of the church, some of the visitors asked the members of the church what they thought of the guest preacher. "Oh, he's all right—but he's certainly not our John Smith!"

Henry Ward Beecher and Harry Emerson Fosdick held court in Petoskey, Michigan, for over eight years. It happened that by 1973, I had become the pastor of the Presbyterian Church in Morristown, New Jersey. The congregation had had an outstanding minister of pastoral care for several years. He decided to retire not because I came, I trust, but because he was over seventy years of age, and he had been wanting to retire for some time.

Gingerly, I called Coke and asked him if he would be willing to consider coming to Morristown as our minister of pastoral care. I thought he was going to leap physically right through the phone line; he was so excited. "Shep and I will be there tomorrow!" he said. Tomorrow was too soon, I told him; I would need to arrange a meeting with the search committee for a new minister. We worked out the details, and Al and Ruth soon came for their visit.

It isn't that Coke was tired of the Petoskey congregation because he wasn't. They were still beloved to him, and he to them. But he had become too psychologically burdened by weekly sermons, and he was eager to give up that ministerial responsibility. As much as I might have hoped it for him, he never found that preaching got any easier than when he first faced the panic evoked by his initial foray into the pulpit in preaching class. He was always an exemplary pastor but an exhausted preacher.

By that point in Coke's life (he was in his mid-fifties), he had been battling diabetes for over thirty years. He had always kept it under control through daily self-injections of insulin. When driving to New Jersey, Coke noticed that he was having some new problems with his vision. He didn't think too much about it, and Ruth and he had a pleasant and exhilarating visit with the search committee for a new minister of pastoral care. The Kalkbrenners seemed very pleased with Morristown and its Presbyterian Church. Ruth especially thought it would give Coke a new lease on life not to have to preach every Sunday. I suggested that they share their honest impressions with one another on the way home and that I would call in a few days to see what they had decided. I secretly assumed the committee would agree to extend a call to Coke, which in fact they happily did after only a short discussion. Nancy and I believed it would be an excellent situation for everyone involved were the Kalkbrenners to come to Morristown.

Before I phoned Coke and Shep, however, they called me. Driving back to Michigan, Coke's vision declined so much and so precipitously that he couldn't even take the wheel. He made an appointment with his doctor the day they returned. As a result of that visit, he was told that within months he would be blind.

To say the least, this was an eventuality on which none of us had given even a remote thought. Thinking out loud over the phone, I told both Coke and Shep that we could make arrangements to have volunteers to drive Coke on his pastoral calls. I truly meant it, and was certain we could organize it. He was an outstanding pastor, and he would be worth the additional effort needed to enable us to make use of his great skills. Without discussing it further though, both Coke and Shep declined the offer but with genuine and heartfelt gratitude.

In less than a year, Albert H. Kalkbrenner Jr. was dead as a result of complications from diabetes. Only a couple of years after that, Ruth Kalkbrenner was dead from cancer.

The communion of saints feels like a very straitened and sober reality in the face of such devastating events. Al and Ruth Kalkbrenner were marvelous human beings. They were remarkably effective servants of the Church of Jesus Christ—both in their many years as lay members before Coke went to seminary and, afterward, when together they admirably served the Petoskey Presbyterian Church. He was a pastor's pastor, and she was a ball of fire as a minister's spouse. They were both lovely people as were their daughters. To my knowledge, neither Debbie nor Jane ever held it against their father that he uprooted them from the familiarity of their young lives in Cincinnati to go into an unknown and perhaps frightening future in Chicago and then only God would knew where after that.

The communion of saints holds out inexhaustible benefits, but it also can involve longstanding unremitting pain. It is often agonizing to remember in detail those we have loved on this earth who are no longer here for us to love.

Nevertheless, if there is any validity to the concept of the communion of saints, it is of immense comfort to believe that we shall see one another again. Surely, it can't be in the persons we were "back then," whenever back then was, but it will be in the eternal "person" and personality each of us shall have. I firmly believe we will recognize one another, but not as we have been in this world, if only because a physical carcass will be of no use on "the other side." We who shall be complete neophytes in death when we first awaken to life eternal should assume the folks who have been "over there" for years or centuries or millennia will be aware of a thing or three which will completely baffle us at first, even though "years, centuries, or millennia" or "at first" have no meaning whatsoever in eternity.

Anyway, I look forward to seeing Al and Ruth Kalkbrenner and everyone in this book "in the spirit," whatever "in the spirit" shall mean, and we won't know till we are "in the spirit."

Saints Paul and Joyce Arnstrom

According to my parents, compared to my brothers, I was old when I was born. Instead of a birthday suit, they claimed that when I emerged from the birth canal, I was wearing a blue oxford cloth button-down-collar dress shirt (although *sans* tie), khaki dress pants, and cordovan wing-tip shoes. My mother strongly objected to those shoes.

Perhaps because of my advanced age at birth, for some reason I gravitated toward more close friendships among the older students in my seminary classes than among those of my actuarial age cohort. *Paul Arnstrom* was the oldest student in our incoming class. He was forty-seven when he started, so he was fifty when he graduated. As I said earlier, for the past twenty or twenty-five years, age is not unusual for people going to seminary; but back in the `60s, it was certainly extraordinary. By virtue of his longevity, Paul was almost the Ancient of Days.

Paul had gone to college when he graduated from high school, but instead of going into business or teaching or some other profession, he became a farmer, following in the footsteps of his father. He had a very fertile and productive farm about thirty miles south of Chicago. If a farmer is properly described as a man outstanding in his field, Paul was an outstanding farmer. He also was an exemplary human being.

Paul's wife, *Joyce*, was a very fine, low-key lady. She was more quiet and reserved than her husband. They had been married for a quarter of a century by the time they arrived at McCormick, but they had no children. Then, lo, and furthermore behold, Joyce became pregnant. This geriatric obstetrical anomaly became the buzz of the entire campus. Since Joyce was about Paul's age, they and everyone else on campus considered they were Abraham and Sarah all over again. We all awaited the Big Day with almost as much anticipation as they did.

Not only was Joyce great with child as it says in the Christmas story in the King James Version, but it turned out she was great with two babies—twin girls, we learned, when the birth occurred. What joy there was for all of us when the babies were born! But then, also what sorrow there was when in a few days, one of the babies died. However, Lisa Joy survived, and she absolutely transformed the lives of her relatively elderly parents with countless blessings. They who had realistically come to accept the fact that they would be a childless couple at last had a daughter to raise.

No doubt, many new parents in exactly the same circumstances would have thought God had been cruel to them in the loss of one of their daughters, but not Paul and Joyce. Without question, they mourned the death of their one child, but they found a theretofore unanticipated immense happiness is their other child. Supposing that they never would be parents at all, now they *were* parents and that they perceived that to be an enormous blessing. As sad as they were for their loss, they were happier still for their great gain in having Lisa Joy in their lives.

There is no requirement, divine or otherwise, which demands that the saints of God must act with grace and gratitude in all situations, but the Arnstroms were the epitome of both virtues in the aftermath of their daughter's death. As the Psalmist proclaimed, "Weeping may tarry for the night, but joy comes in the morning."

The birth of those two tiny babies and the survival of one of them brought unbounded joy into the lives of the oldest geezer in the Class of '64 and his equally elderly spouse.

Joyce and Paul were very sensible if also doting parents to Lisa. When Paul graduated, the Arnstroms Three moved to Gobles, Michigan, where he had received a call to become the pastor of the Gobles Presbyterian Church. He remained there for his entire ministry. We who knew and loved him from the old days always referred to him in the latter days as the Bishop of Gobles, and such he was.

Paul and Joyce Arnstrom were temperamentally very well suited to be the husband-wife team for a parish ministry in a small Michigan town. I presume their hometown of Peotone, Illinois, was similar to Gobles, and both of them would have fit into the life of their church with natural and winsome ease. I never visited the Arnstroms in Gobles, but I have often thought of them and what their lives must have been like. In all my conversations and communications with Paul during his pastorate and after his retirement, he always referred to that lengthy chapter of their existence with pleasure, pride, and deep satisfaction.

The last time I saw Paul was at the thirtieth or thirty-fifth anniversary of our graduation from McCormick. Joyce had died by then. When they retired, they moved back to the farm, south of Chicago. He told me that there was talk of building a third airport for Chicago, and one of the proposed sites was a large plot of land in the middle of which his farm was located. If the decision had been made to establish the new airport there, Paul was going to give the land to McCormick Seminary so that they could benefit from the sale. But alas for both Paul and McCormick Seminary, it did not happen.

Though Paul was the oldest member of our seminary class, he always thought young. He had a nimble and inquisitive mind, and his inner native intelligence always shown through in everything he said. He was a natural optimist. While there were factors about the Presbyterian Church, indeed about *The* Church of Jesus Christ, which did not always thrill him, he was nevertheless always supportive of the Church and its mission.

His language could be occasionally a tad salty, but he used expressions to skirt any improprieties which might be off-putting to people, particularly to ladies. When the cold rains of November swept into the Windy City, for instance, he would loudly declare, "It's damp wet!" And damp wet it was. He was fundamentally a cheerful soul, who never lost his cheerful demeanor as the years went on. In good times and bad, Paul was always Paul, and that was good.

When he arrived on campus in September of 1961, Paul Arnstrom had a full head of dark hair, flecked with gray. When I saw that final time years ago, he hadn't lost a hair in his head, but the color of his plenteous wavy locks had turned to radiant silver.

All of us have a stash of saints tucked into the recesses of our memory. Paul and Joyce Arnstrom will forever stand out in my stash.

SAINTS OF BAYFIELD, WISCONSIN

ALTHOUGH I GREW up in Wisconsin, I had never been to the small town of Bayfield, which is where I was called to serve as pastor of the Bayfield Presbyterian Church. Bayfield is three or four miles south of the northernmost point in Wisconsin. When I met with the pastoral nominating committee, I was greatly impressed by the people. They were salt-of-the-earth folks who exhibited excellent values in all things. Like stereotypical Midwesterners, they neither put on airs, nor did they gild the lily either about Bayfield or its Presbyterian church. Nonetheless, their pride in their congregation and community shone through brightly in the interview process, and I was immediately drawn to them and to their church.

Bayfield itself was also a magnetic attraction. It originally was a lumbering town and then became a fishing port for commercial fishing boats on Lake Superior in search of whitefish, lake trout, and herring. Having grown up hunting and fishing, I thought it would be the perfect place for a beginning pastorate and a happy environment for my wife, Nancy, and our daughter, Amy, who was born a month after we moved into the Presbyterian manse. And thus, we began our communion with the many memorable saints of Bayfield.

St. Dean Johnson

Dean Johnson preceded me as pastor of the Presbyterian Church in Bayfield, Wisconsin. Dean had served in that capacity for seven or eight years before I arrived in that picturesque village on the shores of Lake Superior at the very northern tip of the Badger State.

My going from seminary to Bayfield was largely engineered by Dean and by my Professor of Old Testament at McCormick theological Seminary in Chicago. About George and Nancy Knight, you read earlier. But it is an historical and ecclesiastical fact that together, Dean Johnson and George Knight conspired to convince the pastoral nominating committee of the congregation to extend a call to me to be their minister before any of them had even met me. (In those days, such conspiracies were common. Now they are very rare, and almost always such efforts are unsuccessful. Pastoral Nominating Committees feel free to select any parson to whom, for reasons almost always indefinable and unclear, they take a liking. They assiduously avoid outside suggestions like a pandemic of swine flu, proceeding at their own normally glacial pace and in their own inexplicable process.)

However, because the members of the Bayfield pulpit committee respected their previous minister and the professorial minister who spent his summers among them, they were compliantly willing to have their arms twisted on behalf of a man who would be graduating from a properly-accredited Presbyterian theological school eight months from when we had our first and only meeting in early June of 1964. In the providence of God, I hope and trust that it all worked out well for everyone.

In the spring of 1964, George Knight asked me to meet him after a class I was taking from him on the Old Testament prophets. He said that Dean Johnson had recently left the pastorate of the church in Bayfield to become minister of the Presbyterian-Congregational Church in nearby Ashland, Wisconsin. Dean was shortly going to be visiting the Knights when he was in Chicago for a conference. Would I be willing to meet him, and would I be willing to be considered as a candidate to fill the pulpit of the Bayfield Church?

Even though I had grown up in the capital city of Madison, Wisconsin, I had never been as far north as Bayfield, so I knew absolutely nothing about the community. But I loved hunting and fishing, and I assumed, correctly as it turned out, that one could happily engage in both sports there.

If the truth is told, upon such lofty issues as hunting and fishing are pastoral calls sometimes set in motion. Parsons have all kinds of cockamamie reasons for positively considering certain churches in certain places and ruling out other churches in other places. The process is often much less spiritual and religious than most laity would ever imagine. Lay people loftily suppose that God controls the procedure from start to finish. In fact, few clergy accept invitations to go to churches in communities they presume would be a bad fit for them and their families. Therefore, because of its beautiful and beatific location, I was quite excited to hear more about Bayfield and its Presbyterian church.

On the agreed-upon day and time, Dean came to meet me at the apartment in which my wife and I lived at McCormick Seminary. Dean Johnson proved to be to initial introductions what bulls are alleged to be to china shops. He came bursting into the room as though we had been lifelong friends, scarcely giving me the opportunity to catch my breath after we introduced ourselves. Dean was one of those rare people who simply never met a stranger. He raised the term "hale-fellow-well-met" to an entirely new elevation.

Within ten minutes of listening to Dean, I decided the Bayfield Presbyterian Church was the place for me if I was the man for them. And from that moment, Dean and I became lifelong friends. He was one of the ministers I most valued as a colleague for the more than four decades that I knew him.

On innumerable occasions, previous pastors become the bane of the existence of current pastors. Never mind that current parsons can also drive previous parsons to drink; the problem is almost always perceived to be the predecessors when contemplated by the successors.

Dean Johnson was never once an impediment to me or my ministry in Bayfield. He was always helpful and supportive. Sadly, not all clergy are like that to all other clergy. But Dean was; he always was.

This is not to say we agreed on every religious or theological issue ever to come down the ecclesiastical pike. In those days, I was much more of a traditional evangelical than anyone could now accuse me of being. Dean was far more evangelical than I ever was. We seldom debated our differences. Both of us intuitively understood that we were in agreement on relatively few theological matters. Our politics were very similar, but our religious beliefs were time zones apart, especially as time went on. However, rather than air our differences, we consciously allowed them to lodge beneath the surface, realizing that silence on those issues was probably golden. Many times, that is not a wise policy; but for us, it worked. And it worked for forty years of friendship. We resolved not to let different approaches to faith drive a wedge between us.

Whenever he was able, Dean would come to the funerals of members of the Bayfield Presbyterian Church. Some clergy believe that ought never be done under any circumstances, out of respect to the new pastor. I assured Dean it was not only acceptable to me for him to attend these services, but he was also welcome to participate in the service if the family and he would like him to do so.

Having a previous pastor so close by could seem very threatening to a rookie parson. However, Dean conducted himself in such a way that not only did I not feel threatened by him, but I also always felt supported and encouraged by him. That was not a credit to me, but to him. Of all the ministers I have known throughout my life, he and I were continuous colleagues in a truly collegial sense longer than I have had any other such relationship with any other minister.

As a clergyman, Dean Johnson was pre-eminently a pastor. He loved people, and people loved him. I never heard any parishioners say a single negative word about Dean. As with everyone else, they varied in their thoughts about his personality, but they were uniformly positive about *him*.

Dean cared about people. He recalled minute details about their life stories. He could remember more about them and their families than they could remember about themselves. His God-given gift of memory was truly extraordinary.

Now, through the mists of time, I am reminded of how he used to tell me elaborate, touching, and often hilarious tales about his pastoral dealings with Bayfield folks. I was always immensely impressed with his ability to maintain in his mind a plethora of events and conversations he had had with people from many years before. The "memory button" in his mental computer was astonishing in both its breadth and depth. If every member of the clergy had the enormity of memory of Dean Johnson, we would all serve our flock much more effectively than we do. People are delighted for ministers to recall crucial events from their background, and those recollections create an enduring bond. Dean could do that with everyone he ever met; he was an overflowing fountain of personal and pastoral information.

For most of the time Dean was pastor of the Bayfield church, he was a bachelor. However, a couple happened to move to Bayfield in retirement from Eau Claire, Wisconsin. It was through the Andersons that Dean met and later married their daughter, Diane. Diane was a number of years younger than Dean, but they were very happily married for forty years. He was always the picture of eternal youth; she was the picture of mature womanhood. He was perpetually playful; she was much more reserved and retiring. But they were a marvelous Christian pair.

Their marriage was not without its trials for Diane. As outgoing and gregarious as he was, she was equally determined not to rock anyone's boat. If it is true that opposites attract, their opposite-ness proved to be a major attraction.

Dean's Aunt Irene was a member of the Bayfield Presbyterian Church. By the time I arrived there, Aunt Irene seemed to me to be only a couple of years younger than God. But not only was she old—she was irascibly old. No one was more aware of that sobering reality than her continually beleaguered nephew.

Aunt Irene did not attend church. I would not say it was because she was physically unable to do so. Rather it was because she was mentally unwilling to do so. If the truth is told, probably it was just as well. She was so congenitally ornery she likely would have constantly disrupted the People of God in Prayer. The Aunt Irenes of the Ecclesiastical Realm may well serve Christ and the Church more effectively by their absence than by their presence. They are some of the saints whom the rest of the saints wonder how they can be included among any of the saints at all.

Because she was Aunt Irene to Dean, I also called her Aunt Irene the first time I visited her in her home. I used the term with great hesitation, however. Miraculously, she seemed to appreciate the appellation. Ever after, therefore, she was also Aunt Irene to me. I quite liked the old duck, much to my mystification. Despite her irrepressibly sour nature, I got along with her surprisingly well, even though she always scared the gizzard clean out of me whenever I went to visit her.

Poor Dean never met with his aunt's approval on anything. Nothing he did for her would suit her. Perhaps she expected him to be in her constant thrall while he was the minister of *her* church. After all, she may have deduced, blood ought to be thicker than communion wine. Nevertheless, she was a relative by marriage, not by blood. Dean's uncle had long since given up the ghost, perhaps as an escape from his tart-tongued spouse. And since Dean had not measured up to her satisfaction as pastor-nephew or nephew-pastor, she would make his life as miserable as possible now that he was no longer her pastor, but still in her clutches as nephew.

Whenever Dean would come to see Aunt Irene, which was far more frequently than her behavior warranted, she would give him Holy Ned for not coming more often or for goading her by his relentless good cheer or for failing to say the proper things to a dear and delicate elderly lady. "Why can't you be nice to me?" she would demand to know. "But Aunt Irene, I *am* nice to you!" he would say. "Nice? You don't know the meaning of nice! You only live twenty-five miles away, and you drop in here once every blue moon. I can't count on you for anything."

"You never counted on anyone else for anything," Dean rightly observed, "so why take it out on me? You are the most independent person living on this planet." They probably had many conversations like that.

Indeed, Aunt Irene was unusually independent because she was determined that everyone would fail her; everyone *did* fail her, in her mind. Nobody could succeed with Aunt Irene; she would guarantee it.

A few times after his periodic forays with Aunt Irascible, Dean would drop by the manse to commiserate and lick his wounds. He had taken time out from a busy schedule to see her, and all she could do was to berate him for not coming more often and for not expressing exactly the proper thoughts when he did come. Winning with Aunt Irene was never an option. The sole issue was how badly one was going to lose.

Fortunately, no one else reacted to the ministrations of the Rev. Dean Johnson as did his aunt—and she only was an aunt by marriage, I remind you. With her, no good deed was ever permitted to go unpunished.

With other parishioners, though, Dean's pastoral attention bore much more fruit. Jenny and Henry Zier were two such folk. Both were septuagenarians. Apparently, Jenny had a past. It was alleged by some to be a past that wouldn't ever quite quit. She was maybe like the woman at the well in the Fourth Gospel, whose background I did not study when I preached my senior sermon in seminary before Elam Davies. To this female of a devilishly dubious past, Jesus said, "You have had five husbands, and the one you have now is not your husband." No one ever hinted that Jenny had actually had five husbands, but she apparently had seen a goodly gaggle of males sally swiftly or fitfully through her checkered existence. That didn't deter St. Dean, however. He treated Jenny as though she were the most virtuous woman ever to draw breath.

Somewhere along the line, Jenny had acquired Henry. It happened while Dean Johnson was the pastor of the church. They asked him to officiate at their wedding. Dean being Dean, he was happy to oblige with no hesitation whatsoever. He always did whatever he could to bring happiness into the lives of his parishioners.

A few weeks later, Dean stopped to see how Jenny and Henry were doing in their newly married state. It was about eleven o'clock in the morning. When he knocked on the door, Jenny shouted at him to come in. He called out his name, and she directed him to come into the bedroom.

There was Jenny, still lying in bed with the morning nearly gone. Next to her, pressed up against her, but completely covered up by the blankets, was the form of one whom Dean naturally presumed to be Henry. Dean asked Jenny this and that about this and that, and she said that and this. After they had conversed for fifteen minutes or more, Dean casually asked Jenny how Henry was doing in order at last to include him in the conversation. "Oh, he's right here, Dean," she said. "Come on out, Henry, and say hello to the minister." With that, two beady eyes encased in a very bald head poked out from under the covers. "Hullo, Dean," said Henry, who acted as though only in that moment had the peripatetic parson figured out he was there. Of such gamy stories does every priest or minister have an ample supply.

That Jenny. A man couldn't get enough of her—even at eleven o'clock in the morning. Some gals have it, and some don't. Jenny had it, I guess. Or at least that's how Dean told the story to me. Many times. And always with delight and hearty laughter.

Art and Emily Peterson were an unmarried brother and sister who lived on a farm just north of town. You know how Garrison Keillor tells about Norwegian bachelor farmers? Well, that was Art. And Emily was a Norwegian spinster sister farmer.

A reasonable question you might ask is how anybody of Norwegian descent was a member of a Presbyterian church. The answer, quite simply, is that the Presbyterians were the first to get to Bayfield. By comparison, surprisingly, the Lutherans were Johnny-Come-Latelies. Some of the Norwegians, Swedes, Finns, and Danes of the Presbyterian Church had forebears who had been in the congregation for three or four generations, and they were not about to switch back to the denomination of their Scandinavian ancestors.

Anyway, Dean Johnson had a special place in his huge heart for faithful, steady, and taciturn Emily and Art. Neither the brother nor the sister was blessed with a finely tuned sense of humor. In particular, Art Peterson was to humor what matches are to dynamite: the two just didn't comfortably mix at all.

Knowing this, Dean loved to play practical jokes on Art in a continuous attempt to loosen him up. He told me that one time

Art was on his way out of church after an evening potluck dinner. Although Art never saw anything to be funny, he was not without a willingness to chat a bit. Perhaps more than a bit. When you live out there in the Town of Russell, and there is hardly another living soul other than your sister within five miles, you seize the opportunity to speak to any available human being about any available subject whenever you have the chance.

Well, Dean saw that Emily was still in the church hall talking to another parishioner. Suddenly seized by a fiendish notion, he told Art that Emily was waiting for him out in the truck. Then, he offered to help Art put on his winter coat to ward off the chill night air. Instead of putting on Art's coat, however, he deviously put on Emily's coat. Art trudged out toward his truck. As he did so, he began furiously to swat both sides of his face, as though he were being attacked by a swarm of flies in August beside his manure pile. Emily's coat had a fake fur collar, and the bristles were rubbing against a face which was thoroughly startled by such a sensory offense.

Art glared at the collar, glared down at the coat, and then glared at the chortling clergyman behind him. "Dean Johnson," Art snorted, "you are the very devil!" Dean did take devilish pleasure in playing such a trick but even more so in recalling it. Art Peterson was not amused, although Emily found it quite laughable. To St. Dean, however, it was a memory always to be cherished.

Then, there was the celebrated case of Helen Cease and *TheBayfield Hour*. Helen Cease was a Lutheran lady who was a fixture as a soloist at funerals in all four of Bayfield's churches. *In the Garden* was her funereal *piece de resistance*.

Each morning on the Ashland radio station, which was the only station for many miles around, Helen was featured on *The Bayfield Hour*. She would pass along bits of news, opinions, and gossip. "Haldor and Dagne Norquist motored to Duluth yesterday to see their daughter, Nora, and her three children." Major affairs of state such as that were the usual gripping content of *The Bayfield Hour*.

Helen also would give a daily weather report. She lived up Rittenhouse Avenue on a hill above the town. Nearly everyone in Bayfield lived on some sort of hill; flat places were hard to come by.

112

She broadcast *The Bayfield Hour* from the Bayfield Inn, which stood beside the boat basin near the heart of Bayfield's two-block downtown area.

It was Helen's custom to give a weather report every day, including the daily temperature. Invariably, she would say something like, "It was fifty-two degrees this morning at my little house on the hill, but down here at the Bayfield Inn it is fifty-six degrees."

One morning, Dean and his good friend Jack Lee decided to play a trick on Helen Cease. Jack was a secular Jew who owned the only real clothing store in town. He claimed to be an atheist, but that did not deter Dean from a close friendship with him, despite Dean's evangelical nature. It was an extraordinarily cold January morning. As usual, Helen sat at a desk in the lobby of the inn, glancing at her notes for that day's broadcast. Jack sat near the window outside of which a thermometer was hanging on a cord strung over a nail. Dean Johnson had been huddled there for a few minutes, waiting for Jack quietly to rap on the window just prior to the predictable announcement. In Dean's gloved hand was a cigarette lighter.

Everyone in town, including Jack Lee, was familiar with the prelude to the weather report. When Jack knew Helen was about a minute away from giving the temperature, he quietly rapped on the window to alert the awaiting prankster. Dean reached up for the thermometer, lit the lighter, put it under the mercury, and watched it quickly shoot up to nearly a hundred degrees. Then, he placed the thermometer back on its nail.

"It was twenty-two degrees below zero at my little house on the hill," Helen announced. Then, turning around toward the thermometer, she continued, "But down here at the Bayfield Inn, it is ninety-four degrees. Ninety-four degrees!" she exclaimed, astonished at what her eyes were telling her. With that, Jack Lee began a raucous guffawing.

"Jack Lee!" Helen said. "What have you done?" She never realized Jack had to have had an accomplice in this deception, and neither Jack nor Dean ever told her. But he and Jack Lee greatly enjoyed being the pranksters who engineered the Skyrocketing January Thermometer.

Maybe you thought Lake Wobegon was a fictional small town by a small lake in central Minnesota. It wasn't. It was a real town whose actual name was Bayfield beside a very big lake in northern Wisconsin. In fact, for several years, Garrison Keillor used to come to Bayfield every summer to do a broadcast of *The Prairie Home Companion*. The canny radio comedian knew a good site for his show when he saw it.

Although Dean Johnson had not a drop of French blood in his veins, it was he who fully invented and patented the excellent and useful expression *joie de vivre*. No one found more joy in life than he did. His thunderous abdominal laughter shall live long in happy memory of all those who knew him.

Dean's great passion in the middle years of his life was to establish a retreat center on Madeline Island, just a short ferry ride away from Bayfield in the Apostle Islands. For years, he tried to interest individuals, churches, and foundations in contributing funds for the project. And while there was strong interest, there was never enough financial support to construct the building or buildings he felt the facility would need. Thus, his dream never came to fruition.

Although Dean Johnson was totally committed to northern Wisconsin and its challenging winter climate, his wife, Diane, was not nearly as thrilled by its chilly rigors. Therefore, after her parents had died, she convinced Dean to move to Hilton Head Island, South Carolina. I had accepted a call there as pastor of the First Presbyterian Church several years earlier, and they thought it would be helpful to know someone in the South if they were going to emigrate from a northern clime to live there.

A group of evangelical businessmen gathered funds to establish Dean as the first official island chaplain. He made regular calls on out-of-towners who found themselves in the Hilton Head hospital or on locals who had no church affiliation. He also was available for pastoral counseling for anyone who needed it and asked for his services or for weddings or funerals.

Dean was the ideal candidate to be a minister to folk who had no connection to any church. Though he was as evangelical as ever, he never shoved religion down anyone's throat. His gentle and loving spirit shone through in everything he did. He was, as Luther said we all should be, "a little Christ to his neighbors."

One of the qualities I admired most in St. Dean is that he was never judgmental. He understood human weakness and willfulness. And while he certainly did not condone sin, he did not publicly or privately excoriate it either. He loved people too much to allow their bad behavior to stand between him and them.

My pastorate in Hilton Head Island ended just before I knew my marriage was about to end. It terminated in perhaps the worst way possible for a minister. I will mercifully spare you the highly dubious details.

By that time, I had been married for thirty-five years. Dean Johnson had known Nancy and me for twenty-seven of those years. Nevertheless, though he became well aware of some of the circumstances leading up to the divorce and knew other details from our long friendship, he steadfastly refused to cut me off as a friend; and in fact, he was very supportive of me in my decision when I was somewhat alone in the wilderness.

To be nonjudgmental of everyone in all situations is what the apostle Paul should have called a "spiritual gift"—but alas, didn't. Dean Johnson possessed that gift to the highest degree. Heaven knows I never had it. Although I saw Dean very infrequently after that (he and Diane moved to upstate South Carolina in retirement), I always felt his love and support, despite the way my marriage ended. Because he had known me so long, I enormously valued his continuous friendship. He fully knew me, yet he stuck with me anyway. What a guy!

For years, Dean had heart troubles. A few years before he died, he had a heart attack, followed by bypass surgery. Later, he was afflicted by cancer—from which he eventually died. His sunny disposition sustained him through all his health crises, and he marched proudly into the Church Triumphant.

Good night, sweet prince among the clergy, and flights of angels sing thee to thy rest.

SAINTS OF CHICAGO, ILLINOIS

**FOURTH PRESBYTERIAN CHURCH
MARCH 1968 TO JANUARY 1973**

FOR MOST OF my childhood and youth, I had a close affinity to Chicago. Carl Sandburg's City of Big Shoulders and Hog Butcher of the World was within a hundred or a hundred and fifty miles of Dixon, Illinois, and Madison, Wisconsin, the two places where I lived for a total of eighteen years until I graduated from the University of Wisconsin in Madison in 1961. Throughout those years, our family would occasionally visit Chicago, and I always felt an emotional thrill to go there. The pulsing throb of the Windy City has always captivated me. Chicago is to the Midwest what New York City is to the Northeast. My kind of town it was. And still is.

As I previously explained, when it came time to go to seminary, I considered no divinity school other than McCormick Theological Seminary in Chicago. In those days, it was located on the Near North Side. Nancy taught kindergarten in the west suburban town of Elmhurst, and we lived in an efficiency apartment on the seminary campus. Our seminary years were a delight, and Chicago itself was a major factor in our continuous pleasure, along with attending the Fourth Presbyterian Church each Sunday.

When I received the call to become one of the assistant ministers at Fourth Church, we moved into an apartment in a high-rise building two blocks east of the church, and a block west of Lake Michigan. It was an ideal neighborhood with many other young couples with children in what was called Streeterville, our several square blocks of ten to forty or fifty storey apartment buildings. And thus began our communion with the saints of Fourth Presbyterian Church and the larger Chicago community.

St. John Hastings

John Hastings was one of the first people I met when I returned to Fourth Church as a prospective parson on its staff. Judge Hastings was a member of the Federal District Court of Chicago and also a member of the Fourth Church Personnel Committee. As such, he was one of the people commissioned to make recommendations to the session—the church governing board—for new staff members, including assistant pastors.

Judge Hastings was a uniquely wise, perceptive, shrewd, urbane, and kindly Christian gentleman. As a federal district court justice, he was one step below the United States Supreme Court in the U.S. judicial system. I would imagine that had political conditions in Washington been different, he might have made it to the Big Nine. But he was a moderate Republican, and the White House had Democrats in the nation's highest office from 1960 to 1968, which is when he would have come up for consideration to the nation's highest court. So it was not to be. But the nation's loss was Fourth Church's and Chicago's gain.

Despite his high position in the judiciary, John Hastings deliberately comported himself like an ordinary mortal, albeit a very suave and sophisticated one. He easily met and conversed with other members or visitors to Fourth Church, whether from high positions or low. He treated everyone equally and with respect, regardless of social status. He did not hobnob only with the rich and well-born but with anyone whom he considered a friend, of whom he had a great coterie. Furthermore, he never acted superior to anyone although intellectually and experientially he in fact was superior to nearly everyone. He was a modest giant, a humble titan.

Elam Davies later told me that in the process of seeking an assistant minister, he and the Personnel Committee had interviewed a young minister from a small Midwestern town which had a highly unusual name. Judge Hastings asked the candidate about the origin of the name of his birthplace not because he was particularly interested in the answer, but because he was very interested in how he would choose to answer such an unusual question. Apparently the man launched into a lengthy but misleading and even supercilious explanation, suggesting that he should not be judged by the peculiar moniker or his hometown, which John Hastings had neither intended nor implied. The committee, without Judge Hastings having to add anything to the discussion, judged the unfortunate young man to be someone who might not be a natural fit as a minister of the Fourth Presbyterian Church.

John Hastings was committed to the particular mission of Fourth Church, and he provided ongoing personal and financial support in meaningful but quiet ways. Like many other such stellar people I have been privileged to know in the congregations I served, he lived his faith by what he did much more than by what he said. To many Christians, such exhibits of faith are inferior to spoken or proclaimed declarations, but to most Mainline Protestants, acts trump words in the Christian life. John Hastings lived what he thought by what he did.

There were many attorneys in the congregation at Fourth Church. I never heard any of them utter a negative word about Judge Hastings. He was held in high esteem by virtually everyone who knew him or knew of him. His spoken or written decisions from the bench were paragons of legal justice and clarity.

One of the reasons I thought so highly of John Hastings is because he thought so highly of Elam Davies. I readily confess that people who thought ill of the Boss tended to raise warning flags in my mind. I didn't ignore them or ostracize them from my own mental inner circle, but I did become wary of them. My admiration for Elam may have clouded my assessment of those who did not admire him as I did, but I know that John Hastings was an Elam Davies admirer, and therefore, in addition to everything else about him that I admired, I admired John Hastings for that as well.

Saints Paul and Florence Randolph

Two other people who were strong supporters of the Boss were *Paul* and *Florence Randolph*. Paul was the state representative in the

Illinois legislative district in which Fourth Church was located. He had served in that capacity for many years.

Paul was a Republican as were a strong majority of the members of Fourth Presbyterian Church, regardless of age, occupation, or marital status. Paul was a moderate Republican like John Hastings. He was interested in the welfare and well-being of the less fortunate as well as the more fortunate. He was an excellent member of the state legislature for representing the enormous diversity of the populace of metropolitan Chicago.

Florence, Paul's wife, was his primary if also unpaid assistant in the operation of his elected office. They had no children, so she could go with him wherever he needed to go, whether to meetings or hearings in Chicago or to the state capitol in Springfield. Paul was very politic in everything he said and did. He never spoke quickly but always from measured thought. He always carefully considered everything he said, and he was quiet-spoken when he talked. That was as true at Fourth Church as it was in the political arena of the Near North Side or the halls of the state house in Abraham Lincoln's adopted hometown.

Florence, on the other hand, was far more forthcoming with her opinions on many things or in truth, on nearly everything. She was not mean or catty, but she plainly called it the way she saw it. Furthermore, she was extremely protective of her husband, and she would defend him to the nth degree even if he might be on the perceived wrong side of an issue, which occurred very infrequently. She had a cherubic smile, whereas Paul had a minimalist crooked grin.

Paul had been a commandant of the usher corps for years before we first attended Fourth Church while I was in seminary and when we returned when I became a member of the church staff. He took his usher duties seriously.

It was the responsibility of the ushers to fill the pews with as many people as possible and to move early attendants as far to the front as possible. They all knew there was an optimum number who could fit in each pew, and it was unwise to try to jam more in than were willing to be thus jammed. But on the other hand, they didn't want to leave any unfilled spaces either. It was a weekly test of character and decorum to fit the actual number of worshipers into the space provided for them fifty years earlier by Ralph Adams Cram, the famous ecclesiastical architect. There was to be no seat unused.

When the ushers received the offering, it was with the precision and attention to detail of a military drill team. A key factor in this process was Paul Randolph. After the offering plates were passed through all the pews, the ushers took them to the back of the sanctuary. Then, in strict time, left-right, left-right, they carried them to the front of the sanctuary, where they were stacked during the singing of the doxology. It was a marvel of marching men. And in my day, it was still all men. The striped pants and morning coats gave way to dark suits, white dress shirts, and dark ties, as I mentioned earlier. However, for many years since my time, there have been women ushers, and the formality of attire has been altered as in most other churches in American Christendom.

There was a unique lady who attended Fourth Church on a regular basis for a year or two. We didn't know where she came from or to where she disappeared when she did disappear. She liked to sit on the left side of the nave toward the front. She always wore earrings, pins, and hats which were fashioned in the shape of poinsettias—except at Christmastime, when she wore other feminine accoutrements. It is difficult to get more unique than that. Why poinsettias during the year but not at Christmas was a mystery which remained forever mysterious.

Well, one Sunday she came in later than she normally did, but she went up the center aisle, wanting to get into her usual pew. Paul Randolph was stationed there, and he held out his arms discreetly to prevent her going to where there were no more spaces in her pew. Not to be deterred, she reached into her mouth, pulled out the gum she was chewing, stuck it on Paul's lapel, went to "her" pew, climbed over the legs of astonished people who were unaware of the unusual scene behind them which had just occurred, wiggled her fortunately willowy frame between two startled worshipers, everyone on both sides of her moving left or right to accommodate this very determined lady. By this time, Paul had removed the new badge of honor from his lapel, quickly putting it into his pocket, and he walked to the back of the sanctuary, acting as though nothing had happened. Paul was not a born raconteur, but he loved to tell that story to new ushers-in-training to alert them to the unusual challenges which might be encountered in the service of God in a large and famous city church with a an unpredictable assemblage of worshipers every Sunday.

Like his close friend, John Hastings, Paul Randolph served as both an elder and trustee of Fourth Church. He was always reliable, and if he said he would do something, he did it. He strongly believed in the ministry of his beloved church, and he did whatever he could to reach out to as many as possible with as much as possible. He too was an unstinting supporter of Elam Davies, which made me respect and appreciate him all the more.

Throughout this country, and throughout the whole Western world, I suspect, there are certain congregations of certain denominations which have a certain kind of clientele. Not everyone in these churches is a mover or shaker, but many are. Most of the folks of that variety want their church to operate in much the same way as their business or other such organization, and they provide much of the personal skills to make it happen. Sometimes, they can be a trial to the clergy and others on a church staff; but for the most part, they are a great blessing to the particular ministries of any congregation. Fourth Presbyterian Church has been blessed by numerous such saints through its century and a half of existence. Such individuals tend not to suffer fools gladly, but Paul Randolph did that more gracefully than many of his peers. That troubled poinsettia lady was one he learned to suffer remarkably gladly—perhaps in part because she never again subjected him to the indignity of interrupting his duties as an usher in the house of the Lord. But he and everyone else on the usher team kept a close eye on her ever after.

Not long thereafter, she disappeared as unexpectedly as she had first appeared some time earlier. It has ever been thus in large city congregations. Visitors come and go with dismaying frequency, and after having attended regularly for a few months or years, they may disappear without anyone ever having the opportunity to know their stories. Paul Randolph never forgot a small snippet of her story. It was firmly lodged in his memory as long as he lived.

Florence and Paul Randolph lived in the same building as our family. Because that was so, and because they often met us going up or down in the elevators, they took a special interest in Nancy, me, Amy, and then in Andrew after he was born three years following our arrival at Fourth Church. Perhaps because they had no children of their own, they both oogled and googled our cherubs whenever they saw them although the Randolphs each had their own particular oogling style. But their affection was genuine beyond question, and the children reveled in it, even if Andrew was too young to understand what it was all about.

Saints Ed and Dorothy Gerling

There was a dedicated group of Fourth members who attempted to track down every visitor who permitted themselves to be tracked, and they were called The Invitation Committee. It was my rare privilege to be the staff minister for that committee for three years. *Dorothy and Ed Gerling* had been members of the committee for years before I joined the staff, and they had been members at Fourth Church for many more years than that.

Both Ed and Dorothy were natives of Chicago as I remember. How they happened to join the church in the first place I don't recall. But they were tireless evangelists and recruiters for new members of the congregation as were all the other folks on the Invitation Committee.

The system worked as follows: Every Monday, I would be given a list of people who had been willing the day before in church to identify themselves as first-time visitors. I would write their name, address, and phone number (if they wrote down that information) on a 3x5 card and assign it to a particular person on the committee. We tended to ask married couples to contact married couples, single women to contact single women, and single men to contact single men. As you can imagine, sometimes, it was not possible to know for certain the marital status or gender of anyone by their names. I will say this, however; any member of the Fourth Church Invitation Committee could have been hired by any private detective agency in the city, and they would have done an excellent job for them. They became experts at locating Missing Persons.

On Wednesday evening, the Invitation Committee met together at the regularly scheduled midweek church dinner we had for anyone who wanted to come. Afterward, we would collectively go through the names of our subjects/suspects/quarries to see what, if anything had been learned about them. You might think it goes without saying but it needs to be said that it is no small task even to speak to visitors on the phone who are city folks, let alone to meet them at the coffee hour on a Sunday to have personal introductions. When people live among hundreds of thousands or millions of other people, they tend to be wary of contacts from strangers, even strangers from a church. So in our meetings, we often heard of how deliberately slippery some people made themselves.

The Gerlings were never deterred by this urban phenomenon. Having been lifelong Chicogoans, they well understood and appreciated it. Nevertheless, that did not deter these servants of Christ's Church from attempting to succeed in their appointed rounds. They were thorough, diligent, and determined. They weren't pit bulls exactly, but they weren't Chihuahuas either.

Ed and Dorothy Gerling both had fulltime jobs. They were not captains of industry or commerce, but they were hard workers. So when they served on the Invitation Committee, theirs was obviously a labor of love. They loved Fourth Church, and they loved The Church. They were happy to give their all to advancing its mission in their particular form of service as low-key evangelists and new-member recruiters.

No one on the committee was an evangelical in the way many contemporary evangelicals are evangelicals. There were no "Are you saved?" inquiries, no overpowering testimonies to the way God had worked miracles in their lives or in Fourth Church. Instead, the Invitation Committee people did what the committee title implied: They invited people to join what they believed was an outstanding congregation in an outstanding setting in an outstanding city. Many evangelicals would be offended by the gentleness of that approach, but it worked at Fourth Church. We had three thousand members, and every year, we needed to receive three hundred new members because every year three hundred current members—*ten percent*—moved away, died, or became inactive. And every year, we managed to add about three hundred new saints to the church rolls.

Dorothy and Ed Gerling were naturals in this process. They were warm, witty, and willing servants of God, Jesus Christ, and Fourth Presbyterian Church. They didn't wear their religion on their sleeves; they wore it in their hearts and heads. They were tireless in their devotion in what could be a challenging and deflating responsibility. Probably not one in five of the people they were able to talk to ever joined the church. But if they and the other committee members hadn't made the contacts, probably not one in ten or one in twenty would ever have joined the congregation. As every professional church consultant will attest, the way to acquire new members into a church is to invite them to come to church.

Some people might ask, should that really matter? Is church membership all that important? It probably isn't in the Kingdom of God, but in the Church Militant and therefore the Church Triumphant, it is. The church's one Foundation is Jesus Christ her Lord, as the hymn declares. And the Gerlings and everyone else on that crucial committee worked very hard on behalf of their church to strengthen and broaden the Christian foundation. Without their services, Fourth Church would be much different than it was and less than it was. Because of all those folks, and hundreds of others like them, it was one of the strongest congregations in the Presbyterian denomination, and one of the most influential congregations in Chicago and the entire Midwest.

Perhaps Ed and Dorothy Gerling were not irreplaceable cogs in the mechanisms of their weekday workplace. They were Ordinary Folks. But in the mechanism of Fourth Church, they were Vital Folks, Important Folks, people whose unstinting service in recruiting new members helped to make that great congregation what it was and is. Mighty oaks from little acorns grow, and they were the advanced guard in searching out and nurturing any likely little acorns they could find among the visitors at Fourth Church.

St. Reba Staggs

When I wrote earlier about the Boss, I noted that it was under Elam Davies's wise early-years leadership that Fourth Presbyterian Church elected the first female elders and trustees in its then hundred year history. In the Twenty-Teens, that may not seem like such a massive undertaking; but for the 1960s, in such a tradition-bound church, it was no small matter.

Reba Staggs was one of the two women who, together, were elected as elders in a new group of church officers in the late '60s. Reba was a southerner by birth, and she never lost a syllable of her soft southern accent during her sojourn in Chicago.

Reba had a very responsible position in the meat industry. She had graduated with a bachelor's and master's degree in home economics, but her focus was not on the home per se but rather on the industry which supplied meat to homes and restaurants around the country. She was the head of the National Meat Board, the trade association which oversaw the entire process of meat production—from the farm to the feed producers to the packing houses to the refrigerator, whether that refrigerator was in an efficiency apartment or a huge food supplier or restaurant chain. She believed in meat. She believed meat was good for people—not too much, but in proper amounts. In those days, there was almost no concern about the potential problems of red meat in the human diet.

Reba Staggs was a large woman—not obese but regally somewhat stout, like Queen Victoria although she was much taller than the Queen. Reba's physiognomy may have reflected her commitment to the primary product of her profession. As such, she was imposing. In a business dominated by men, she nevertheless managed to work her way to the top. I doubt that she ever would have been coarse in her leadership style; she was too much the refined southern lady for that. On the other hand, I'm sure she was no pushover either. Years later, I met a professor in the School of Agriculture at Purdue University who knew Reba well in her professional capacity, and he spoke very highly of her and her ability to shine in a male-dominated industry. I am confident she was widely admired and respected in the work she did for a living.

She certainly was respected in the work she did as a key member and leader of the Fourth Presbyterian Church. She shared Elam's concern for the least, the last, and the lost. As chairman of one of the session committees charged with community outreach, she applied her vast organizational skills to ways the congregation could assist children and adults nearby who were far less fortunate than the affluent members of the Gold Coast Fourth.

Reba never married. Was her personality too imposing or challenging for the vast majority of men, or was it that she did not choose to be married? I don't know. She would have been a wonderful wife to someone; of that, I have no doubt. However, perhaps she was too married to her church and to her work to have time for any man to whom she might also have been married.

The word, "spirituality," came into wide usage in the `90s and has remained in vogue ever since. Reba Staggs was deeply spiritual before the idea became popular. Whether in session meeting discussions over various issues or serving communion or simply sitting in the pew in worship, she exuded a genuine glow of inner Christian faith. If a matter of principle was being debated among the elders, she would forthrightly state her convictions, hoping they would prevail. But if not, she was a team player, and she would support the majority decision, even if she disagreed with it.

In my opinion, all church people are Christians, to one degree or another, but not all Christians are church people. In other words, I believe it is quite possible to be a committed Christian without being a member of any church. Millions of Christians are convinced they fit into that category. But as a card-carrying parson of fifty years, "church people" will always have a special place in my heart because the most dedicated of church people are an absolute necessity to the successful operation of any congregation of any denomination.

Reba Staggs was one of the most wonderful and supportive church people it has been my privilege to know. There is no one who could have been a better candidate to break the glass ceiling to become an elder at the Fourth Presbyterian Church.

St. Beulah Scott

Beulah Scott was the other woman to be elected an elder at Fourth Church in that pivotal year, along with Reba Staggs. But Beulah represented a different kind of church member from Reba.

Beulah had lived in Chicago far longer than Reba and had been a member at Fourth Church much longer. She was a little older than Reba, I think, although I couldn't correctly guess how much older. A male in his late twenties or early thirties is a notoriously poor estimator of ages of women two or three decades older than him. Looking back, I would suppose Reba was in her fifties, and Beulah in her sixties. Since they both have entered the Celestial Church, I can't get into trouble with either one by misjudging their ages. But my main point in writing about this is to say that they both were outstanding women for cracking the glass canopy which theretofore had prevented anyone of the female persuasion from becoming elders in a very traditional Presbyterian city congregation.

Beulah had retired from her employment before we arrived at Fourth Church. As such, she was able to participate in many of the daytime women's activities of the congregation and did so with enthusiasm and dedication. She was one of Grace Davies' best friends because Grace also was involved in several of those groups. They not only enjoyed what they did, but they also did well and did good at the same time while doing it. The outreach of those women's groups to the immediate community, the city of Chicago, the nation, and the world was extraordinary, and Beulah Scott played a major part in making those things happen. It is probably inevitable that "women's ministries" in churches have dwindled in the past half-century, but it also is sad. A power of work was performed by those powerful ladies.

Like Reba Staggs, Beulah Scott never married. She had gentlemen friends, and she spent time with them. But for whatever reason, either the right man did come along, or the right man never popped the right question. And what a miscreant he was not to have done so, whoever the poor sap may have been. Or so says I.

For many millions of people in thousands of churches all over the world, "the church," meaning a particular congregation, is a major part of their lives. There have been people like that in every church I have served as a pastor. But there was a higher percentage of such people in Fourth Church than in any other of the congregations I have served. One of the reasons may have been that over half of the members were unmarried, and therefore, they may have felt they had more time to devote to their church than did their married co-members. Fourth was a beehive of Christian endeavor.

Beulah Scott was a unique "church person" among hundreds of unique church people. She quietly served in many capacities and in many groups prior to becoming an elder, and when she joined the session, she became as quietly effective as an elder as she had been in all her other organizations and relationships.

There are some church officers who are talkers as well as doers, there are others who are doers but not so much talkers, and there are still others who are talkers and doers. Beulah was both, but she was more of a doer than talker because she did not like the spotlight to shine on her, even though she was her own incandescent spotlight.

She had somewhat of a tentative gait when she walked. It may have been the result of an old injury or an orthopedic problem. As such, it signified a slight hesitancy in her behavior as contrasted to her fellow first-female elder Reba. But Beulah was no less effective or influential. She was known to and knew hundreds of Fourth folk, especially the old timers. And despite her old-fashioned name, she was not old fashioned. She was the epitome of a with-it older (or so it seemed to young me) lady.

Quality people are quality people in whatever type of community they exhibit their outstanding qualities. Beulah Scott was such a person. She was a regal gem of reserved dignity, a lady among a whole host of marvelous ladies.

Saints Virginia and Arthur Wirtz

Most people who knew *Virginia and Arthur Wirtz* would probably automatically identify them collectively as "Arthur and Virginia Wirtz." Arthur was a major Chicago developer of commercial real estate, and he was most definitely a power to reckon with in Windy

City business. Besides his business interests, he was also the owner of the Chicago Blackhawks of the National Hockey League. In his time, Mr. Wirtz would likely be considered one of the most influential businessmen in Chicago.

However, to most of the staff members of Fourth Presbyterian as well as to many church members, the Wirtzes would be identified as "Virginia and Arthur Wirtz." That was in no way to try to diminish Arthur, but rather to elevate Virginia. Because from the congregation's standpoint, Virginia played a unique, if also very quiet, role in the church's life.

First of all, she was very regular in her church attendance. In the days of rented pews, she and her husband had procured a pew very close to the front of the sanctuary. After it was no longer permitted to rent pews, Virginia came very early to take "her place" in "her pew" so as not to be dislodged from her customary perch of many years. If she was miffed by the session decision to eliminate pew rentals, deftly maneuvered by Elam Davies, she never expressed her miffitude. But because she respected Elam so much, she likely concluded that it was just another example of inevitable change in the life of the *Ancien Regime*. The *ancien regime* always experiences some kind of a challenge to the old ways. That is as certain as the rising of the sun tomorrow.

In the Broadway musical, *Hello, Dolly!*, two of the characters sing a song in which they proudly declare of themselves, "We are elegant, we are oh so elegant." Well, Virginia and Arthur Wirtz were, from my vantage point, genuinely elegant, especially Virginia. They exuded *elegance* and *"class"* and *good breeding* from every pore. If I ever knew their backgrounds as children and youth, I have long since forgotten it although I think they both were native Chicagoans. But it appeared to me, as a rather distant observer, that they also were "to the manor born," as Shakespeare expressed it, as well as to the manners born because they had elegant manners.

Both of the Wirtzes were highly gracious people in the "social sense." That is, they treated everyone at every level of society with grace and dignity. That was especially true of Virginia. They did not behave as Eliza Doolittle proclaimed of Henry Higgins in *My Fair*

Lady that the imperious professor treated "every princess as though she were a flower girl, whereas Colonel Pickering treats every flower girl as though she were a princess." Arthur and Virginia Wirtz would be categorized in the upper-upper class by virtually everyone who knew them or knew of them, but they both seemed genuinely open to everyone at every level of the social structure. They were not at all imperious in their behavior toward those who were of a lower level of society. In truth, nearly everyone was at a lower level.

Among the four clergy of Fourth Church, Arthur, as a trustee, was much closer to Elam than the three assistant ministers. That was not only understandable but perfectly acceptable. He probably had less time for idle chit-chat with us than with Elam because his mind was a high RPM engine of thought about matters commercial. And if he was less involved in the daily or weekly activities at Fourth than his wife, it was because he had innumerable entrepreneurial fish to fry which Virginia didn't need to worry about.

Virginia, on the other hand, had as much time for Fourth as Fourth had time for her, which was a considerable amount. Every Friday, she would arrive in her chauffeured Rolls Royce at the Delaware Street entrance to the church, immediately inside which was the John Timothy Stone Chapel. The chapel was a small worship site seating perhaps thirty or forty people. For many years, she had made it one of her ecclesiastical obligations to provide an orchid from her sizeable home collection for a small vase at the front of the chapel. Thus, every weekend, there would be a fresh orchid to grace the space for any who might be married in the chapel on a Saturday or who preferred to hear an audio broadcast of the service there instead of sitting in the sanctuary. I strongly doubt that anyone ever asked her to do it; she just did it. She was that kind of a lady. And her connection in Fourth Church went all the way back to John Timothy Stone, who had been the pastor in the 1910s and `20s when the present sanctuary was built and in whose honor the chapel was named. Later, he became the president of McCormick Theological Seminary.

Without Virginia's quiet but firm influence on her husband, Arthur Wirtz probably would have been less involved in the mission and ministry of Fourth Church. She well understood what she needed to do to get him to do what she wanted him to do. In that, she was like millions of other wives or husbands. However, it has been my experience, after half a century of observing this phenomenon, that more wives inspire their husbands to become more active in church than husbands similarly inspire their wives. It works both ways, to be sure, but the sober truth is that were it not for women in general, the church in general would have shriveled into oblivion long ago. Virginia Wirtz was a *grande dame* of a grand church, and she turned her husband into a grand Fourth Church man as well.

Virginia and Arthur Wirtz could have offered themselves to many very worthwhile causes other than that Church of Jesus Christ or the Fourth Presbyterian Church in particular. My guess is that Virginia kept Arthur more involved than his nature otherwise would have directed—only because he was such a genius in business matters. But both of them were part of the magnificent tapestry of the members of Fourth Church.

A Brief Interlude Regarding Christian Stewardship

It was assumed by countless numbers of people in the wider Chicago community, and even among many Fourth Church members themselves, that there must have been hundreds of people of similar financial standing to Arthur and Virginia Wirtz in the Fourth Presbyterian Church. Well, *many* Wirtzes there simply weren't—a few dozen perhaps or three score at most. Compared to most Chicagoans, most Fourth Church members were affluent; but compared to the 1 percent of the 100 percent at Fourth, the majority were simply well off but certainly not off the charts.

Through five decades as an ordained minister among mainly affluent Christians, I have discovered that truly wealthy people are much more likely to contribute substantially to specific projects in the church than to the general church operating fund. Without question, that too is very helpful; but overall, it would be a far happier situation ecclesiastically if Mainline Christians were as generous in general as evangelical Christians. However, such an eventuality is not likely to occur in this world; and in the next, I am certain it will be of no consequence.

One of the things that always mystified me about Elam Davies is that he resolutely eschewed giving stewardship sermons and, in fact, almost never did. By the third year I was there, I noted this apparent aversion, so I asked him if he would mind if I preached a stewardship sermon on a Sunday morning. He seemed absolutely delighted with my offer, which frankly shocked and surprised me. He didn't mind someone else carrying the banner, but stewardship banner waving was not in his makeup. Who knows? Maybe it was a Welsh thing.

Anyway, when I was preparing my sermon, I asked the financial secretary to tell me at what level the pledge for Nancy and me stood in the ranking of the potential of about two thousand five hundred "giving units" in the membership of the church. This was before computers were in wide usage, so alas, Martha had to go through the hundreds of pledges by hand to see how ours stacked up against others. When at last she finished her calculations, she discovered that we were eighteenth—*eighteenth!*—highest. I was more appalled than amazed. How could it be that an assistant minister and his wife who was a full-time homemaker have the eighteenth highest pledge in the Fabulously Fortuitous Fourth Presbyterian Church? That convinced me as nothing else had previously done that almost no Presbyterians seem to have grasped what a tithe is.

I asked the Boss if it was okay in my sermon to say that we had the eighteenth-highest pledge in a congregation of three thousand fairly affluent souls. After some careful thought, he gave me permission.

By now, you may have concluded that it does not seem to be strongly woven into the warp and woof of my character to avoid controversy at all costs. In truth, by the time I was born I already had gallons of chutzpah coursing through my veins. Through the years, I acquired many gallons more. So, throwing caution to the winds, about two-thirds through my one and only Fourth Church morning stewardship sermon (I did it annually in evening sermons), I casually announced that as tithers, the Millers' pledge to the church was the eighteenth highest among all the pledges. I had no intention to brag about that but rather, quite frankly, to try to shame anyone who might feel appropriately shamed. I don't recall an enormous inhaling of oxygen when I made this surprising observation, and in fact, hardly anyone ever said anything to me about it afterward. But I was pleased that for the next year, there was an increase of almost 8 percent in total pledges and 12 percent in the total amount pledged. Whether it had anything to do with my exercise in shaming stewardship, I cannot say.

I will conclude this interlude about charitable giving by stating that in general, Mainline Christian saints are not as committed in Christian stewardship as are evangelical Christian saints. Does that make Mainliners less Christian? I don't think so. But if you, dear reader, in reading these unsolicited musings, conclude that you perhaps should contribute more to your church than you do, my heart will not wither for having gently assaulted your contributions conscience. Amen, dear heart, and amen.

Saints Ben and Eunice Howiler

Eunice and Ben Howiler were another Fourth Church couple who lived at 850 DeWitt Place, where our family lived. Because there were relatively few children in our building, and because the Howilers knew us from the church, they took a particular interest in our family. Further, because the Howilers had a friendly elderly cocker spaniel named Myrtle, our children developed a particular interest in the Howilers and in Myrtle. We all became a mutual admiration society.

Ben was the chief pharmacist in what then was known as Wesley Memorial Hospital. Later, it merged with Passavant hospital across the street and became Northwestern University Hospital.

Ben also was an elder on the Fourth Church session. Like many other women her age, Eunice was unusually active in several of the women's organizations of the congregation. Eunice and Grace Davies were good friends, as were Ben and Elam Davies.

The Howilers were both natives of California. There were many people under forty who had been born in California and had ended up at Fourth Church in Chicago, but there were almost no others of the Howilers' vintage in that category. They had come to Chicago because Ben had been recruited to take the post at Wesley Hospital.

Our family felt very close to the Howilers because we all lived at 850 DeWitt. (Incidentally, when the Fourth Church staff referred to members, we often said where they lived by numbers in order to better place them in our minds: 260 E. (Chestnut), 1100 (Lake Shore Drive), the Carlisle (intersection of Lake Shore Drive and Michigan Avenue), 30 East (Elm Street), 1400 (Lake Shore Drive). Only in a large city and in a large city-church staff would—or could—such ecclesiastical shorthand be employed to help pigeonhole parishioners.) The Millers became ever closer to the Howilers during our five years at Fourth Church. Because we did not have a dog, Myrtle was a major assistance in cementing the relationship for our children. She seemed, in some small measure, like our dog too.

Eunice Howiler always looked the part of a stately woman. She comported herself with dignity, and she was friendly to everyone in a reserved way. She wasn't gushy, but she was quietly effusive. Back then, ladies of Eunice's age were called "matrons" by many people, both female and male. She was one of the multitude of Fourth Church matrons who had multitudes of friends in the congregation because of her participation in the women's groups.

Ben Howiler was an unusually affable chap. He always had a ready smile whenever he saw anyone he knew or whenever he met someone in the hospital who quickly needed a prescription for some medication or another. He did not frequently engage in session meeting discussions, but when he did speak, his words mattered. He was one of those reliable church officers who make the work of ministers ever so much easier. If everyone elected to ecclesiastical office were as thoughtful and helpful as Ben Howiler, the clergy would have much smoother sailing on the churchly seas.

After we moved to New Jersey from Chicago, we continued to keep in touch with the Howilers through Christmas correspondence. Then, a year or two after we went to New Jersey, the Howilers moved to Hilton Head Island, South Carolina. Wesley Hospital had a mandatory retirement policy at age sixty-five, and Ben wanted to continue working for several more years as a hospital pharmacist. He loved his work, and he was very good at it. The Hilton Head Hospital needed a pharmacist; he applied, and he was immediately hired. Our family vacationed on Hilton Head Island a couple of times when we lived in Morristown, New Jersey, and both times, we spent some time with Eunice and Ben. It seemed like old times, except in another time and on another shore.

The second time we visited Hilton Head, I called the Howilers at home, but neither of them was there. So I went to the hospital, hoping I might find Ben in the pharmacy, which I did. After a few pleasantries, he asked me in a conspiratorial tone if I wanted "a new job." Those were his exact words. As it happened, I had begun the process of seeking a new pastorate. I shall go into more detail about this in the next chapter, but suffice it to say that Ben and Eunice Howiler were major factors in how we ended up in South Carolina— where, in a million years, we could never have imagined we would live. And so the communion of saints transferred for all of us two blocks from the shores of Lake Michigan close to the shores of the Atlantic Ocean.

SAINTS OF MORRISTOWN, NEW JERSEY

THE PRESBYTERIAN CHURCH IN MORRISTOWN
JANUARY 1973 TO JULY 1979

THE PRESBYTERIAN CHURCH in Morristown, New Jersey, has two separate buildings that are three blocks apart. The building where the congregation worships is on the Green, or square, in the center of the town; and thus, many refer to it as The Presbyterian Church on the Green. The offices, social hall, and Sunday school rooms are in the old South Street Presbyterian Church building, which is called the Parish House.

It has the two buildings because two separate Presbyterian congregations of two separate Presbyterian denominations merged in the 1920s. The two denominations split in the mid-nineteenth century over theological issues too petty and too embarrassing to try to explain. The Presbyterian Church in Morristown also split at that time because a small group of dissatisfied dissenters managed to divide the congregation in two, and they left to form the South Street Presbyterian Church. Suffice it to say that Presbyterians are outstanding splitters and have been for more than four centuries.

The Presbyterian Church in Morristown was founded in 1733, which is to say, forty-two years prior to the shot heard round the world. In 2033, it will be three hundred years old.

Morristown started out as a village in the hills of northern New Jersey. By the time of the American Revolution, it had become a center of resistance to British rule. George Washington spent two winters in Morristown with the Continental Army during the Revolution.

By the turn of the twentieth century, many wealthy people from New York City and northeastern New Jersey constructed large summer homes in and around Morristown because of the cooler "mountain air." (Most of the town is about six hundred feet above sea level although there are places close by that are over 1300 feet in altitude. That doesn't provide mountain air that is much cooler than at sea level thirty miles to the east, but apparently they thought so.) Thus, there have been wealthy families in Morristown for well over a century and a half. They became known as the Quiet Millionaires.

Not many of those folks were ever members of the Presbyterian Church on the Green. But following World War II, Morristown and the surrounding Morris County became the center of new regional or national corporate offices, and the area population grew rapidly. Eventually, the New York City and Newark suburbs reached out as far as Morristown and beyond, and so it became part of the greater New York metropolitan community. Many of the members of the church commuted into the city to work as well as to surrounding suburbs. So the Morristown community and its Presbyterian church inevitably became very cosmopolitan.

About four years after I came to Fourth Church in Chicago, Elam Davies decided I had learned as much from Fourth and from him as I needed to absorb, and staying longer might be somewhat superfluous. Neither Nancy nor I were sure we wanted to be shoved out of the nest so quickly; our sojourn in Chicago was an unusually happy and fulfilling time for us. Nonetheless, I did have to admit to myself that with the experience I had acquired, I believed I was ready to become pastor of a fairly sizeable congregation somewhere. (Whether such a congregation would agree remained to be seen.) Therefore, the Boss suggested I start looking for likely churches which might be willing to risk my becoming their pastor.

All along, I have assumed it is "church people" who would read this brief tome, if even they had any interest in it. I can't imagine that anyone unfamiliar with any church would ever have the inclination to peruse what kind of folks church folks are, if only because they have no connection with such peculiar individuals, except perhaps as friends or acquaintances.

Therefore, I want again quickly to explain how the clergy move from one parish to another. There are basically three different methods illustrated by the three basic forms of church government: episcopalian (where there are bishops), presbyterian (where there are collective "bishops," known as a presbytery or classis), and congregational (where each congregation chooses it own clergy by whatever means it selects.)

The primary denominations with bishops are the Roman Catholics, Eastern Orthodox, Episcopalians, Lutherans, Methodists, and any split-offs which have evolved from them. The denominations with presbyterian government are the Presbyterians and the Reformed. The congregational churches are the Baptists, the United Church of Christ (sometimes, although not quite correctly, called the Congregationalists), and all nondenominational independent congregations that need no permission from any ecclesiastical authority above the congregational level to call whatever minister they want. (I never thought about it until I was writing this paragraph, but to my knowledge, the clergy in congregationally governed churches are never called priests, but only ministers. That is because, so I presume, only bishops can ordain priests; there is no official priesthood where there is no episcopacy.) All of this is to commend the remarkable diversity of the Church of Jesus Christ. The communion of saints exists despite all these human-created and oft-convoluted divisions over how churches opt to govern themselves.

The main question I want you to think about is this: Does God move the clergy from one parish to another, or do the clergy move themselves? It is, fundamentally, a theological question.

Some people believe God alone moves the clergy around. I understand why they say that; it seems ever so much more spiritual and religious to have that conviction. However, if that is the truth, the whole truth, and nothing but the truth, then it has been evident for hundreds of years to millions of Christians in thousands of congregations the world over that God made a huge mistake when He sent the likes of that noted misfit Rev. Mr. Smith to dear old First Church or the mystifying Ms. Jones to St. Stephen's-by-the-Shore. It becomes obvious in a few weeks or months that certain clerical ecclesiastical matches are actually disruptive mismatches, and if God is the ultimate arbiter of all this, obviously it must be He who made the ultimate mistake.

The fact is that in those denominations or traditions that have bishops, the bishops are pivotal in who goes where as pastors of churches. Methodist bishops have the most influence, followed in descending order of influence by the Catholics, the Orthodox, and the Lutherans. Surprisingly, the Church whose bishops have the least influence in assigning the clergy to particular parishes is the one whose very name is based on the reality of bishops, the Episcopal Church. Go figure. One of the best features of Episcopal church government is that where there are genuine problems in the match between the clergy and the churches, the bishop can fairly quickly rectify the situation by sending someone else to become the pastor and moving the troubled pastor to another charge, where it is eagerly hoped by everyone that things will work out much better.

Congregationally governed churches can act with astonishing dispatch in securing a new minister. They also can dispatch what they consider a mismatch very quickly. It all depends on how rapidly the congregation wants to move on such important matters. But there is no higher ecclesiastical authority either to prevent them or to force them to do what they want to do.

In the Presbyterian system, nothing happens quickly, either in calling a new pastor to a church, or in transferring out a mismatched parson. "Glacial" would be a good description for the Presbyterian call system. When a new minister is sought, a pastoral nominating committee of church members is named. That process itself can take several weeks to a few months. Then, they must fill out certain forms to the satisfaction of the presbytery, which also might take months. A presbytery consists of all the clergy in a given geographic area (much like a diocese or district), plus an equal number of lay people who are elders from the various churches in the presbytery. No Presbyterian congregation can call a minister without the approval of the presbytery. By itself, the presbytery part of the Presbyterian call process can take up to a year or more. Nowadays, Presbyterian churches often call an interim pastor to fill in on a temporary basis until a permanent pastor is called. Forty or fifty years ago, that was rare because both congregations and presbyteries were able to move much more swiftly. But the Presbyterians have progressed into a much slower process.

The national headquarters of the Presbyterian Church provides a list of "vacant" churches to clergy who are seeking a new call. When I was sent that list while we were still in Chicago, I engaged in a host of geographic fantasies. Where should we go: East, West, North (although in Chicago we were fairly far north already), or South? The South was out because the Southern Presbyterian Church, officially called the Presbyterian Church in the United States, had split from the rest of the Presbyterians at the beginning of the Civil War, and they didn't reunite until 1983. Anywhere in the Midwest was perhaps the best likelihood because I had spent all but one year of my life in the Midwest.

However, I noticed that the Presbyterian Church in Morristown, New Jersey, was looking for a minister. I knew nothing about New Jersey and had spent only a few hours driving through it several years earlier on the way home from Scotland. I asked Elam Davies if he knew anything about the Morristown church, and he did. On reflection, he thought I might be a good "fit" for them. The pastoral nominating committee sent a deputation of three or four people to come to Fourth Church to meet me, and Elam arranged for me to preach a sermon on a Sunday morning for them to hear me. I had an enjoyable if also nerve-wracking visit with them, but they spent more time with Elam than with me. With good reason, they trusted his assessment of me more than mine of me. As a result of that visit, and especially because of their time with Elam, they issued me a call as their pastor.

On every pulpit committee I ever met with, I had an individual who was my "champion" with that group. In the case of Bayfield, It was Prof. George Knight, who was not even a member of the committee. In the case of Fourth Church, I choose to believe it was Elam Davies, whether or not that in fact was true. In the case of Morristown, it was an elder named Dave Wilson. For whatever reason, from the first time he met me, Dave was convinced I was the parson for their pulpit, and I sincerely hoped he was correct.

Therefore, I want to repeat a question I asked earlier: Does God move the clergy from one parish to another, or do the clergy move themselves? Surely, God is involved in the process because God is involved in everything in the world. But the clergy also are an obvious factor in how the process ultimately manifests itself. No parson is a pawn on a chessboard. Probably, Nancy would have been happier for us to remain in Chicago for a few more years, but I was ready to stretch my wings as the pastor of a congregation which turned out to be at once local, regional, and suburban all at the same time. Therefore, it was with excitement, anticipation, and not a little anxiety that the four Millers moved to New Jersey.

Saints Tom and Mildred Mutch

The man who preceded me as pastor of the Morristown church was Robert Holland. Bob was an outstanding preacher whose skills in the pulpit led to a call from the Shadyside Presbyterian Church in Pittsburgh as their minister after only five years in Morristown. For generations, Shadyside had been one of the premier preaching pulpits in the denomination.

I was told that theretofore, no pastor of the Presbyterian Church in Morristown in its more than two-hundred-year history had ever left that pastorate except by either retirement or death. That chronological reality speaks volumes about what an outstanding congregation it is and why all but one of its clergy had stayed there until they decided to retire or until the roll called up yonder had their name on it.

The man who served as pastor before Bob Holland was *Tom Mutch.* Tom had served the congregation for thirty years, and he and his wife *Mildred* continued to live in Morristown in retirement until they died. Mildred was always "Mildred" to everyone, and never "Millie." Tom was never "Thomas" but always "Tom"—unless he was "Dr. Mutch" to some of the younger people or the less-involved members.

Tom Mutch's father had been a well-known Presbyterian minister who came to America from Scotland, bringing his brrrrisk Scottish brrrrogue with him. He was pastor for many years of the Bryn Mawr Presbyterian Church in suburban Philadelphia.

Unlike either Andrew Mutch or Robert Holland, Tom Mutch was not widely recognized as a great preacher. But there has never been a better pastor, particularly of a large church, than Tom. He knew everyone in the congregation, and he knew their backgrounds and their personal and family stories. Most amazing of all, at least to me, is that he remembered everything about everybody. He had an encyclopedic memory for pastoral care. Would that I could have recalled 20 percent of what I needed to remember as a minister about parishioners, but Tom Mutch remembered it all. And he remembered it well into his eighties. He might block on a name or two, but on the circumstances of the lives of the people he had served, he never missed a beat.

When parishioners were in need, Tom was there. When they were sick, he was there. When they were in the hospital, when their marriages were dissolving, when someone in the family died, he was there. "There" could have been Tom Mutch's double-entendred middle name: Thomas There Mutch.

Sometimes retired ministers who remain in the community and who continue to attend the church can be a major obstacle for new pastors. That was never the case with Tom Mutch, and Bob Holland also corroborated that for me on several occasions. Tom was perennially supportive and complimentary. It was not in his nature to interfere in anything where he knew it would be unwise to do so, and he assiduously refrained from becoming involved in church activities of any kind. There could be no finer Pastor Emeritus of any church than he.

Mildred was an ideal minister's wife, especially considering that much of his ministry occurred in the first half of the twentieth century. In those days, there were no female Presbyterian clergy, so all clergy spouses were female. Therefore, Mildred was, in effect, an unpaid very active pastoral assistant. She frequently accompanied Tom on pastoral visits, and they created many close friendships in the congregation and community. If any church members ever felt they played favorites, I never heard it.

What they accomplished in their thirty years in the church was truly extraordinary. They were the human glue which firmly held the congregation together. It wasn't Tom's preaching which did it. It wasn't the nature or breadth of the programs. It wasn't worship per se. It was Tom and Mildred Mutch, the Team. They were wonderful, warm, caring people, and it showed in everything they did and said. Neither was effusive, but both knew how to exude Christian love and concern.

The Mutches had three children. Their daughter, Patricia, died at age twelve; and of course, that was a huge blow to them at the time. But they adjusted to her death as they adjusted to all things and went on with their lives. Their other daughter, Betty, married an attorney, and they remained in Morristown. Betty opened a bookstore and gift shop in an old Victorian house next door to the South Street Parish House. Their youngest child, Thomas A. (Tim) Mutch, became a renowned professor of geology and planetary science at Brown University. He also became an expert mountain climber. Another great sorrow in their lives occurred in 1980 when Tim was killed in a fall in the Kashmir Himalayas. But they bore up in that tragedy with quiet grace and dignity, never accusing God of neglect nor bewailing the fact that their son died before they did.

By then, sadly, Mildred had fallen victim to what now would likely be diagnosed as Alzheimer's disease, but then was called merely senility or dementia. Perhaps it had begun before we came to Morristown, but it certainly became evident while we there. And it progressed fairly quickly. Tom was a loving and attentive caretaker. He did not make excuses for her behavior, which on occasion could be a tad unusual; he assumed everyone knew what was the cause of the peculiarities. But he carried on as long as he could, doing everything he could. They were an immensely admirable couple, and that never ceased to be evident as long as they both lived.

If I tend in these recollections to focus rather heavily on the clergy and their spouses, it is because the clergy and their spouses have had a profoundly positive effect on my life. Without question, several ministers in my youth inspired me to go into the ministry; and since my ordination, I have been blessed to have had many close and edifying friendships among other clergy and their spouses.

Old age became Mildred and Tom Mutch. That was true even for Mildred in the infirmity of her dementia. They were marvelous pair. I suspect they always had a soft patina about themselves, but as I got to know them better, that patina had reached a luminescent glow of elderly admirability.

St. Phil Thayer

Phil Thayer was the chairman of the Morristown pastoral nominating committee. He was a high-level executive at Bell Laboratories in Murray Hill, New Jersey. The congregation had many scores of men and women employed by what then was affectionately known as "Ma Bell." A major component of the AT&T corporate complex of companies was located in nearby Basking Ridge, New Jersey, and many others worked for other Bell Labs installations, New Jersey Bell, New York Bell, or the AT&T headquarters in Manhattan.

The people serving under the umbrella of Ma Bell were unusually bright and talented. Certainly, Phil Thayer was one of them. He was a gifted administrator with a scientific mind, but he also was a very dedicated churchman as illustrated by the fact that the PNC elected him as their chairman. Phil and his wife, Marjorie, were regular attendants at worship, although perhaps Phil was more interested in church activities than Marge. He had served on the session a few times before we arrived in Morristown, and he was re-elected again while I was there.

Phil Thayer was very definitely a right-brained man. In this case, I take that to mean that with his scientific and mathematical mind, he was very meticulous about everything, including how a church should be operated. To Phil, it should very naturally run like, well, like Bell Labs. Thus, it should be orderly, functional, and efficient, with little time devoted to speculative issues or extraneous discussions, which, while perhaps interesting, were likely to extend the time of session meetings to no discernible purpose.

Like many scientific-mathematical-engineer types, Phil was more concerned to come quickly to decisions and therefore to implement them as soon as possible. Lengthy discussions were not his favorite ecclesiastical pastime. Furthermore, diplomacy in debate was not high on his agenda. In meetings, he was fairly reticent; but when he said something, he came straight to the point. To him, "the point" was the point and not the thoughts or feelings of others. He knew others had their thoughts and feelings, but to Phil Thayer the issues were the issues. And they should be thrashed out on that basis.

Of the five congregations I served as pastor or assistant pastor, the Morristown church had the greatest percentage of Phil Thayers in its membership. With all those Ma Bell folks and the people who worked in the financial industry in New York and Newark and the high-level management corporate people from hither and yon, many of our elders and trustees wanted to get things decided as soon as possible when they attended church meetings. Educators, artistic types, attorneys, homemakers, and middle-management people are willing and maybe even happy to debate issues till the cows come home, but the Phil Thayers of the ecclesiastical realm like to get right at it and get it done ASAP.

This is not to suggest that Phil was not a warm personality, because he was. He always had a ready smile. He did not guffaw, but he did chuckle. He was genuinely interested in the lives of the people around him. He was fairly soft-spoken, but in conversation, he was prepared to speak with anyone about anything that interested them.

In the years after we left Morristown, I kept in closer touch with Dave Wilson, my "champion" on the pastoral search committee because he and his wife Norma often drove south to Florida, and they would stop in Hilton Head Island on their way to or from the Sunshine State. But I have also always had a special place in my heart for Phil Thayer because ultimately, he as chairman of the pulpit committee had to affirm the committee's decision to nominate me to the congregation as the new pastor. I knew then as I know even better now that there was a risk in accepting a thirty-three-year-old pastor of a two-hundred-year-old church with two thousand members. From a personal standpoint, Phil Thayer was the man who personally most personified that risk. As far as I know, he never looked back with any hesitancy about the decision of the committee; and for that, I shall be forever grateful.

St. David Wilson

As I stated in the previous paragraph, *Dave Wilson* was the member of the Morristown pastoral nominating committee who, for whatever reasons, concluded I was without any question in his mind the clergy candidate the committee should present to the congregation in nomination. Dave was a native of northern New Jersey. He and his wife, Norma, had known one another since childhood in the Newark suburb of Verona. Dave established a very successful insurance agency which had business and individual clients all over northeast New Jersey.

In the initial contact I had with the PNC (pastoral nominating committee), I suggested that someone should have a conversation with Elam Davies to get the most honest and the broadest summary of my strengths and weaknesses as a person and parson. Dave was either the committee member designated or the one who volunteered to call Elam. From what the Boss told me, they established an immediate rapport, and that greatly enhanced my candidacy.

Incidentally, the Presbyterian "call process," or any other call process for that matter, may seem for too human-dominated and far too little divine-dominated by way of my presentation of the process. Christians who believe that the clergy move from one parish to another in a wholly idealized and wholly holy procedure may be scandalized to hear this particular minister's version of how he thinks the system really works. I have absolutely no doubt that God is involved in the process because God is involved in everything, if for no other reason than simply because He is God. Nevertheless, He is not a God who leads by direct intervention as much as by indirect inspiration.

In any case, the clergy, the bishops, the district superintendents, the pastoral nominating committees, and entire congregations all feel a divinely mandated responsibility to do their best to engineer the best clerical matches possible; and thus inevitably, there is a very large and inescapable human element in determining who moves where and why. If God intended for human beings to be mere pawns in His hands, He wouldn't have given us brains, wills, and powers of discernment. Nor, on the other hand, does He give us untrammeled autonomy either. Or so says I.

The small group of three or four members of the Morristown PNC came to Chicago to meet with me and to hear me preach. But they also intended to spend some time with Elam Davies. There is no one who is in a better position to assess the true capabilities of an assistant or associate minister than the pastor with whom that person (parson) has worked for several years. Frankly, I do not know specifically why Elam Davies thought I would be well suited to become the pastor of the Morristown Presbyterian Church; but apparently, he did think it. And he communicated that to the committee members, and especially to Dave Wilson. Thus, in effect, I choose to believe that a trio were particularly instrumental in the process which led the congregation to call me as their next pastor: God, Elam Davies, and David Wilson.

Dave was serving on the session, the governing board of the church, when I came to Morristown, and he was re-elected to serve during my pastorate. He was genuinely devoted to the health and well-being of the church, and he was a supportive and active elder and session committee member and chairman.

Because Norma and Dave Wilson had been members of the Morristown church for a number of years, during which time their children had all grown up in the church, they were aware of the unique challenges represented by having two separate church buildings more than three blocks apart and how that especially affected parents and children because of the children going to Sunday school while many of the parents were attending worship at the same time. Wouldn't it be better, the Wilsons and others wondered, if all church activities were located in a single enlarged building on the Green?

Dave sought the permission of the session to engage an architect he knew to draw schematics of how such a concept might be accomplished in bricks and mortar. Dave Wilson was nothing if not both a dreamer and a doer, and he set out with unbounded enthusiasm to try to bring the dream of one building into reality. Without going into detail, it involved constructing a long, narrow educational facility and offices in the long, narrow parking lot behind the sanctuary. By moving just a few graves in the centuries-old cemetery behind the parking lot, the proposed addition would provide everything believed to be necessary for all the programs of the congregation, and in one location.

There were two major potential obstacles to be addressed, however. By that time, the Presbyterian Church in Morristown had operated out of their two buildings three blocks apart for over half a century, and many wondered why they now needed to change that reality. Secondly, but truly perhaps primarily, there was the question of money. This idea would cost a considerable amount of money. Could it be raised with certainty, and would it be worth the potential backlash among some parishioners if it were raised?

After much reasoned and dispassionate discussion, the session ultimately voted not to present the concept to the congregation for a vote, and the idea died a dignified and well-pondered death. The architectural firm and its primary partner won an award from the American Institute of Architects for unusual creativity in suggesting an innovative solution to an ongoing ecclesiastical logistical impediment, but the session decided it was too big and expensive a step to undertake. No one was more saddened by the decision than David Wilson and John Miller. Might the congregation have been better served for the future if an affirmative vote by the membership had been promoted? It is impossible to make accurate conclusions one way or the other. But the entire matter was given a full and fair hearing by the session, and in a close vote, they decided not to present the possibility to the whole congregation.

The Church and *the churches* are wonderful, powerful, exhilarating and inspiring institutions. They also are somewhat unpredictable, if only because they consist 100 percent of members of the human species. The Church must trust its members to do the right thing, and even if some might argue they might not do the right thing, they must trust that it will all work out right in the end. As the apostle Paul declared, "We know that in everything God works for good with those who love him, who are called according to his purpose" (Romans 8:28). The Presbyterian Church in Morristown, New Jersey, has existed for almost three hundred years, and it has operated successfully out of two separate buildings separated by three-plus city blocks for almost a century. As the French say, *C'est la vie; c'est la guerre.*

My close relationship with Dave Wilson may raise a potential problem in the minds of readers. Is it possible for the clergy and particular parishioners to become too close? Without doubt. And God—and many others—know it has happened far too frequently. For fifty years, one of the ways I have tried to avoid that problem has been to avoid close social relationships with church members. But I do not deny that Dave and I were two peas from one ecclesiastical pod. In many ways, we thought alike. On nearly all church matters, we agreed. I greatly admired Dave and his ever-warm humanity. I loved his enthusiasm, his generosity, his invincible sense of humor, his deep-voiced chuckle, his unfailing positivity, his way of turning what might sufficiently be a ten-minute chat into an hour chat, his love of people, his natural gifts as a born salesman. What a piece of work was David Wilson, how noble in reason, how infinite in faculty, in form and moving, how express and admirable!

Dave died of an acute form of lymphoma shortly before the manuscript for this book was completed, and thus did he meet the requirement to make it into this collage of members of the Church Triumphant. I am saddened by his death, but I was greatly blessed by his life.

St. Elena Sedano

Elena Sedano was not a Presbyterian. She was a Methodist. When our church instituted a shortened midweek service on Wednesdays at noon, followed by a luncheon, Elena began to attend those services every week.

She had long been familiar with the Morristown Presbyterian Church because for many years during July and August, the Methodist and Presbyterian congregations held joint services. For one month, they were in one church, and for the next month in the other. It was an excellent arrangement because so many people in both churches were gone for long periods in the summer that each church would look like an ecclesiastical ghost town if they didn't combined forces in the good old summertime.

By means of those joint services, Miss Sedano became familiar with me, and then some time later with Nancy and our children. Although she attended our church with increasing frequency, especially for the Wednesday noon services, at my urging she retained her membership in the Methodist church. By the time we moved from Morristown, she had become quite close to our family.

She had a very interesting if also somewhat sad background. Her parents had moved to New Jersey from Cuba before she was born. Apparently, her mother was a cold and aloof woman; and both as a child and as an adult, she never felt close to her. Her father, on the other hand, was the apple of her eye. She would often explain in detail the difficulties she and her brother had with their mother, but in her mind, her father was a man without flaws.

Elena never married. She became a kindergarten teacher and happily taught young children for over forty years. When we first became well acquainted with her, she was in her late seventies, and she lived into her late nineties.

She was one of the gentlest souls I have ever known. She was soft spoken, and her whole manner was one of respect, kindness, and compassion. She felt things deeply. Once anyone was her friend, that person was a friend for life. She cultivated her friendships and all her close associations with other people.

Unfortunately, she had a marked tendency to idealize those whom she chose to idealize. By no means did she idealize everyone, but she felt that way about some. Equally unfortunately, I was one of those whom she led herself to believe was without human flaw. Perhaps she saw in me some characteristics which reminded her of her father; I could never figure it out. As hard as I tried to convince her that I had shortcomings by the multitudes, she seemed incapable of hearing any of it. Her poorly considered adulation of me still makes me feel guilty, even though she has been gone for a quarter of a century.

Elena also idealized our family. To her, our children were above reproach, and Nancy and I were the perfect couple. They weren't, and we weren't. But that did not deter Miss Sedano from supposing it to be true.

On one occasion, Elena was a member of a tour group from Morristown that I led to Israel and Egypt. The group flew up the Nile River from Cairo to Luxor to visit the Temple of Karnak and the Valley of the Kings. Due to a glitch in the plane reservations (and oh, did that whole sojourn in Egypt have glitches!), the entire group did not make it onto the return flight to Cairo. We sent as many ahead as could fit on the plane, and I implored Miss Sedano to go with the main group. She refused, insisting she would stay with Nancy and me until we and the remaining few got on the next flight. There was no way she would be separated from us, even for a couple of hours. Well, what can I say?

We actually became much better acquainted with Elena after we moved to Hilton Head Island. She would fly down to the island for a week once or twice a year and stay for a week at a time at one of the resort hotels. Then, she would come to our home for dinner or we would join her at the hotel for dinner during each stay. In between times, she would come to the house for tea on the weekends, and Nancy and I individually would stop to see her daily at the hotel. And of course, she always attended church.

It was during those visits that she explained in detail the circumstances of her upbringing, her love of teaching and young children, and her outlook on life. She experienced a genuinely deep and abiding joy in her teaching career. Because Nancy also had taught kindergarten, she felt a unique kinship with her. And while Elena definitely expressed her distance from her mother, she regularly voiced the utmost devotion she felt toward her father.

Elena was as pure as the driven snow, and in that regard, she also was a bit of a puritan. She did not approve of bad behavior in anyone. She was especially repulsed by any notorious sexual improprieties that might make it into the news headlines. However, like the excellent teacher she was, she would always truly forgive the sinner while at the same time excoriating the sin to a fine fare-thee-well. Despite her disapproval, she never said anything really nasty about anybody, no matter how nasty these miscreants may have been. But sometimes, she did make her thoughts known on such occasions.

If you have deduced that I think Elena Sedano was a complex person who lived her ninety-plus years with considerable psychological and emotional complexity, you have deduced what—in fact—I deduced. Would she have benefitted from some in-depth psychological counseling? Perhaps. I am not sure.

Do other clergy encounter parishioners such as the saintly Elena Sedano? Perhaps. I am not sure. However, I suspect many do. Maybe it is a vocational given.

Elena was essentially very stable; of that, I have no doubt. She was a lady through and through and an incandescent Christian. Her personal beliefs were very deeply held, but perhaps not as deeply pondered. In that, she was like many if not most Christians. Elena transformed her ideas of the Christian life into how she lived her own life; she was thoughtful, generous, caring, loving, and unfailingly kind. If her over-the-top adulation of yours truly made yours truly nervous, that certainly was not her intention. But that was its result anyway. Around her, I always felt like the man who could never become the one she believed me to be, and it made me more than a little uncomfortable, especially when Nancy and I separated and then divorced after thirty-six years of marriage.

I wonder: If Elena had been a card-carrying Presbyterian, would I ever have allowed her to get as close to us as she did? Do I need some counseling to try better to understand why I have always held parishioners at arm's length but let down my hair with other Christians of other denominations? Perhaps. I am not sure. The older I get, the less sure I am of many things. Maybe such uncertainty attends the aging process. Perhaps. I am not sure.

St. Ed Vogt

Edward L.C. Vogt was a lifelong resident of Morristown. His forebears had lived in Morristown almost as long as there was a Morristown. He, his wife, Mollie, and their children lived in a large Victorian frame house on Miller Road, which was a residential street of large and impressive homes dating back to the final two or three decades of the nineteenth century.

Ed was not "Edward" to anybody, and the "L. C." in his name stood for "LeClerc," which was a family name. He was known to everyone as Edward L.C. Vogt, but few knew what L.C. stood for, and everyone called him just Ed.

Ed was a stocky, jolly, happy, contented soul, who, as far as I know, did not have an enemy in the world. On the other hand, because he was one of the town's leading attorneys, no doubt there were some folks who did not think Ed had "hung the moon" as they say in the South. No attorney can practice law effectively and for a long period of time without locking horns with somebody or other over something or other.

The law firm in which Ed had long been a partner was one of the largest in the state and perhaps the largest outside Newark. Over the decades, a few members of the New Jersey State Supreme Court came from the firm.

Ed Vogt was the very epitome of integrity, the soul of superior traits and values that are and should be represented in the legal profession. He was widely respected, admired, and loved in the community. And if ever anybody was a pillar of any church, Ed Vogt was a gargantuan upholder of the figurative framework of everything in the Presbyterian Church in Morristown. He first became a church officer as a young man, and when I knew him in his fifties, he had participated in almost every church activity sponsored by the church.

Because Ed was a lifelong member of the congregation, he knew nearly everyone, and everyone knew him. One of the features of his Christian discipleship which I most valued is that he frequently attended the funerals or memorial services of old timers. Being at funerals is a very visible means for the communion of saints to be perceived and enacted. If they gave out little emblems for attending funerals to be hung on one's lapel like they did for children attending Sunday School in the `40s and `50s when I was a boy, Ed Vogt would have had his whole front glittering like a Christmas tree and looking like the one of the brightest stars among the Soviet commissars. He believed in the communion of saints, and he displayed his belief by how he lived.

The article of winter clothing which most identified Ed Vogt from a distance was a dark green-and-grey woven herringbone topcoat. He had worn this topcoat for perhaps a hundred and fifty years. I suspect it came over on the Mayflower. It was so well made that it never occurred to him to purchase a newer model. Why waste money on something so frivolous when the old coat still had years of wear in it? Well, if the truth was told, the Ed Vogt memorial topcoat had seen better days. Probably it was his wife, Mollie, who convinced him to break down and buy a new coat.

The first time he wore his new overcoat, the word went out like wildfire across the community. People all over town were heard to mutter to one another, "Ed Vogt got a new coat, did you hear?" It was astonishing news. Everyone had gotten so used to seeing Ed in his antique winter wear that they hardly recognized him when he sauntered down the street in his new topcoat.

There was a tradition represented by that old coat, and its owner was a uniquely traditional man. In ecclesiastical matters, he knew the value of tried and true traditions, but he also was willing to try new things to fit new circumstances. He reveled in proven patterns of church activities, but he was open to hearing about new ideas.

Ed had been a good athlete in his youth, and he was a member of several different teams in his prep school. He continued to play a few sports in his older years, and found much enjoyment in it.

One of the things he most loved was surf casting for bluefish and striped bass. He and Mollie owned a cottage close to the beach on Nantucket Island, off the southern coast of Cape Cod. One summer, soon after we came to Morristown, the Vogts invited us to use the cottage for a week, and that is how I became hooked on surf casting myself. When the bluefish are in the surf and are hitting hard, the fishermen might throw in a sardine can or a broken piece of a toy car and they will strike at it. But if the fish aren't out there, or if they are not in a feeding frenzy, they can be very hard to catch. Thanks to Ed and Mollie Vogt, Nancy and I liked Nantucket so well that we bought a time-share there, which our family happily used for the next twenty-five years.

Almost every evening on Nantucket for all of those years, I fished. And that very pleasant chapter of my life was made possible only because of the kindness and generosity of Ed and Mollie Vogt.

The English word, *person,* comes from a Greek word, *persona.* The *persona* was the clay-pottery mask worn by actors in the classical Greek tragedies or comedies. The characters in tragedies wore masks with frowns and downturned mouths, and those in the comedies had laughing masks fastened over their faces. The two kinds of masks have become the symbol for the theater ever since.

Etymologically, are we person *masks*, or are we *persons*? Are we merely facades that cover flesh and blood, or are we ourselves real, genuine, true flesh and blood?

Ed Vogt was the real deal of the human species. He was what Jews would call a *Mensch*, and what many of his young colleagues in the legal profession would call a mentor. He was what all lawyers— and Christians—ought to be.

Because Ed had always been a member of the Presbyterian Church in Morristown, he had come to know many hundreds of fellow church members and to observe many of the issues, both enormous and minuscule, which affect the life of every congregation. He possessed great wisdom in sorting out the ecclesiastical wheat from its inevitable oodles of chaff, and his quiet observations in session meetings were welcomed by everyone on every side of every matter under discussion.

This is not to say that Ed suffered fools gladly, because he didn't. But he always sounded very calm and reasoned when he spoke, and his was such an irenic spirit that he never ruffled anyone's feathers, even if they strongly disagreed with him. That is a singular gift which, if we all had it, would make human existence infinitely more peaceful, but which, unfortunately, shall never happen. Ed was like the poet in Robert Frost's poem *Mending Wall.* He liked "to put notions" into the heads of neighboring folks, things they might never have thought or thought of before, and perhaps should consider before making important ecclesiastical or other decisions.

Ed died shortly after we moved to South Carolina from Morristown. It was a distinct honor for me to be asked to come back and assist in his memorial service and to recall some of those unique characteristics which made Ed such an outstanding Christian, churchman, family man, attorney, and friend. My eulogy included the mention of his old, and new, topcoats. May his tribe ever increase!

St. Jane Winthers

Jane Winthers, like Ed Vogt, was a lifelong Morristonian. She too grew up in the Presbyterian Church on the Green. Her father had been the clerk of session, which is somewhat akin to being the senior warden in an Episcopal church or the president of the congregation in a Lutheran church. Besides being a Christian, which is the more important status, she was Presbyterian to the core, which it is hoped in many cases is an added, unsolicited bonus—unless you believe in the incorrect understanding of the doctrine of predestination in which case such an added status is thought to be foreordained, except that it isn't because that is a fallacious reading of predestination. What is correct, however, is outside the purview of this brief tome, so you'll just have to guess or read up about what predestination truly means.

Jane was a character, a free spirit, a lover of life, and a laugher at funny occurrences. She always had a twinkle in her eyes. And to her eyes we shall return presently.

Like her father, Jane served as an elder on the session. Unlike her father, she was not clerk of session. That isn't because she was not capable of serving well in that office, but rather because she might have been considered too flighty to serve well as the primary lay officer of the congregation. Flighty she wasn't; quintessentially Jane she was.

What, in her case, did that mean? It meant she was far more likely to see humor than pathos in people and situations, not that she was incapable of perceiving pathos. It meant she was a tad scatter-brained, but not exactly flighty. It meant she personified *joie-de-vivre*. It meant she got a full twenty-four hours out of every day.

156

It also meant she could be a bit saucy and spicy. She reveled in the racy and luxuriated in the lasciviously laughable. By no means was she like that all the time, but neither was she never like that. She was captivated by the folly and pratfalls of our species. She clearly saw herself in the folly and the pratfalls, and she could and did laugh at or with herself as much as at or with anyone else.

She and her husband, Tommy, had a happy and productive marriage, so far as I could tell. But I didn't know them as a couple nearly as well as I knew Jane. Jane was far more church-oriented than Tommy. She also seemed to be the more dominant personality, but that may be only because I saw her so much more because she was on the session. Coincidentally, you may be wondering why there are so many elders in these brief parishioner bios. It is because I got to know church officers better than most members in general, simply because I spent more time with them in meetings and at other church functions.

When I came to Morristown as a thirty-three-year-old whipper-snapper, I made the grievous announcement that I intended to visit in every home in the membership. Counting families with children, married couples, and single people, that represented about a thousand homes.

After reading this bold proposal in the church newsletter, Jane stopped by my office soon thereafter, loudly chortling over the brash notion of a wet-behind-the-ears ministerling. She was not mean about it; she was just humorously realistic. "It can never be done," she insisted. "Many people won't want you to come, and you won't have time to visit everyone who does want you to come." Jane had been around the ecclesiastical block many more times than I, and she found the enthusiastic if ill-informed greenness of my thinking most amusing. She didn't come right out and accuse me of being naïve, mind you, but in the space of a very few months, I realized she was absolutely right. I would never achieve my idealistic goal. Had I managed to do that, I would have neglected other responsibilities which would have been even more important. In a congregation of two hundred members, a pastor might accomplish an every-house-hold visit, she said, but not in one of two thousand members.

I wonder what Phil Thayer and Dave Wilson, the chairman and vice-chairman of the pastoral nominating committee, thought of my proposed initiative. They never said. But Jane did because Jane was Jane. Human foibles were her meat and potatoes.

Earlier, I mentioned the twinkle in Jane Winthers' eyes. As the years went on, her eyesight began seriously to fail. She couldn't see well when we lived in Morristown, but after we left, she became not only legally blind but almost totally blind. Everyone and everything became a diffuse and indistinct blur to her. After her husband Tommy died, life closed in on her as never before. But it didn't stop her. She kept right on going. And her Jane-ness never failed her. She did not bemoan her condition; she just lived through it and with it.

Years after we had gone to South Carolina, the Morristown church had a special anniversary to which I was invited. During the brief visit at her invitation, I was invited to be a guest in Jane's home. An amazing transformation had occurred for her. In the intervening time, some outstanding ophthalmological advances had made it possible for Jane to have surgery to restore almost all of her vision. Without a second thought, she opted to have the surgery performed. She couldn't see anyway, so what would be lost if the operation failed?

Lo and behold, it was a resounding success! But it had a typically Jane Winthersian side-effect. The results of the surgery were almost immediate. Naturally, everyone was thrilled with her good fortune. They congratulated and hugged her. But she who had not been able clearly to see anyone or anything for many years now could see everyone and everything. And the thing which instantly struck her was how old everyone had become! She who could not discern faces let alone facial characteristics, could now perceive waves of wrinkles and legions of lines etched into the visages of people whom she had not seen distinctly for two or three decades. It was a hoot to see all these geezers she had known before as youngish contemporaries!

But then, Jane also realized she also had joined the ranks of the oldsters, and that was an even bigger hoot for her. She told me she laughed and laughed at her never-before-observed wrinkles, through which, she said, typically, you could drive a small motorcycle.

Jane Winthers, like so many other Mainline Protestants, was an always-active church member. However, like many of her fellow Mainliners, she was not an ethereal, other-worldly Christian. She was a woman who perceived God in other people, particularly in the unusual, winsome, or bizarre. She was a character who loved characters and lived life to the fullest. The disability of her extremely limited vision did not slow her down. She almost was a centenarian when she died. And like the Energizer Bunny, she kept going and going and going.

St. Richard Cadmus

Dick Cadmus had been an active member and leader in the church in Morristown for years before I came there as pastor. His wife and children were also very involved in church activities.

It became evident to me within a short time that I was not the most admired parson Dick had ever encountered. After a while, I asked the two associate pastors and other staff members if my perception was correct, and they affirmed that it was.

No minister can appeal equally well to every member of any church. The plethora of human psychological patterns and personalities render that an institutional impossibility. Anyone who sets out to be well liked by everyone in any occupation or endeavor shall soon discover that lofty goal can never be accomplished. Because it is based so strongly on interrelationships, the ministry of all vocations is guaranteed to produce people with whom parsons simply fail to connect for whatever host of reasons: the sound of the minister's voice, the accent, the way his or her hair is combed, the lack of hair, the abundance of hair, the content of the sermons, the manner of attempting to provide leadership—whatever.

Well, it was obvious from the get-go that I was not high on Dick Cadmus's clerical leadership list. Without being able to put my finger directly on any part of why that was so, I sensed that nothing I might ever do would meet his expectations. Perhaps my primary failing is that I was not my predecessor, Bob Holland, to whom and with whom Dick felt very close.

Nevertheless, Dick never stopped coming to church because I was the primary preacher and the pastor. He was there nearly every Sunday, sitting in his customary pew with his wife and children. And he continued to participate in many of the activities. Dick Cadmus was committed to the *church* even if he was not committed to its pastor, and that is both understandable and acceptable. Good marks to him for that.

Now for a parenthetical comment. For the fifty years I have been a minister, I have always made a point of knowing what members contributed to the church. Many readers might be scandalized to read that. You may feel it is none of the pastor's business to know what amount of money people give to the church. In that opinion, you would have a great deal of support, especially from most church members, but probably also from a majority of the clergy.

Without trying to convince you of why I have followed that policy, let me at least try to explain it to you. Finances are a primary means of achieving the broadest possible mission in any congregation. A church that struggles barely to exist is not likely to be involved in much outreach to the community or world or to be able to support specific forms of congregational ministry that require money to operate. Sadly, thousands of American churches are in that category. Recently, I read that every day, on average, nine churches close their doors forever, passing out of existence. Declining membership is the main reason for that, but it is followed closely by declining finances, which is a direct result of declining membership.

What should be reasonable expectations for the stewardship of financial resources in any church? The answer to that depends on many factors: the demographics of the congregation, its specific location in whatever community it finds itself, the estimated average income of the membership, and so on. It is my firm conviction that if a minister ignores those factors, she or he does so at the peril of the congregation he or she serves. A church cannot reach its fullest potential without also reaching its fullest financial potential. It needs to be noted that no church ever reaches that goal, but it should strive to do so. And it can do so only if it is known by the clergy and officers what the level of contributions actually are. "Receipts" are as important to the success of a church as they are to a corporation or any other form of enterprise, even if the means of receiving them are altogether different.

So what were the receipts in the Presbyterian Church in Morristown, and what should they be? Not long after we arrived in New Jersey, I read in the local newspaper that Morris County, New Jersey, was one on the ten wealthiest counties in the nation on a per capita basis. That was a very important statistic, at least from my parsonly perspective. A look at some of the annual contributions in the top 10 percent of receipts would bear that out—many in the middle 80 percent and a few in the lowest 10 percent. But as in every congregation, *where* people lived and visibly *how* they lived might appear to have little relationship to *what* they contributed. I believed I needed to know that in order to know in what way and how hard to press the matter of Christian stewardship.

Eleanor Perry, the church financial secretary, was surprised and perhaps shocked when I asked her to show me the contribution records. I gather that had never happened in her thirty-three years as the church's financial secretary. But she graciously opened the books, and there I discovered, as in every other congregation I have served, a wide variety of interesting and inscrutable information.

When I came to the name of Dick Cadmus, I noted that in the previous year, he had given very minimally to the church. But in addition there was an odd recorded contribution of $968.28. I asked Eleanor what that strange figure meant. "Oh," she said, "for years, Dick has paid the premium on a life insurance policy on his life. Our church is the sole beneficiary."

Instantly I thought to myself, "How clever! And how kind." But then, already having become somewhat skeptical regarding Dick, I almost instantly reconsidered. "Is that *truly* kind? Dick Cadmus financially helps us a great deal if he dies, but while he is alive, he contributes almost nothing." I decided to call him to invite him to lunch to discuss this matter. Instead, he invited me to lunch at his country club. It was a beautiful clubhouse, and it also was a very good lunch.

After bantering for a few minutes about this and that, Dick asked what was on my mind. I appreciated that he made no effort to beat around the bush, whatever bush there might be to beat around. I told him that it had come to my attention he had given very little in cash to the church the previous year but that he had been contributing a fixed amount each year toward a life insurance policy which designated the church as the sole beneficiary. "How did you learn that information?" he asked, a quizzical if not dark frown sweeping over his face. I told him I asked Eleanor Perry to see the record of contributions. "For *everybody*?" he asked, incredulously. I told him yes, for everybody. In that declaration, I suspect Dick's assessment of me as a minister precipitously declined further; and already, it was in the lowest tenth of a percentile. I then took several minutes to explain why I did what I did, and why I would likely to continue to do for as long as I was to be a minister. He listened and asked some questions, but it was obvious he was not affirming one scintilla of my rationale.

"I understand your strong disagreement with my philosophy, and I acknowledge it. But Dick," I said, "you're a far better steward for the mission of the Presbyterian Church in Morristown if you're dead than if you're alive." He agreed that might appear to be true, but some day the congregation would receive a very substantial amount of money, and at that time, they could do with it whatever the session decided. (Dick had served on the session when Bob Holland was the pastor, so he knew how session decisions were made. Probably he assumed the elders would use their windfall for something they might otherwise be unable to do.) I countered that if everyone took the position he had taken, currently the church would be poorer than a church mouse, but that at some unspecified point or multiple points in the future, it might have enough funds to endow a small denomination. In the meantime, however, it could not function at all, should everyone do what he had chosen to do.

"Not everyone does what I do," Dick correctly observed. "No," I answered, "you're the only one in the whole congregation who pledges the annual premium of a life insurance policy." Once again, an even darker frown creased his brow as he realized I had secured that brief bit of intelligence from what he considered either an unethical or unwise breach of contributions confidentiality.

Dick Cadmus and I probably left that luncheon more estranged than we had been beforehand. Our level of cordiality with one another, never warm, became distinctly cool. As long as I was the pastor of the Morristown church, he and I spoke to each other—but sadly, only superficially and never at depth about anything.

I wanted Dick to understand why I, as the pastor of the church, objected to him putting nearly all of his annual contribution into the insurance policy, and almost nothing into the operating budget. I didn't assume he would agree with that, but I did want him to understand my objection.

Do I recall this situation almost forty years later because either Dick Cadmus or his unusual stewardship idea irritated or befuddled me, or because the constant distance I felt from Dick hurt my maybe too easily assaulted feelings? Perhaps "yes" to both possibilities. But I still stick by what I tried to explain to him: If anyone's primary contribution to any church is to pay the premiums on a life insurance policy in which the church is the sole beneficiary, his contribution is valid only when he is dead, and not when he is alive.

Nevertheless, I respected the fact that Richard Cadmus remained a regular attendee the whole time I was at the Morristown church, and he participated enthusiastically in many of its activities. He was a good, motivated, and able man, both as a human and as a Christian. He was also tough-minded and very firm in his convictions. Once he made up his mind, there was no dissuading him. Several years after we left Morristown, he became disenchanted over something in the church, and he transferred his membership to another congregation close by. And he probably changed the sole beneficiary of his insurance policy to that congregation. Thus, he was true to himself and to his unique form of delayed Christian stewardship. Whether he was totally supportive of the Presbyterian Church in Morristown while he was a member there, I will leave for you to decide.

Saints Kit and Ed Taylor

Ed Taylor was born "Edward," I presume, and I also presume his wife, *Kit,* was born "Kathryn" or "Katherine." But to everyone who knew them, they were always Kit and Ed.

The Taylors both were born in Mt. Vernon, New York, which is an inner ring suburb of New York City in Westchester County. They both grew up in the Mt. Vernon Presbyterian Church. Prior to World War II, they both went off to college. Then, when the war began, Ed went into military service. On his first furlough back home, he and Kit were married. They ultimately produced six outstanding children, of whom one became a Presbyterian minister.

Ed Taylor was a hospital administrator, working in several locations before they came to Morristown. When they lived in suburban Philadelphia, Kit was involved in the administrative office of Conwell Seminary before it merged with Gordon Seminary in suburban Boston to become Gordon-Conwell Seminary. Wherever they found themselves, Ed and Kit were active in Presbyterians churches close to them. Certainly, they both were mainstays in the Morristown church.

The Taylors were affable, outgoing, warm, and interested people. Unfortunately, they seemed increasingly not overtly to display those characteristics toward one another. They never publicly were unkind or sharp with one another, but they appeared to follow two quite different sets of personal operating principles.

As church people, however, they were unusually responsive and hardworking. Each would do well whatever they were asked to do, and often, they did things they didn't need to be asked to do. They were the kind of folks who can make the pastoral ministry a very pleasurable vocation. If everyone in every church were like the Taylors, church life for everyone would be a perpetually glorious experience.

Sadly, Kit and Ed could not be to one another what they were to everyone else. It was never abundantly evident that their marriage was severely strained, but reading between the lines, careful observers could deduce that perhaps all was not well.

I always had the impression that Ed may have felt somewhat overshadowed by Kit. It is not at all that he was incapable or inept. He could be and was very confident and charming. But he may have lacked the stick-to-it-ive-ness and follow-through that Kit naturally possessed, and he might have felt diminished by that.

Having grown up together, and having known one another for their entire lives, did they think they had the commonality which is a main ingredient in a successful marriage but eventually discovered they evolved into two quite different persons and personalities? Did the similarities of their youth undermine the differences they acquired in later adult life, and could they not figure out how to adjust to their growing differences?

I had a deep admiration and affection for both Ed and Kit Taylor. They were lovely people and harder workers for Christ and his kingdom could not be found anywhere. Nevertheless, there always seemed to be an unexplained and perhaps unspoken strain between them, and that supposition saddened me.

Decades after our family moved from Morristown, I happened to see the name of their minister, son, George, in a publication. I called the church he was serving to relive old times with him. Partway into our conversation, George told me that his parents had divorced not long after we left Morristown. I was not surprised, and yet I was also somehow shocked. They had maintained the façade so well during the years I knew them that I was genuinely sorrowful to learn of their divorce. George told me that both his parents remarried— Kit first and then later, Ed. George said that his father married an ex-nun who was twenty-five years his junior. But, he said, their second marriages turned out to be very happy and fruitful—not in the production of more children. They both no doubt concluded that six offspring was a sufficient number for both of them together, and more were not required once they were with new marital partners.

Since that conversation, I have wondered about Kit and Ed Taylor. Were they too young when they married? Did the war affect them adversely? Countless thousands of couples married during World War II—some in haste, but others not so. If they had waited until a few years after to hostilities had ceased, would they have encountered fewer hostilities between themselves? Or were they ever truly hostile? That seemed impossible to imagine because they both were such wonderful and kind human beings.

Then, another thought occurred to me. Were Ed and Kit Taylor such outstanding church members because they could not be outstanding spouses to one another? Do some people pour themselves into the positive activities of a church or volunteer organizations because they feel incapable of pouring themselves into a marriage they believe can never become fundamentally positive? It's that chap, Paul, way back there twenty centuries ago all over again: "All things work together for good for those who love God, who are called according to his purpose." I am very sorry that Ed and Kit did not succeed in their marriage, as I am when anyone divorces, although they were great successes in other aspects of their lives. But I find consolation that they who were such stellar members of the Church Militant are now again united in the Church Triumphant—however we might understand that complex concept and that complex reunion.

SAINTS OF HILTON HEAD ISLAND, SOUTH CAROLINA

HILTON HEAD ISLAND is the southernmost and largest of the barrier islands along the Atlantic coast of South Carolina. It is located at the southern tip of the Palmetto State, just north of the mouth of the Savannah River, where the river empties into the ocean.

The island has a long and fairly complicated history. Prior to the Civil War, its land was devoted to long-staple, sea-island cotton plantations plus other plantations for rice and indigo cultivation. For the duration of the war, Union troops occupied the island, and Union ships controlled the entrance to Port Royal Sound just to the north of the island. Then, for nearly the next century, Yankees abandoned Hilton Head Island altogether. It was given over to the people who had long lived there, namely, the ex-slaves.

When the northern troops captured Hilton Head, they freed the slaves who had been tending the plantations. The freed slaves established the town of Mitchelville, which is thought by some to be the oldest settlement of freed blacks in the country. Once the soldiers left the island at the end of the Civil War, for the next several decades, the native islanders established small farms, fished, collected oysters, and engaged in a barter economy which lasted into the 1950s and `60s. That was the Gullah culture, as they called themselves, until northerners began to re-discover Hilton Head Island.

In the 1920s, wealthy Northeastern businessmen began to purchase some of the land on the island for hunting preserves. Then, in the 1940s, some lumbermen from Georgia began to buy land for logging purposes. Two of them were General Joe Fraser of the Georgia National Guard and his friend Fred Hack. In 1949, together, they and a few others bought the southern end of the island; and in 1950, Fred Hack bought the northern end, establishing the Honey Horn Plantation.

General Fraser's younger son, Charles, had graduated from the Yale Law School in the early 1950s. Charles was an entrepreneur, environmentalist, and consummate dreamer. He believed that Hilton Head Island could be developed as a resort community, with hotels, restaurants, golf courses, beachfront homes, homes along Calibogue Sound between the island and the mainland, and homes along the fairways of the golf courses—which would be cleared in the forest primeval. Before long, his dream evolved into the nascent Sea Pines Company with Sea Pines Plantation as its first and primary enterprise.

In the meantime, the Hack family—who had been very active members of the Presbyterian Church in Hinesville, Georgia, from whence they came—wanted to found a Presbyterian church on the island. The previous owners of Honey Horn Plantation had built a small chapel under a cluster of large live oak trees on the expansive property. Some of the earliest white settlers on the island used the chapel as their place of worship, arranging for visiting clergy to conduct the services. The congregation of the First Presbyterian Church was chartered by the Charleston Presbytery in that chapel in 1957.

A few years later, Fred Hack and a business partner donated land upon which a permanent church building could be constructed close to the center of the island. The first structure was built in 1965, and—as they say—the rest is history.

It is important to note, however, that the earliest history of First Presbyterian Church was accompanied by a natural rivalry which sprang up between Fred Hack and Charles Fraser, the founder of the Sea Pines Company. Charles wanted to give land for the new congregation along the main thoroughfare at the southern end of the island. It was where the Methodists, Catholics, and Episcopalians were given land. Charles Fraser's older brother, Joseph Junior, and his family were very active in First Presbyterian Church, but Charles much less so. His enthusiasm for things Presbyterian may have diminished markedly after the decision was made to locate the church where it still stands—in the center of the island and not on the south end. In light of later major developments on the northerly end, that may account for much of the rapid growth of the congregation, evenly serving as it does the entire island population.

Then, there was the matter of the naming of the congregation. More than any other denomination—except perhaps Southern Baptists—Presbyterians have traditionally been eager to call the first Presbyterian church in any town "the *First* Presbyterian Church." It may be neither catchy nor classy, but it does certify a certain historical solidity. This pattern held true for both the original Presbyterian and Baptist congregations on Hilton Head Island. The Episcopalians have St. Lukes and All Saints, the Methodists have St. Andrew By-The-Sea, the Catholics have the Holy Family and the St. Francis By The Sea (no hyphens) Churches. But the Presbyterians and Baptists have the First Presbyterian and First Baptist Churches. These other congregations have more descriptive monikers, but the Baptists and Presbyterians of Hilton Head Island can luxuriate in their historicity, even though it is of relatively brief duration compared to many other First Churches elsewhere in much older communities of the country.

When our family arrived on Hilton Head Island in the summer of 1979, the church had 650 members. Within eight years, it had 1,800 members. That surely was due to good luck as much as to good management—or ministry. The island population was growing very rapidly in those years, and the First Presbyterian Church, courtesy of the Hack family, was propitiously located to take ecclesiastical advantage of their location.

And who were these new residents on what one of those new residents once disgustedly described to me as "this godforsaken sand pile by the sea"? Yankees, mostly. Interlopers from the North, like the Miller family. There were many "new" retirees of varying ages, from their mid-fifties to their mid-eighties. Some of the people who established small businesses were young southerners, but the majority of the new residents since the `70s have either been from the Northeast or the eastern Midwest – or increasingly from other parts of the world, but especially Europe. And a sizeable percentage have continued to be retired folks.

Because I served far longer in the First Presbyterian Church of Hilton Head Island than in any of the other congregations with which I was associated, at least up to this point, there will be a far larger collection of Hilton Head saints than those from anywhere else. And as with all the other churches, there could be hundreds more brief biographies than I shall include; but time, space, and book length prevent other very deserving folks from gracing these pages. However, to paraphrase the writer of the Fourth Gospel, these saints are written about that you may believe in the communion of saints and that believing you may perceive yourself also to be a saint, surprising as that may be to you (see John 20:30–31).

St. Billie Hack

St. Billie Hack's husband, Fred Hack, had died before we arrived on Hilton Head Island. Two of their children, Avary and Byron, moved away from the island in their early adult years; but their oldest child, Frederick Hack Jr. (Frederick, not Fred), has lived on Hilton Head Island for all but the earliest few years of his life. By the way, Billie Hack told me I should always call the sceptered isle "Hilton Head *Island*" and not just "Hilton Head," to which its shortened name is designated by the great majority of people. Whenever I hear others say "Hilton Head," or when I myself say it, I still feel a twinge of guilt for them as well as for myself because of Billie. "It's an *island*," Billie quietly informed me, "it isn't just *Hilton Head*." But it isn't easy to say "Hilton Head Island" every time, particularly if you are from certain parts of the South. Some southerners pronounce it "Hee-yul-ton Hay-yud," and by the time you make five syllables out of three, and then add two more, Hee-yul-ton Hay-yud Ah-land is almost too much of a mouthful.

Further by the way, it is called *Hilton* Head Island in honor of William Hilton, an English sea captain who sailed by Hilton Head (Island) in the 1660s. The Spanish and French had been in the vicinity many times in the 1500s. But when William Hilton showed up, sent there by King Charles II (they aren't called the *Carolinas* for nothing) he noted a *headland* (a bluff) on the north end of the island. Thus, it became Hilton Head Island. Strange, but true.

Billie and Fred Hack moved with their three children to Hilton Head Island in the early 1950s when there were only two or three other permanent white families living there. These few families were the first post-Civil War permanent pioneers among twentieth century island palefaces.

Billie gave singular meaning to the words *gracious* and *gentle* and *genteel.* She was the epitome of a quiet, thoughtful, determined southern lady. I never heard her raise her voice about anything, and I doubt that her husband or children did either. She was uniformly soft-spoken.

This is not to say that she was a pushover who could be convinced of anything of which anyone wanted to convince her—no indeed. She well knew her mind, her thoughts, and her beliefs, and she stuck by them, but always, always, *always* quietly. Invariably, she came across clearly but never combatively. She would have been an outstanding diplomat, except that those upon whom she was attempting to exercise her diplomacy might incorrectly suppose her low-volume, measured words belied a mushy inner core. Not on your life. Billie was *tough*, but in the gentlest conceivable manner. She knew who she was, which is a great advantage to those who want fully to become what God wants them to be. In my opinion, Billie achieved that to her utmost limit.

Billie had oodles of friends. They were southerners and northerners, young and old, black and white, serious (and she herself was nothing if not serious) and not-so-serious, conservative and liberal, Republicans and Democrats, old-time islanders and just-arrived islanders. She was not cosmopolitan in the sense that she adopted and adapted to the mores and folkways of everyone she came across. She was always a *southern* lady; of that there could be no doubt. Nonetheless, she got along with everyone of every region and origin and culture. She had respect for all people, regardless of their strengths or weaknesses as she perceived them.

But Billie was also very reserved. She was not someone who could easily chat with anyone for hours. She was a listener more than a talker. She wanted to understand others and where they were "coming from" as we, but not she, would say. She didn't approve of everyone's values; and occasionally, by a slightly arched eyebrow or downturned mouth, she might indicate a smidgeon of skepticism about something someone said about something. But she would never rip into anyone as a lion would rip into a fallen gazelle; that would have been utterly unthinkable to her.

Sometimes, because Billie *was* so preternaturally mild-mannered and she *was* so naturally soft-spoken, it might be difficult to know exactly where she stood on certain issues. But if she could be coaxed out of her gentleness, she would offer her well-reasoned opinions in measured words and tones.

I always had the feeling that northerners were either enigmas to Billie Hack or, often, that we were hard pills for her to swallow. By her standards, we, or at least folks such as I, were so brash and rash and outspoken. To her, some of us surely must have come across as bulls in china shops.

Well, to her we probably *were* bulls in china shops. We wanted every unresolved issue addressed instantly. With us china-shop-bovines, there was no time for velvet banter, no inclination toward circuitous caution. But Billie knew that feelings could be hurt and psyches could be assaulted if words were spoken too directly or loudly or pointedly.

With two other southern ladies, both of whom were also members of First Presbyterian Church, Billie started what evolved into a long-admired island institution called the Bargain Box. It is a thrift store, but a thrift store with an exclusively community-minded purpose. The basic idea is that people would give used clothing and furniture and appliances and books and other goods to the Bargain Box. Nearly everyone who moved to Hilton Head Island discovered within minutes or hours of the moving van being unloaded that they had brought far too much stuff with them. The Bargain Box would take their stuff, sell their stuff to those who needed or at least wanted their stuff, and give the proceeds from their stuff to the growing number of charities and non-profit organizations that found their place in the expanding island community. (Hilton Head has more stuff than it knows what to do with them. It always has.)

Everyone benefitted: The people who donated their things to the Bargain Box were pleased they could be recycled for good purposes. The lower-income people who purchased quality goods at very reasonable prices were far better off than they would be if there were no Bargain Box. The people who staffed and volunteered in the charitable organizations and the people in the Bargain Box itself who volunteered to keep the growing amount of re-salable items flowing smoothly and quickly out their doors also benefitted.

The three ladies started out in a very small one-room building near the First Presbyterian Church, and most of their early financial grants went to the church. When they outgrew their small store, they built a building on the church property, which expanded over the years. As their sales grew, they concluded other churches and institutions should benefit from their grants. By now, the Bargain Box has contributed millions of dollars to many organizations on Hilton Head Island and in the Lowcountry of southern coastal South Carolina. Their gross sales each year approach a million dollars, and their net contributions after expenses amount to well over nine hundred thousand dollars.

By now, there are several other charitable thrift shops on the island—each with a storehouse of stuff for sale. Because that is so, every year, a few thousand tourists come to Hilton Head Island for a day or week not for the beaches or golf or tennis or for fishing, but for the thrift stores. Hilton Head must be one of the best places in the world to purchase very high-quality used stuff at very low prices. If the thrift stores don't keep the prices low, they can't compete with the other thrift enterprises. It is capitalism at its smoothest, except that it isn't capitalism at all. It is charity at work, benefitting everyone: donors, "owners," churches, community organizations, and medical foundations.

Were it not for Billie Hack and her concern for the fiscal well-being of a new congregation on a newly-discovered resort island into which new residents and new low-paid workers were streaming, First Presbyterian Church and the other island churches and other charitable groups would not be what they are. She and her friends had a vision of how much good could come from people giving away what they didn't need to those who could afford to pay or wanted to pay but little for it. Yet that "little" amounted up to a huge "much."

Billie was heavily involved in the women's activities of the church, in its study programs, in its social groups, and especially in its worship. She was an every-Sunday Christian, even though she had been widowed for some time and generally came to church by herself. She was sufficiently an old-fashioned southern lady that she had ineradicable doubts that women should ever be elected as elders of the church. Though she was approached many times about serving on the session, she always politely but firmly declined. No one could sweet-talk Billie Hack into anything she opposed and for whatever reasons she opposed them.

I never had the opportunity to know Billie's husband, Fred. Together, they were a strong and vibrant couple; that I deduced very soon after coming on the island and into the church. I am sure Fred was far more outspoken on issues than Billie, and no doubt, she deferred to him more than most wives thirty to fifty years younger than she. Besides, she was southern; and decades ago, southern women were taught that the husband was to be the head of the household. Fred was likely the head outside the household, but Billie was the head inside the household itself. At least that is how I perceive it must have been.

Though Billie was low-key, she was not meek. Though she was refined, she was not easily manipulated by anyone. Though she was soft-spoken, she was never silent—particularly when she felt strongly about something. She was a classic steel magnolia. I have never known anyone else who had exactly the same traits and attributes that she had. Like many Mainline Protestants, she held her deepest beliefs close to her vest, but no one could ever doubt that her beliefs were deep. She was a lovely lady and a true pioneer in the modern development of Hilton Head Island. With her husband, Fred, she was a trailblazer for what contemporary Hilton Head was intended to be.

St. Richard Bowen

Dick Bowen was a womanizer. Anyone who knew him and didn't know that didn't really know him.

Dick had built up a manufacturing business in Buffalo, New York, and it became a thriving corporation. When he was still a relatively young man, he sold the business to his son—his only child—on a long-term financing plan, which provided him a very good stream of income for the rest of his life. Then, he retired to Hilton Head, presumably to live there happily ever after.

Before Dick moved to Hilton Head Island, however, he had been married to a woman he deeply loved. That marriage ended in his wife's death, which was an enormous psychological and spiritual blow to Dick. Of all his women, and there were many, she was truly what he often described as "the love of my life." Probably no one else could ever measure up to her, which was unfortunate for that ever-lengthening legion of ladies. He married again shortly thereafter, but that did not work out.

After I came to know Dick much better, I wondered if his first wife was his favorite wife because she *was* his favorite. Or was it because she had died and was gone forever, and therefore, he missed her more. It is conceivable, really, that monogamy was not strongly etched into Dick's genetic code. Or so it seemed to me.

When I first met Dick, he had been associated for some time with a capable and independent-minded businesswoman who was a member of the First Presbyterian Church as was Dick himself. They did not live together, but they spent many hours of every week together.

Dick Bowen was a charmer. He was handsome and generous, he liked good food and drink, and he liked to treat the women in his life to what he and they liked. They knew it, and he knew they knew it.

Among Dick's weaknesses, of which there were more than a couple, is that he drank too much. When I would ask him if he was an alcoholic, which I felt compelled to do from time to time to see if I could jar him out of his addiction, he always denied it. Nevertheless, he would readily and regularly admit that he drank too much. The bartenders in the clubs of which he was a member and the wait-staffs in the restaurants he frequented were delighted with him. In addition to being a big tippler, he was also a big tipper.

I suspect Dick's primary problem with women is that he wanted to possess them. Most of them, wisely, did not want to be possessed. In his own way, he loved women, many women, but he wanted to love them on his terms, which meant they were to be "kept" women. Dick was not a bad man, but he was a stereotypical engineer-type (if such a type there be) who had little self-understanding and even less understanding of others and human psychology. He wanted what he wanted when he wanted it, and he did not have an overabundance of patience to nurture a relationship with a woman and allow it slowly to grow and mature. He wanted the whole nine yards quickly, if not instantly.

Dick didn't have coveys of women at one time; he usually had one woman, with perhaps another woman or two on the side. Needless to say, if the main squeeze discovered there were others who were being squeezed, it proved problematic. Usually he could convince her to stay connected to him because he really was charming and generous. For whatever reasons, however, he seemed incapable of establishing a permanent healthy relationship with any woman, especially after he seemed to have decided to forego another marriage altogether.

Nevertheless, he always had someone with whom he "kept company." The first of these ladies I knew the best because they both came to church quite regularly. They even came occasionally to other church functions together. They didn't live together, as I said earlier, but they spent many hours of every week together. In the end, I believe she broke off the relationship because of the drinking. It may be that Dick was a "mean drunk" although I never personally observed that. That may have been because almost always, I saw him during the daytime; and usually, he was fairly circumspect about the volume of his imbibing in front of the minister.

After Dick and Betty parted, he would call me now and then to have lunch. He spoke of his loneliness, and I have no doubt he was lonely. Dick Bowen without a woman was like a car without wheels.

By himself, he was going nowhere, and he knew it. Therefore, I would patiently urge him to find someone to establish a permanent and committed relationship with her and only her and to settle down by taking the matrimonial plunge again but this time, making sure it would be until death would them part. He was happy to try to find someone, but the rest of the parson's formula was more of a challenge for him. And he never appeared seriously to try to follow my entire advice. But he still came to church regularly, even if for extended periods by himself.

After a while, Dick came to church with a new lady. They seemed to hit it off very well. As with previous relationships, they spent a lot of time together. Then, much to my astonishment, Dick told me they planned to be married, and they wanted me to counsel them. The best counseling I could give the prospective bride was to recall Dick's history with women and to urge her to be cautious. This I did with Dick present; I didn't want him to think I was doing anything behind his back. They were married despite my hesitancy, and it was I who officiated at their wedding. And they were happy—for a few years. And then, the same patterns recurred: excessive drinking, which led to bad behavior, which led to excessive drinking. And then, that marriage also ended.

Eventually, Dick met a much younger woman who had a teenage daughter. I couldn't imagine anything ever coming of this new relationship, if only because of the girl. By then, Dick was in his late sixties or early seventies, and he was old enough to be the young girl's grandfather. Never having claimed great success as the father of his own son, it seemed unlikely he could become a successful stepfather or "my mom's nice boyfriend" to the teenage daughter. Nevertheless, as nearly as I could discern, he was basically kind to both of them when he was not under the influence of his favorite liquid substances. They lived with him for a few years until the same lethal patterns loomed up again. When Mary could stand it no longer, she and her daughter moved off the island to try to start a new life.

No one could ever accuse Dick Bowen of being cheap. He had made a great deal of money in his business, and he was always happy to relieve himself of some of his assets on behalf of jewelry, clothes, cars, travel, and other amenities for his lady friends.

Did he try to buy love or at least affection or maybe more likely, sexual favors? Perhaps. But if so, he seemed to do it lavishly. My impression, as an interested outsider, is that the women in Dick Bowen's life had certain undeniable advantages as well as some inevitable disadvantages.

The last female with whom Dick Bowen spent time together probably perceived him to be a super-sized sugar daddy, which in many respects I too had always perceived him to be. As with all the previous women in the Bowen stable, he was very generous to her. Finally, in a weak moment, he reluctantly acceded to her unsubtle suggestions that they should become matrimonially attached. He sent her by herself to a jewelry store to choose a diamond as only he would do. He was romantic but only as he chose to be romantic. She selected a much-larger-than-average rock, which, when he learned the price, he reluctantly and ruefully paid for. Their engagement lasted for a couple of years or more. He didn't want to rush into anything. "Marry in haste; repent…"

In the meantime, however, he became ill with a constellation of medical problems that ultimately took his life. He had always driven Mercedes automobiles, none of which was ever among the cheaper models. His newest paramour had begun to drive the much more expensive of his two expensive cars. Dick concluded that he wanted the diamond and the Mercedes back. After a protracted and bitter confrontation, however, death intervened, and neither the ring nor the roadster was ever returned.

I will now confess to you that I have forgotten countless details in the personal vignettes I have written in this litany of saints. In trying to determine whether I had all my facts straight about Dick Bowen, I phoned a friend on the island I have known since she moved to Hilton Head. (I did this as well with other people for other saints whose memory I trusted far better than I trusted my own, in case you are wondering.)

My friend knew Dick nearly as long as he lived on the island. She corroborated that many of my recollections were correct; a few were not. And she reminded me of other features in the colorful life of this gifted, able, and addicted man, who was addicted to women as much as to distilled spirits. She reminded me of something I had entirely forgotten. At Dick's memorial service, she recited to me my opening sentences in my meditation about this flawed parishioner and friend. She said that I said (and I have no reason to deny that I said it, but I didn't remember saying it until she recited it), "Dick Bowen loved women, and women loved Dick Bowen. If you don't believe it, look around you." And with that, she said, everyone laughed. She remembered that there were only two men in the large room in the funeral home and a whole host of women, most of them of a certain age. As much as they might have liked to ring his neck while he was alive, they were there properly to see him off now that he was dead. Included among them was the big rock and big Mercedes lady.

Dick Bowen a saint? Come on! How could a man like this be a saint?

But as I have said, he was kind and generous and charming. He was solicitous and concerned. He displayed all those characteristics to women more than he did to men, to be sure, but he was all those things to everyone he knew to one degree or another. I am convinced that his primary failing was that he could exercise no control over his intake of alcohol, and he took in many gallons or barrelsful during his lifetime. Perhaps because of that form of excess, he also became addicted to women as well. Who knows? He was just like the title character in Edward Arlington Robinson's poem:

> MiniverCheevy, born too late,
> Scratched his head and kept on thinking;
> Miniver coughed, and called it fate,
> And kept on drinking.

Certainly, Dick Bowen was a very magnanimous steward. He gave millions of dollars to his alma mater, Bucknell University in Lewisburg, Pennsylvania. Over the years, he gave tens of thousands of dollars to the First Presbyterian Church of Hilton Head Island. I was away from the island serving in four interim pastorates after I left the First Presbyterian pastorate. I returned and inaugurated The

Chapel Without Walls in 2004. For unknown reasons, Dick never once attended The Chapel; but one year, his accountant informed him that it would behoove him to give away a sizeable amount of money to avoid paying a much higher income tax than he usually paid, which was always more than sufficiently sizeable.

Dick called and asked me to come to see him. By this time, he was no longer very mobile. He explained his problem (a very nice one to have) and asked my advice. I suggested he should give a large contribution to Bucknell University since it had meant so much to him. No, he said, he had given them enough. "Well then," said I, "give some to First Presbyterian and some to the congregation you attended for a while with the last of your wives. And while you're at it," I opined, "you could also give some to The Chapel Without Walls, which probably could use it more than the other two congregations that after all, do have some walls." In a few days, he told me he had sent $25,000 to each of the other two churches and an equal amount to The Chapel.

Dick Bowen made a great deal of money in his working career, and he gave away a large part of it to various institutions, churches, and other charities in his retirement. He was a very loving brother to his sister as she was a loyal, loving sister to him. He was estranged from his son, and I seriously doubt he did all he could to narrow that gap. But oh, the women he loved! He could never get enough of them, even though—sadly but understandably—eventually, most of them felt they had more than enough of him.

Through it all, he continued to believe in God, and he served God in his own unique if also not-always-admirable way. He attended church regularly, and he supported Christ's Church in a uniquely Bowenian financial style.

I have known other men who were similar to Dick Bowen with respect to women, but no one exactly like him. But then, no one is exactly like anyone else. Is that not true? We are all God's chillun, and in many different ways, none of us is precisely like any of the rest of us. Dick Bowen, womanizer, was definitely one of a kind. He was also always a good friend. RIP, Richard.

St. Bee Lane

Bee Lane was a certifiable pistol. She was a smoking six-shooter, a blazing Beretta, a loaded Luger.

When Bee first started to attend First Presbyterian Church, I didn't know she was there. Bee being Bee, that was surprising because those who knew Bee always knew when she was in their presence. In a large congregation, anyone, even the most noticeable, can go unnoticed for a while; so for a while, Bee was unknown to me. However, I, along with many others, became well acquainted with her when she began to attend some weekday adult education classes I was teaching.

In order to understand Bee, you need to understand her background. For the first five years of her life or so, Bee was brought up in a Presbyterian family in rural north-central Florida. She had a sister who was ten years older than Bee and a brother who was somewhat closer to her in age and of whom she thought very highly. Her parents' relationship, on the other hand, might charitably be described as troubled.

Her father was a womanizer and left home for another woman when Bee was just a young child. Eventually, when both of her siblings had left home, Bee was raised by her mother as an only child. Bee saw her father almost never again.

At some point in her youth, she and her mother moved into the small college town of northern Florida called DeLand and, in a few years, to Bradenton. They became Episcopalians, and an Episcopalian she remained until she wandered into the First Presbyterian Church of Hilton Head Island some sixty years later. Exactly why she and her mother switched from John Calvin to Henry VIII I cannot say. I do know why she switched back to the Episcopal Church at the end of her life. But we shall come to that presently.

People who live in South Florida are, for the most part, northerners. People who live in North Florida, however, are usually southerners.

Bee was a southerner. She talked southern, she thought southern, and she *was* southern. She lived all her life in the South: first in North Florida; then in Charleston, South Carolina; then in

Savannah, Georgia; and finally, in Bluffton, South Carolina—on the mainland side of the bridge from Hilton Head Island. In between, she lived a year with her two young daughters in Switzerland. South Switzerland. Sort of.

Life wasn't easy for St. Bee Lane. There were the early troubles between her parents. Her brother didn't get along with her father. But then, I gather many people didn't get along with her father.

When Bee married, life became easier and more pleasant for Bee. She and her husband had two daughters. They were very active in the social swirl of Savannah, and they both established a place for themselves in the social life of one of the South's fine old cities.

Nevertheless, things in their marriage began to deteriorate. After more than two decades of trying to make things work, Bee and her husband were divorced. Perhaps neither was happy, but maybe they were less unhappy afterward than they were before. And that at least was something.

For a few years, Bee and her daughters continued to live in Savannah, Georgia. She became very involved as a volunteer for the Girl Scouts, which had been instituted in Savannah decades before by their founder, Juliette Gordon Low. She was the chairman of the board of directors for the Girl Scouts.

Inevitably, Bee became a social butterfly. She was a party girl. She well understood how to party and was devoted to all aspects of the avocation. No one ever had more fun than Bee Lane, nor did anyone know how to do so better than she.

In the Savannah years, Bee sent her daughters to one of the finest private schools in the city. I assume that she had financial independence by means of the divorce. She became a realtor—more perhaps to keep herself occupied than to earn lots of money. She was a real estate dabbler more than a crackerjack sales agent. But she had many contacts, and she maintained many friendships by means of introducing prospective home buyers to prospective homes.

I have known many people such as St. Bee who were too committed to Good Times to be committed to the Good News as well. Not Bee. She was always a committed believer, and she always went to church, taking her girls in tow with her. And the church, as I said, was Episcopalian. There is something about Episcopalianism which leads its adherents to suppose it is unique among all branches of Christendom, which it surely is. So is every other branch as well, but the Episcopalian variety of Christianity has a hold on its members which the rest of us envy. It is a psychological-sociological-ecclesiastical tie which is impossible adequately to define but also impossible to ignore.

In the midst of her Savannah sojourn, Bee Close met and married Preston Lane. Pres became the manager of the Savannah Wildlife Refuge a few miles outside Georgia's oldest city. The refuge was located in the tidal marshes and low-lying islands where the Savannah River slowly sloshes around before finally depositing its pale brown waters and suspended pluff mud into the Atlantic Ocean.

There was a large old house which was the official residence for the game refuge manager and his family. By that time, Bee's two daughters were off on their own, so it was the two getting-ever-older no-longer-youngsters who lived there. They had many a swinging party through the time they lived there. She and Pres spent several happy years in their mansion in the marsh until Pres retired. Then, because Savannah no longer had the attraction for Bee and Pres it once had held, they moved to a house in Bluffton, South Carolina, where both of them had some previous connections. Not too long afterward, Pres died.

Bee continued to be a regular attendant at her Bluffton Episcopal church until they called a new rector who had two major shortcomings in Bee's eyes. He was too evangelical, and he was too high-church. She loved to claim the clouds of incense nearly choked her to death. Thus, it was that after many attempts to make her peace with the new ecclesiastical regime she found her way denominationally into the Church of her childhood by means of the First Presbyterian Church of Hilton Head Island.

She became a live-wire valued member of the weekday morning classes I taught. If the discussions became too heavy, she had a way of lightening them with her humor. She loved to make slightly off-the-wall observations about this and that, especially if there was a moderately off-color tinge to what she said. It seemed to me she liked to try to shock the rest of us. As time went on, however, we learned not to be shocked; instead, we all concluded that was just Bee being Bee. And Bee being Bee was a delight.

One time, we were talking about prayer and specifically what was wise or unwise to bring to God in prayer. Bee said, "I used to pray that God would change people who tend to drive me crazy, but now I just pray for God to help me to put up with them." It was an excellent observation all of us would do well to remember. Some people will never change, but with divine assistance, we can change how we relate to those people. Being a saint is often not an easy or instantly evident business. Nonetheless, God helps us along in the difficult lifelong process.

The youngest member of those classes was Lois Landis, who later was to become my wife after Nancy and I were divorced. Lois became a close friend of Bee Lane, who was one of the oldest members of the class. In some ways, they seemed an odd pair, but they shared many of the same views on many things. And each enjoyed the company of the other.

Years later, when I left home and then eventually married Lois, Bee was very put out with both of us as no doubt were many other people in the congregation. By that time, however, I had moved away from Hilton Head Island to do some interim ministry pastorates in Virginia, Minnesota, and Ohio, so we did not see Bee at all during that six-year stint.

When Lois and I returned to South Carolina in late 2003, we moved into Bluffton, the mainland community adjoining the bridge to Hilton Head Island. We learned that Bee had gone back to her Episcopalian church in Bluffton but that she was not in good health. Both her daughters lived elsewhere—one in New York City and the other in the mountains of western North Carolina. Bee had help who came to her home each day to take care of her. She being the independent soul she was, that was no easy assignment for those ladies.

Because Bee lived close to where we lived in Bluffton, and because both Loie and I had been close to her during our years at First Presbyterian Church, we started to visit her on a regular basis— not as a pastor and his wife but as longtime friends from days gone by. And on that basis, whatever animosity she had felt toward us appeared quickly to dissolve after Loie's first husband died and Loie and I were married two days after my divorce was finalized.

It was always an experience filled with unanticipated disclosures to talk to Bee about North Florida and Savannah and Bluffton in the old days. She loved to entertain with captivating stories about her colorful, event-filled life. We felt blessed to be with her in many of her final days as she slipped away—not with a bang but certainly not with a whimper either. She was closing in on a hundred years, and she, the perennial pistol, had packed a heap of living into every single day of her unique existence. She was a Christian, but a distinctively Bee Laneian Christian to the core.

St. Bert Yancey

Bert Yancey was a professional golfer on the PGA tour for a number of years. He also was afflicted with bipolar illness.

Bert was a graduate of the United States Military Academy at West Point, where he was captain of the golf team. In his senior year, he encountered his first bout with severe mood swings. He was hospitalized for nine months and was given an honorable discharge shortly thereafter. Once he was sufficiently stabilized, Bert joined the PGA tour. Later, he married, and they had a son. Bert did quite well in the dozen years or so he competed on the tour. He won seven tournaments and had six top-five positions in the four major tournaments. Eventually, no doubt due largely to the stresses and strains of his bipolar illness, Bert and his wife divorced.

I well remember him telling the Men of the Church at a breakfast meeting about how he almost won the Masters. The "almost" was one approach shot on either the last or the second-to-last hole at Augusta in the fourth and last round. He was leading at the time. He selected his club, took careful aim, and struck the ball. It landed on the line he wanted, and it hit the lip of the green, which is also what he wanted. But instead of bouncing forward onto the putting surface for what likely would have guaranteed him the winning putt, the ball perversely trickled backward into the trap, where it became lodged too close to the wall of the trap to allow him a clean shot out of the bunker. In that moment, he told us he knew it was all over.

His illness didn't badly engulf Bert again for the first part of his career as a touring professional. But then, in the mid-`70s, it returned—this time, with a vengeance. Like many who suffer from bipolar disease, Bert's behavior was far better when he was depressed than when he was in the manic phase. When he was high, he was beyond the clouds in a world only he could see or imagine. For a few years, he had several hospitalizations plus short incarcerations for a variety of offenses of varying degrees of seriousness. All the while, he was trying to regain sufficient composure to return to the tour. His medication, however, gave him the side effect of hand tremors, which meant he could not putt for sour apples, and his golf game therefore soured in the process as well.

Thus, it was that he ended up on Hilton Head Island, where he became a teaching pro at one of the local golf clubs. And thus, he became an active member of First Presbyterian Church. And thus, I came to know Bert quite well, both as a pastor and friend. He became close to a sweet young woman named Laura who was also a member of the church. For a few years, she came to represent steadiness and moderation for him; and for most of that time, he did not experience many debilitating mood swings.

Bert joined a group of teachers I taught who became teachers themselves in a national interdenominational Bible study program. He enjoyed the discipline needed to keep up with the material, and over the course of the two-year preparation, he made many interesting and thoughtful comments about biblical passages we were studying. Occasionally, his comments seemed to come from somewhere out in the neighborhood of left field (or the left rough perhaps more appropriately), but everyone in the group knew Bert and knew about his illness, and so it was all okay. When he became a teacher, he performed very well with his own class, and his class members respected and loved him.

One early winter evening, Laura called me to say that Bert had plummeted into a deep depression. He had not emerged from his apartment for three days, nor had he eaten much, if anything. She thought I might be able to talk him out of his funk. I went immediately to see him. When he did not answer the door, I walked in. There were no lights on, and with the coming night, it seemed like Sing Sing Prison in a power outage.

At first, it was difficult to get him to talk at all; but finally, he began to speak in short, clipped sentences. He said he knew he was drifting into a mental decline, but he felt there was nothing he could do other than to take his medication and try to ride it out. I phoned him a few times each day for the next few days to check on his progress. The depression was gone, and he appeared to be back to normal, whatever "normal" meant for this tortured saint. Then, he asked me to come visit him again at his home, which I did.

This time, it was evident within a few seconds of seeing him that he was on a rapid rise toward the manic phase of what was then unhelpfully called manic-depressive illness. I asked him if he was taking his meds, and he, like many others who are assaulted by this cruel mental aberration, said he did not want to do so because he was exhilarated by the high his manias always provided him. He knew highs were even more destabilizing than lows, but the feeling they gave him was so wonderful he wanted to experience it all again.

Then, he told me about other times his highs had lifted him out of his depressions. He recounted one incident in particular, which had made national headlines in the sports pages. He was in the LaGuardia Airport in New York City when he felt compelled to climb to the top of a tall stepladder in one of the terminals. He ordered whites to one side of his makeshift pulpit and blacks to the other side. Then he announced that God had declared to him he should preach against racism, which he did—for as long as anyone was willing to listen to a somehow-familiar preacher perched on a stepladder in a terminal in LaGuardia Airport. It was not long before his listeners had disappeared into the distance, however, and the airport security personnel were there to coax him down from his makeshift elevated platform.

People don't expect to hear sermons about racism from noted golf professionals standing on stepladders anywhere, let alone in busy urban airports. As he recounted the bizarre incident, Bert laughed about how peculiar it must have seemed to those whom he managed to collar for his homily. But at the time, he said, he fully believed he had been commissioned by the Almighty One of Israel to do what he did, and who was he to refuse to follow a divine mandate?

Because Bert Yancey was so well known in a community with thousands of happy and not so happy golfers and because nearly everyone in church knew Bert's condition and because he was such a gentle southern gentleman, he was widely accepted and acknowledged as one of the mainstays of First Presbyterian Church as long as he was part of our congregation. Then, he turned fifty years of age, and he decided to give golf another whirl on the Seniors Tour. He moved back to Florida, where he had grown up; and there, he re-married. And there, he and his wife had a child. A few years after he left Hilton Head Island he had a massive heart attack while competing in a senior tournament, and he died almost instantly.

It is not possible for anyone who has been a member of the clergy for many years not to have had parishioners with various forms of mental illness. Mental illness is one of the most complex and perplexing of all diseases, and it can and usually does affect everyone who comes into contact with those who are thus afflicted by it. The web it spins is very difficult, exasperating, and profound. St. Bert Yancey managed to maintain a positive relationship with his fellow members of First Presbyterian Church because his situation was so widely acknowledged, and he was such a genuinely good guy. I expect that all who knew him remember him with admiration and affection. He was among the straightest of shooters, despite that one shot that bounced back into the bunker at the Masters. But Bert supremely saw himself as a servant of the Master, and that was what meant the most to him. He was an evangelical Christian to his core. In retrospect, however, he readily admitted, with his sunny grin and a twinkle in his eyes, that maybe it was neither God nor Jesus Christ who ordered him to the top of the LaGuardia ladder on that day which unfortunately gave him the most notorious headlines of his whole lifetime. But I guess a man's gotta do what a man's gotta do.

Those who are afflicted with mental illness have an unusually heavy cross to bear, both because of how they perceive themselves and how others perceive them. Bert Yancey truly bore the demons of bipolar illness as well as he could. Sometimes, he was clearly out of control, but he also was always Bert. And that was more than enough. *Requiescat in pace, frater.*

Saints Jim and Evelyn Mitchell

Jim and Evelyn Mitchell moved to Hilton Head Island long before most of the many thousands of other immigrants who landed upon its sandy shores. The Mitchells arrived in the late `60s, when there were just a few thousand residents, half of whom were native island blacks. They built a house on Brams Point when there was almost no one living on that narrow peninsula and back then, was far removed from where nearly everyone else lived.

The Mitchells came from suburban Chicago. Jim was in the airplane insurance and reinsurance business long before most people had even thought of it. He had been a pilot from his early days, and during World War II, he was instrumental in forming the national Civil Air Patrol. With others, Jim helped form a company which specialized in insuring private and commercial airplanes. He was very successful in the business, managed to be able to retire early, and he and Evelyn lived happily ever after. However, no one who knew them knew whether they had two nickels to rub together. They were very frugal, which was in keeping with Jim's Scottish parents. Though they had more than sufficient assets, it would never have occurred to them to flaunt it.

The Mitchells had been Lutherans in Naperville, Illinois. Because there was as yet no Lutheran church on Hilton Head, they became Presbyterians. Both Evelyn and Jim eventually became elders in the First Presbyterian Church. Like most others who were to join the first Presbyterian church on Hilton Head Island, the Mitchells were not dyed-in-the-wool adherents of a particular denomination. Instead, they affiliated with the congregation for a host of other reasons, having little or nothing to do with theology or tradition or ecclesiastical propriety but rather, with proximity or "feel" or "fit."

The Mitchells were the kind of church folks who were active in virtually everything except the choir. Whether that was because they couldn't sing well or they chose not to sing in the choir, I don't know. But they participated in everything else. Evelyn also became the president of the Bargain Box, the charitable thrift shop which St. Billie Hack and her two friends had started years previously.

Friendship was one of the longest suits played by the Mitchells. They made friends easily. Because they came to the island much before nearly every other immigrant islander, they knew most of the old timers as did few others, even though Spanish Wells Plantation, as the Brams Point area came to be called, was one of the smallest residential developments on the island. Evelyn and Jim got along well with everyone. Anyone who couldn't get along with them couldn't get along with anyone.

Dependability was another of their long suits. Whatever they chose to do, they could be counted on to do it. They were quiet, as opposed to flamboyant, believers. As they were private about their assets, they also were private about their faith. They did not trumpet their convictions; they just lived them daily in their own low-key way, like many other Mainline Protestants.

The Mitchells having been old timers, they also attended many funerals and memorial services of other old timers whom they had known. One of the greatest illustrations of Christian friendship is to give others, Christian or otherwise, a proper send-off when the time comes. I still have a clear mental picture of Jim and Evelyn, and then Evelyn after Jim had died, sitting in the sanctuary, paying their respects to the memory of people they had long known and loved. It is an incalculable comfort to family members to have a large gathering of friends when the departure from this world of Dad or Mom is respectfully noted. The Mitchells were friends up to, and beyond, the end for all of their host of friends.

Jim Mitchell happened to be a member of the pastoral nominating committee who presented my name to the congregation as their candidate to become the new pastor of First Presbyterian Church. Tom Wamsley was the chairman of the committee. Tom telephoned me to see if I would be preaching on a particular Sunday in late

March of 1979 and if two members of their group could attend a service in the Morristown church on that day. I said it would be an honor to me if they were to come, which they did.

Thus, it was that on that long-ago cold and cloudy day I looked down from the pulpit, and there were two men, dressed in the light tan suits which then—and to a much lesser extent—are still worn by southern gentlemen in the house of the Lord on the Sabbath. However, no other soul in Morristown, New Jersey, was wearing that semi-tropical garb in the chilling grip of a New Jersey March Sunday going out like a lion. Jim and Tom may as well have had signs in large, thick letters around their necks proclaiming, "We're Members of Another Church PNC, and We're Here to Check Out Your Parson." It was one thing that they were attired as they were, but they also were sitting in the exact middle of the second-to-front pew in a four-aisle sanctuary, where no one had ever sat in the previous three-quarters of a century.

Nevertheless, in view of others things written in this sanctified memory book, it should be evident that one thing led to another, and I ended up on the Sacred Sand pile by the Sea. The two gentlemen in tan were the initial vital step in that process, and St. James Mitchell was one of those very visible visitors.

Evelyn Mitchell lived on for many years after Jim died. To the end, she was involved in many church activities. Eventually, she moved to one of the retirement communities where she expanded her huge stable of friends. Evelyn had literally hundreds of people, mostly women, with whom she cultivated close friendships. She and Jim were participants in some of the church tour groups I led to Israel and the Middle East, Europe, and Britain. After Jim was gone, she went with friends to places in the U.S. and elsewhere. She loved to travel, and she loved doing it with friends.

True friendship is one of the greatest gifts that God's saints can give to God's people. In Evelyn and Jim Mitchell, that talent was well and lovingly nurtured. Greater love has no one than this, that the friends lay down their lives for their friends. The Mitchells offered themselves to their community, and their community loved them for it.

Saints Bob and Dorothy White

Robert White and his wife, Dorothy, were the two people to whom I was pastor for the longest period in my half century of ministry. I first met them in 1973 when we moved from Chicago to Morristown, New Jersey. They were very active members of the church there.

Bob was the vice-president for manufacturing of the Warner-Lambert Company, which was headquartered in Morris Plains, a community adjacent to Morristown. Warner-Lambert was a pharmaceutical firm which also sold other kinds of products. They had plants all over the world, and Bob's job was to see to it that everything in all those facilities was done as it was supposed to be done.

Bob was a very able but also remarkably low-key administrator. I have known a number of high-powered businessmen, but Bob was not in that category. He had great talent for what he did, but he did it in a quietly efficient rather than a visibly authoritarian way. He was a gentleman's gentleman.

Dorothy was also a quiet person in her own way, but she didn't have the same sort of persona as Bob. She was very gregarious and could talk to anyone about anything until the proverbial bovines turned homeward. However, she was not into production as was her husband; people were her vocation. She cultivated friends like fertilizer cultivated plants. Dorothy White had oodles of friends.

Bob was a quiet speaker, but Dorothy spoke with a uniquely frenetic and breathless intensity. And as given to staying on subject as he was, she was given to leaping all over the conversational map. Dorothy has a wonderful sense of humor. She loved to laugh and also deliberately to promote laughter. Furthermore, she often was the epitome of humor without intending to be. Her sometimes scattered thinking led her to make hilarious statements which she neither meant to verbalize in the manner from which they emerged from her mouth nor did she necessarily see the humor in her unintended double entendres once she had uttered them. If you're old enough to recognize this analogy, she was Bob White's Gracie Allen to his George Burns. Or she was Edith Bunker to his Archie Bunker, except that neither was really Edith or Archie, nor was she really Gracie or Edith.

The Whites attended church regularly in Morristown. Bob served on the session there frequently through more than twenty-five years they lived in New Jersey, and Dorothy was with him every Sunday in worship. Dorothy was not as involved in ecclesiastical organizational activities as Bob. Her involvements were more in the community, in golf, and in playing bridge. Both of the Whites were experts at duplicate bridge, and they participated in many tournaments all around the country and even abroad.

It was through the Whites that our family became acquainted with Hilton Head Island. They owned a vacation villa on the island to which they retreated for a couple of weeks each year. In 1976, they graciously allowed us to use it for a week after Easter, and that was our introduction to coastal South Carolina. Subsequently, in following years, we traded a time-share week we owned on Nantucket Island, Massachusetts, and returned to Hilton Head Island.

The third time we were on Hilton Head, in 1979, we went to a time-share resort. While there, as we always did, we visited former parishioners we had known at Fourth Presbyterian Church in Chicago, Ben and Eunice Howiler. Ben had been the chief pharmacist at a large hospital there. The hospital had a mandatory retirement policy at sixty-five, and Ben had no intention of retiring, perhaps ever. He saw an ad in a trade magazine for a pharmacist at the new Hilton Head Hospital, and he and Eunice moved to the island a few years before we made our first visit there, courtesy of the Whites.

When I stopped at the hospital to say hello to Ben and to arrange for the four of us to get together, the first thing he said after the initial greeting, was to ask if I would be interested in a new pastorate. We spoke very briefly about it then and later in more detail when Nancy and I met the Howilers for dinner. I said I wanted to talk to the Whites about it because Bob was about to retire, and they were going to move permanently to Hilton Head. I was sure the Whites' advice would also be very helpful.

Whenever Dorothy and Bob had been on Hilton Head, they attended the First Presbyterian Church, so they were fairly familiar with the kind of congregation it was. When I mentioned the pulpit vacancy to them, Bob and Dorothy became very enthusiastic about my considering being interviewed by the pastoral nominating committee. On their recommendation and that of Eunice and Ben Howiler, I expressed an interest to the committee; and three months later, the PNC selected me as their candidate for a vote by the congregation. That was in 1979. In 2016, that process would be more likely to take three years. The system for calling Presbyterian ministers is nothing if not very thorough—and very slow.

Thus, when our family moved to Hilton Head Island in July of 1979, we already had known the Howilers for eleven years and the Whites for six years, and we felt especially welcomed by all four of them. The friendship and pastoral connection with the Howilers lasted until 1996 when I resigned from the Hilton Head pastorate and they moved to Atlanta to be near their daughter. Bob White died in 2003, and Dorothy died in early 2015.

As Bob White had served on the Morristown session several times, so also did he serve as an elder for the Hilton Head church for two separate terms. When the sanctuary was expanded to seat a thousand people rather than the four hundred it originally held, and a new Christian education building was constructed, Bob was the chairman of the fund-raising committee. He and Dorothy always were very generous in their stewardship, and there was no one more qualified to lead the campaign to secure the necessary pledges for the building project than Robert C. White.

Dorothy and Bob both grew up in St. Louis. They met after Bob came home from the war. He was several years older than Dorothy. They had an unusually happy marriage, and their personalities meshed very well, even though they had two quite different personalities.

My wife, Lois, is from Pennsylvania. In the nearly twenty years we have been married, she has met hundreds of Midwesterners in the churches I have served, especially when we lived in St. Paul and Cleveland—but also on Hilton Head Island. Lois is convinced that in general, Midwesterners are more open and honest, with less artifice than most other Americans. Having been raised in the Midwest myself, I am naturally but also very humbly (of course) inclined to agree with her. There is something uniquely appealing about the quintessential Midwesterner, whoever that person might be. Such a stellar American is Martha or Martin Midwesterner!

Bob and Dorothy White were stalwart, salt-of-the-earth, what-you-see-is-what-you-get Midwestern human beings. In different ways, each was an outstanding and committed Christian. Every church has its "pillars," and they, particularly Bob, were pillars of the two churches in which I was privileged to be their pastor. When Lois and I returned to Hilton Head Island in 2004 and I started The Chapel Without Walls, Dorothy attended with some regularity, even though she retained her membership at First Presbyterian Church until she died. In her final couple of years, she lived in a retirement home, and she was not as mobile as she had been. Her two daughters and their husbands also lived on Hilton Head, and they toted her hither and yon, including to church at The Chapel.

When I officiated at Dorothy's memorial service, I said in the homily that it represented the end of an era for me. I was associated with Bob White as his pastor from 1973 to 1996, and with the exception of the seven years I was away from Hilton Head Island doing interim pastorates, I was Dorothy White's official or unofficial pastor for thirty-four years. She was subjected to my pastoral peculiarities longer than anyone else I have ever known. For that, if for nothing else, she deserves much praise, or more appropriately, sympathy. But there are many other attributes in Dorothy and Bob White worth noting, for they were an exemplary Christian couple. My life has been immeasurably enriched by having known them. They are both tightly woven into the tapestry of my existence.

St. Edie Scott

Edie Scott was one of the most narcissistic, self-centered, self-absorbed, and off-putting people I have ever known. She also was one of the most faithful in worship attendance and participation in other church activities.

These two factors are not mutually exclusive. There are multitudes of what my mother would call "real pills" in the Church of Jesus Christ. Not every church member has a highly admirable personality, nor is that a requirement for membership. I suspect if some people were not affiliated with a church, they couldn't fulfill the necessary qualities to be allowed into any other voluntary organization. Fraternal or "sororal" orders can blackball prospective members as can, card groups, or other social organizations. They have a way of weeding out those considered undesirable, but churches—at least Mainline Protestant ones—let virtually everyone in who wants in. And once they're there, nobody ever suggests they should be ejected from the sacred precincts because they are pills. Churches put up with pills as best as they can. It goes with the ecclesiastical territory.

I doubt Edie Scott ever realized that for most of the members of the First Presbyterian Church, she was a pain in the body part which connects the head to the shoulders. If the truth is told, she wasn't a pain to most members; it was only those members with whom she came into close contact that she could be a trial to one's Christianity.

And it wasn't that Edie intended to drive people away like an unclaimed suspicious-looking package in an Israeli department store or an Iraqi mosque would provoke people instantly to flee. As the late Governor Ann Richardson said of a certain political personage from her state, "He was born with a silver foot in his mouth, and he just can't help it." Edie Scott seemed incapable of helping the fact that she constantly came across as a narcissistic, self-centered, self-absorbed, off-putting person, and she just couldn't help it. That was true, I think, because she never had enough self-realization nor did she come to grips with just how irritating she could be. If she had agreed to psychological counseling, which I doubt ever would have happened, she might have learned how to overcome some of her most vexing traits. But because she could not grasp how easily, quickly, and thoroughly she drove people round the bend, she was highly unlikely to imagine that she needed any assistance in mitigating the negative tendencies which were obvious to everyone except herself.

Edie was not naturally nasty. She didn't have a nasty bone in her body. On the contrary, she was quite friendly and urbane and sophisticated. I am certain she would do anything for anyone, including giving them the shirt off her back, except that that wouldn't be very urbane or sophisticated. However, she would go the extra mile—or two or three—for people she knew well as well as for total strangers. Kindness of a sort was knitted into her being. Unfortunately, however, she had a knack for putting people off so rapidly that they wouldn't give her the opportunity to be kind.

Edie's husband, Charlie Scott, was a genuine prince among men. He was as positive as Edie was negative. For him, the glass was never half-full. It was completely full, always. For Edie, the glass was never half-empty; it was completely empty.

Charlie travelled a lot in his work. I mean a *lot*. I never talked to him about why he did that because I think I knew why he did that. Furthermore, merely for me to address the issue might be taken by Charlie to mean that I questioned why or how he had stayed married to Edie for so many years. It was obvious that she drove him to distraction because many times, I heard him indicate that reality beyond any doubt as she managed to do to nearly everyone else as well. To his everlasting credit, however, Charlie Scott remained as married to his physically attractive bride as would be humanly possible for any man.

I remember driving Edie and two other ladies to a church retreat which was held several hours away from Hilton Head Island. By the time we arrived at the retreat, the other two women seemed prepared either seriously to contemplate boiling her in oil or to avoid her at all costs during the entire retreat. When we returned to the island, I was not surprised that I had two different passengers plus Edie.

Both going and coming, there was constant conversation (oh, what a joy). And no matter what the subject was, Edie always was able to turn it into an episode about herself. Was the subject elephants? She would tell us at great lengths how she saw her first elephant when she was at the circus as a five-year-old child and what her thoughts and feelings were about elephants and whether it is true that elephants never forget anything. Was it about Trivial Pursuit? She would tell us in chapter and verse about why she detested Trivial Pursuit and could not comprehend how any sane person of any merit would waste two milliseconds playing it. And then, she would tell us when and where she played it for the first time and how dreadful was the experience. And what about the baked ziti we had at the retreat? Well, she said, it was all right, but not nearly as good as her mother's. Then, she told us in enormous detail how she herself was a better-than-average ziti baker, regaling us precisely what to do to make it just the way they make it in Milan, which she then told us she and Charlie had visited in 1967, along with Rome (a complete tour), Venice (ditto), and Florence (double ditto). Four fine females of the First Presbyterian Church informed me in no uncertain terms that never again were they to be toted anywhere for anything with Edie Scott.

I am not telling you anything about Edie that is not absolutely factual. (Well, the part about the drive to and from the retreat had a modicum of artistic license; I have long since obliterated whatever we [which is to say *she*] talked about, lest I carry some unpleasant baggage around with me for the rest of my born days.) Anyone who knew Edie even moderately well would corroborate every word I have told you while telling you hundreds or thousands of their own words just to get their own baggage extricated from resting heavily on their chests.

Nonetheless, it is imperative for you to understand that Edie never once intended to be a thorn in the side to anyone. It's just that, totally unintentionally, she could be a thorn to virtually everyone. Her narcissism was classic; her self-absorption was boundless. And the truly sad reality is that she never understood why people so assiduously avoided her. She knew they did; she just couldn't imagine why.

Edie was not a bad person. She truly was not. She was good person—in some respects, an exemplary person—and most assuredly a beloved child of God. But she was also a constant trial to everyone with whom she came into contact, including her ever-committed husband and her ever-maternally-tested children.

Remember this, however: Edie Scott was *Saint* Edie Scott because she had faith in God, and she lived that faith as best she could, given the personality deficiencies she possessed. Is narcissism a mental disorder? No doubt it can be, if it takes control of every facet of life. In Edie though, I think it was simply a major part of who she was, like a big person is big or a little person is little. Without help, she could no more control her self-centeredness than Melissa McCarthy could transform herself into becoming Tina Fey. And Edie being Edie, she seemed incapable of, as Robert Burns might have put it, "seeing herself as others saw her."

In the last few years of her life, I saw Edie a few times in a nursing facility in which she was living. Some of her "Edie-ness" seemed to have dissipated. Was that because she had mellowed? Perhaps. More likely it was because she had simply aged, and her focus on herself had lost some of its focus. Growing old can do that. And maybe, in some instances, that is a good thing, especially for St. Edie.

St. Neil Pruitt

Neil Pruitt was one of the most influential members of the First Presbyterian Church. But his influence was mainly second-hand and in an unusual sort of way. It was his wife, Nancy, who was ecclesiastically the more influential half of this marital duo, but Neil was always very supportive of Nancy in her ministry as an active and dedicated member and elder of the congregation.

Neil and Nancy Pruitt both grew up in the mountains of North Georgia. They were among the relatively few folks in First Presbyterian who sounded like genuine Southerners, born and bred. Most of the rest of us sounded like we had just gotten off the boat which had just arrived from Boston or New York or Philadelphia or some other godforsaken Yankee community "up there."

Neil also was one of the smartest and most enterprising entrepreneurs in my long acquaintanceship with such men. He owned a number of pharmacies, nursing homes, assisted care facilities, and hospices in Georgia plus a nursing home which he bought on Hilton Head Island relatively late in his business career. The Pruitts had owned a second home on the island for several years before Nancy moved there more or less on a fulltime basis. By that time, their daughters were grown and were away from home. Their son, Neil Junior, was still in high school.

I say that Nancy moved to the island fulltime. Theoretically, Neil did too, except that Neil travelled throughout Georgia during most weekdays and sometimes on weekends as well, visiting his various medical facilities. He was never anyplace "fulltime." Thus, he was not on the island much because his business responsibilities put him in his automobile so much of the time. When he was in town on Sundays, he came to church with Nancy, but he was fairly frequently gone on many Sundays.

You know how some very successful men are vociferous, voracious, and volatile? Neil wasn't like that. He seemed somewhat quiet and reserved and introverted. He was as successful as he was low-key and as low-key as he was successful. He was never the hale-fellow-well-met type of man or the life of the party (at least any church party at their house I can ever remember him attending). He was instead the strong, silent type.

To my way of thinking, Neil Pruitt lived out his sainthood in part by not reluctantly allowing but by actively encouraging his wife to participate as fully in the life of the congregation as she wanted to do. And Nancy was so warm, friendly, and able that she constantly offered her time and talents to the church in as many ways as she felt qualified. She was a loyal and dependable elder, and she gave time and effort to other church activities with as much energy and enthusiasm.

Neil always seemed to take a quiet pride in what his wife did in and for the church. For all I know, subconsciously, he may have concluded she could do many things for the church which time prevented him from doing; and therefore, he felt that vicariously he also was accomplishing the mission of Christ's Church through Nancy. Whether or not he actually believed that, it was true; his gifts as an entrepreneur were reflected in her gifts as a gracious and loving member of the church.

That reality was always evident to me in a particular aspect of the Pruitts' collective church membership. They were very generous stewards. Neil grew up in a very poor family, and it was Neil who amassed their assets. But it was Neil and Nancy who made the pledge to the annual fund or the building fund or whatever else, and they were always very generous in their financial support.

As the family business grew, Neil and Nancy set up a foundation to benefit children associated with hospices in Georgia, Florida, and North Carolina. Neil arranged for these youngsters to go to a camp in the summertime, where specially trained counselors were available to them. They had not only lost parents or siblings to illnesses, but also to family violence or other such tragedies. The Pruitts believed they needed support and encouragement in very difficult circumstances, and they provided it for them through the camp experience. It was called Camp Cocoon, and at the end of their stay, butterflies were released, symbolizing that the children also could fly away from the cares which had weighed so heavily on them.

Neil also instituted a program via the foundation where young children were paid to read books through the summer. His mother had read to him when he was very young, and he was convinced it would be helpful to them in their future education to be able to read more proficiently.

I have known spouses who seemed to resent the deep involvement of their spouse in the life of the church or other philanthropies. Usually, it was a husband who was unhappy that his wife spent so much time at church; but sometimes, it was a wife who felt that way about her husband. I can readily comprehend that resentment, particularly if the unchurched spouse is not only unchurched but also antichurch. It must be a psychological and philosophical trial for anyone who is genuinely antireligion to have a wife or husband who is demonstrably proreligion. In some cases, I suspect, the properson may have become involved in a church just to get a weekly or more frequent reprieve from the antiperson. But in most instances, these kinds of marriages represent a spoken or unspoken decision by each spouse to follow a "live and let live" policy regarding the other spouse.

With Neil and Nancy Pruitt, however, Neil was not a passive accepter of Nancy's church commitment; he was an active promoter of it. He knew it meant a great deal to her, and so it meant a great deal to him. He supported whatever she supported in whatever way he could support it. And because he was so successful as a businessman, and because financial success was one of the most obvious indices of that success, he was always happy to contribute financially to whatever Nancy wanted to do on behalf of the First Presbyterian Church.

In time, all three of the Pruitt children came into the business with Neil after they graduated from college. Because of that, and because the entire family were devoting increasing amounts of time to travelling through the Southeast to oversee the various medical facilities the family owned, Nancy and Neil moved back to Toccoa, Georgia, where the home office for the corporation was located. They retained their home on the beach on Hilton Head Island, but they came to it with increasing infrequency.

Neil continued to put many thousands of miles on his car each year, traversing the roads of Georgia and South Carolina to maintain the close personal connection he wanted with each of his nursing or assisted care homes. Several years ago, not long after he left home to go on yet another of his countless road trips through the mountains and hills of the Peach State, he drove into a sudden thunderstorm which dumped an incredible amount of rain into a narrow valley over a very short span of time. Coming around a curve, he encountered a fairly deep pool of water which had covered the surface of the road in a matter of minutes. The car began hydroplaning across the basin of rainwater and slammed into an oncoming truck. Neil was killed instantly.

As I would have expected, Nancy recovered from the loss of her husband with remarkable inner strength and resolve. They had always been an unusually close and committed couple, but Nancy made the best of a very trying situation and went on with her life. She is as active now in her church in North Georgia as she was in her church in Hilton Head Island.

It is impossible to know whether those who have died are aware of what still goes on this side of the veil of eternity. Frankly, I hope they don't. But if they do have any knowledge of what we earthlings are still doing, I am certain that St. Neil Pruitt is still as proud of Nancy's church involvement as he was when he was on this side of the veil but was unable to do much himself other than to support her in her ecclesiastical labors. My mother used to quote the old line of poetry, "They also serve who only stand and wait." Neil Pruitt never stood still for very long waiting for anything, but he always served the Church by means of his loving wife, Nancy. May God bless them both and in both time and eternity.

St. Joann McCreight

Joann McCreight was married to John McCreight, and John is a retired Presbyterian minister. The McCreights moved to Hilton Head Island in the mid-1980s. They became mainstays of the congregation at First Presbyterian Church from the first day they arrived on the island. Later, John came out of retirement five times to serve on the staff of First Presbyterian or other close-by Presbyterian churches in various capacities. Still later, after Lois and I returned to the island to inaugurate The Chapel Without Walls, John became one of our most faithful and supportive attendants. He also preached in my absence several times, and he preached what he determined would be his final sermon in The Chapel when he was ninety years old.

Joann and John both came from a long line of Presbyterian ministers. His father and two cousins were ministers, and their son, Bob, is a minister. Joann's father and brother were ministers. As I told them on numerous occasions, the whole family history seems somehow vaguely incestuous.

Joann and John met their first week as freshmen when they were students at Muskingum College in New Concord, Ohio, a Presbyterian school. They became, as they say, "an item" immediately and remained so for the rest their lives. Joann's father was president of Muskingum, and John's father taught there. They were married the day after they graduated from college, and in fairly short order, they had three sons and a daughter. While their children were still young, Joann was employed as a social worker. She was very gainfully employed for most of their married life, while also serving as the ever-loyal and helpful spouse to her minister husband.

I didn't know the McCreights during the time John was the pastor of various churches and Joann was working as a social worker. It was when they came to the island and became so involved in almost every aspect of our congregation's life that I really came to know and appreciate them.

Joann had the naturally rosy cheeks of a person of British ancestry. She always had a cherubic smile, which otherwise might indicate she was a peaceable pushover. Peaceable she was; a pushover she wasn't. She had definite ideas about everything, and she was always willing to express them in a clear but noncombative manner. She was a tireless volunteer in the Hilton Head Planned Parenthood group, and she became president of the afore-mentioned and wonderfully community-minded Bargain Box.

Joann also was a feminist from her youth onward. Though she was a typical minister's wife in certain respects, she was not a doormat—either to her husband or to the congregations they served. She made it clear that she was not an unpaid associate pastor nor could she be relied on to support every decision John made if she did not approve of it. She was never confrontational, but she never allowed anyone to be uncertain of where she stood on issues either. She was active in Planned Parenthood in the communities where they lived, and she inspired their daughter, Tina, to become a Planned Parenthood staff director. She was, in my opinion, one of the best examples of being a feminist: direct without being adversarial, strong without attempting to overpower, and honest without ever being deliberately ambiguous about where she stood.

It is an unwritten understanding that the spouses of Presbyterian clergy do not serve on any of the boards of the congregation, and that applied to Joann while John was the pastor of the churches he served through the years. However, when she was the wife of a retired minister, she was very quickly elected to the session of the First Presbyterian Church; and there she served with distinction, being the chairperson of one of the most important committees. Having lived through some tight spots during the many years when John was in the pastoral harness, Joann well understood what it was like for yours truly when I was in tough spots. If she agreed with me on any particular issue, she backed me to the hilt. If she disagreed, she publicly voiced her objections and told why she objected, but she never made disagreements personal. She had a natural knack for the give-and-take of ecclesiastical politics, which no doubt she learned at her father's knee as well as having been the mistress of the manse for lo those many years.

Without going into the historical background, both Joann and John McCreight grew up in the United Presbyterian Church, which was somewhat more conservative theologically than the larger Presbyterian Church in the United States of America. The two denominations merged in 1958 to become—whoever could have guessed it?—The United Presbyterian Church in the United States of America. I tell you this very brief summary of denominational history to suggest that both John and Joann McCreight were, by nature and background, theologically somewhat more conservative than I, which might be true of almost everyone alive. Nevertheless, never for a moment did I feel any animosity from either of them over theology or belief for any positions I elucidated from the pulpit or elsewhere. They were outstanding friends and unstintingly supportive of both First Presbyterian Church and myself as its pastor.

A church can become quickly entangled in damaging controversy if certain individuals make it their business to provoke discord. Joann McCreight had a deeply intuitive sense of how to engage in discussion without engaging in discord. She had great understanding and love for *The* Church and *our* church, and it showed in her cherubic if also straightforward demeanor.

Having been an actively employed parson for so many years, I have observed many traditional and untraditional ministers' wives. Three of the most admirably traditional were Grace Davies, Mildred Mutch, and Joann McCreight. Because the first two were older than Joann and had been young and then older women a generation before Joann, they were more "traditional ministers' wives" than Joann. Joann was part of the bridge-generation which made both the "new traditional ministers' wives (or husbands)" and the "contemporary less traditional ministers' spouses" possible. All that explanation notwithstanding, all three of these exemplary women were stellar spouses to their stellar husbands, and I was the beneficiary of their marvelous personalities.

When we returned to South Carolina after having been gone for over six years, we of course saw the McCreights socially on occasion. During those visits, it appeared as though Joann was not quite herself. Eventually, it became obvious that she was suffering from some sort of dementia. The doctors were never able to pinpoint it, which is often the case with dementia. Was it Alzheimer's disease, or not? No one could say definitively. But it was obviously both real and unavoidable.

Like many unusually intelligent people, Joann was able quite deftly to mask her disability for a few years. Then, it became clear that it was sweeping her into that shadowy, remorseless world to which dementia consigns countless millions of people—most of them in advanced age. John took marvelous care of her as long as he could, but she finally was moved into the memory care unit of the nursing facility of their retirement home. There she lived in a steady, slow decline for the last three years of her life.

I visited Joann once a week while she was there. Even at the very end, when I would come into her room, her face would light up, and that glowing smile would come across her instantly revived visage. I often thought to myself, "You don't know who I am, do you? But you're going to play the warm and affectionate lady you have always been anyway, aren't you?" And for all I know, she was thinking to herself, "You think I don't know who you are, but I do, you perfidious doubter, you! It's just that I can't remember your confounded name. But be glad I'm glad to see you, you skeptic, you!" At the last, she was totally unable to speak, and mercifully, after literally only God truly knows how many years dementia had assaulted this lovely lady, she slipped away into the silent (but I seriously doubt they are silent, Mr. Bryant) halls of death.

Throughout this entire meander down memory lane, I have written frequently of the clergy and their spouses. Being a minister is one of the highest privileges afforded to any human being, but it also has its own unique if also manageable burdens. One of the ways those burdens are best managed is to associate closely with other clergy and their other halves. Long ago, I discovered that sharing war stories is wonderfully therapeutic. In my own declining years, John and Joann McCreight were invaluable allies in maintaining at least some measure of equilibrium in a seemingly increasingly unbalanced world.

Saints John and Lois West

John and Lois West had been affiliated with First Presbyterian Church for several years before we came to Hilton Head Island. John was an attorney from Camden, South Carolina, and he and Lois retained their membership in the Presbyterian church in Camden. But they also became associate members in Hilton Head. It was very characteristic of the Wests that they kept their connection with their roots while at the same time establishing a new identity in what in many respects was a relatively new community largely inhabited by an ever-growing crowd of Yankees. Though John and Lois West were Southerners in every fiber of their being, they were equally Americans to the core.

John became one of the last Democratic governors in South Carolina. But he was not like many other Southern Democratic politicians in the `50s and `60s who were really Red-State Republicans, waiting to burst out of the closet. He was more like a Jimmy Carter Democrat. In fact, he was later named the U.S. Ambassador to Saudi Arabia by Jimmy Carter.

After the Supreme Court ruled that public schools must racially integrate, Governor West was one of the first Southern governors to do everything he could to make that decision effective. As is easily imagined, this did not meet with universal acclaim by all the citizens of the Palmetto State, especially those of the Caucasian persuasion. Had the Court not ruled unanimously on *Brown vs. Board of Education*, the South Carolina governor could have made no headway whatever in ordering the schools to be united racially. As it was, John stood his ground and took his expected lumps, of which there were more than a few.

In these strife-ridden times, many people consider most politicians to be unprincipled opportunists. John West certainly was not of that political ilk. He was man who put his faith and his beliefs into action every day of his life: as a husband and father, as an attorney, as a governor, as an ambassador, and as someone who perceived himself to be a child of God. No one who knew him could ever manage to miss the fact that he was a politician, but he was a gentle one, a gentleman, and the kind of politician who used to give politicians a deserved good reputation.

Like everyone else I have cited in this book, the Wests were very regular in their attendance in church. They seldom came to any other church activities because they both had many other fish to fry in the community, state, and nation. They were on numerous state and national boards, and they very generously donated their talent and their financial resources to these causes.

It would be a considerable stretch to imagine that a Presbyterian attorney and his wife from rural South Carolina could fit in well with the international jet set of the king and princes and business barons of Saudi Arabia, but that is exactly what they did. They were particularly close to Zaki Yemani, the Saudi Oil Minister whose influence on petroleum markets was so pivotal for so many years and perhaps continues even to the present day. For the rest of their lives, the Wests numbered many Saudis among their closest friends, and they kept in touch with them with the most genuinely gracious Southern hospitality they could muster. And in the commodity of hospitality, they were among the most gracious.

One time, Lois and John had a group of Saudi businessmen at their home for dinner. They invited me to join the group. The Saudis were all impeccably dressed, either in traditional Arab garb or in suits from Savile Row or Fifth Avenue. With a short glance at their sartorial elegance, it appeared to me that we were in the presence of men who collectively were worth many millions or even billions of dollars, but they were as open and friendly as they could be to this relatively-young Presbyterian parson in their midst. When he extended the invitation, John had asked if I would say the blessing before we sat down to dinner. Needless to say, I gave considerable thought to what would be appropriate. Prior to beginning the prayer, I gave what in essence is the essential creed of Islam, to which I also could truthfully add my affirmation, *La illaha il' Allah*: There is no God but

God. And I ended the prayer with another Arabic declaration, *Allahu Akbar*: Praise God.

Neither John nor Lois West said one word about what I should say in that blessing, but I think they knew what I was likely to say. And they wanted their Saudi friends to hear an American clergyman acknowledge the legitimacy of their religion and their culture (or at least parts of their culture). I have never been to Saudi Arabia, nor am I ever likely to get there; but at the behests of the two Wests, I did what I could in a minute or two to try to bridge the gap between East and West. It was typical of John and Lois to offer me such a unique ministerial opportunity. And the Saudi gentlemen (there were no ladies with them) seemed pleased that an American clergyman on a small island at the western edge of the Atlantic Ocean knew a couple of Arabic-Muslim phrases.

When the first service of The Chapel Without Walls was held on the first Sunday in January of 2004, John West was in attendance. He was there as often as he could be for the next two or three months. By then, he was afflicted with what proved to be terminal cancer. Knowing that, but also despite it, he agreed to be one of the founding members of our first board of trustees, adding the cachet of his name to our nascent congregation. It was the last such new board membership out of the scores or hundreds of such associations that he maintained throughout his long and exceedingly fruitful life.

When John West died, he had made arrangements for his body to be taken back to Camden, there to be buried alongside many others in the West family. It was there where I went to help officiate at John's committal service as I had earlier for the Wests' daughter-in-law, Sue, and later for their son, Doug, Sue's husband. Family and roots: South Carolina and Camden: Presbyterians and place—John and Lois West.

Like many other politicians, John West kept his cards close to his vest while any sort of political game was being played, including ecclesiastical or social politics. On all issues, he always maintained his quiet demeanor, never raising his voice about anything. But once he was certain of what other players thought, how the tide of thinking was running, and what he could add to the discussion, he would express his convictions in his forever soft-spoken, courtly way.

To me John West was a senior statesman, a mentor, and a friend. Whenever I asked for his advice, he would offer it. And sometimes, when I didn't ask for it but he thought I needed it, he would give it anyway and always gently, of course. He was more conservative on some political or social issues than I, as one would expect. But he never tried to make me out to be a fool, even when I was foolish. He was the best of the South and a genuine American patriot. He and Lois were a magnificent team, each supporting the multitude of talents and causes of the other. RIP, dear hearts.

St. Elizabeth Grant

Elizabeth Grant was always Elizabeth to everyone else. She was never Betty or Lizzie or Liz although sometimes she referred to herself as Liz or Lizzie, but no one else did. She was an excellent artist, particularly in portraits and especially in watercolors, and she always signed her paintings "Eliz Grant." Not "Elizabeth Grant" or "Eliz. Grant," but Eliz Grant. Nevertheless, she wasn't Eliz Grant; she was Elizabeth Grant.

Elizabeth had been married to Ben Grant for almost forty years when they moved to Hilton Head Island in retirement. Ben was the managing editor of *US News and World Report*. Ben was a Republican because *US News* was a basically moderate Republican magazine. Elizabeth, on the other hand, was fairly apolitical. If she was anything, she was a social liberal. Essentially, she was a people person. People fascinated her, particularly off-beat, off-the-wall, out-of-the-ordinary people.

Despite her abiding interest in human beings in all our faults and foibles, Elizabeth was not much of a joiner in any kind of human organization, except artistic ones. Her art was her thing, and she pursued it—as they say these days, but not in those days—passionately.

So how did she ever become a member of First Presbyterian Church? That, I suspect, occurred via her husband, Ben. Ben probably had always been a devoted churchman, going back to his boyhood in North Florida. He graduated from the University of Florida in the old days when it was an all-male college. For the past century, North Florida has been Southern and South Florida has been Northern. It was out of that Southern ethos, I suppose, that Ben Grant grew up in and fairly naturally continued in the Church of Jesus Christ; and it was into that Church that, by dint of his winsome personality, he enticed his free-spirited wife to go to church. Without Ben, Elizabeth likely would seldom if ever would darken any church's door. She was "spiritual-but-not-religious" before anyone knew what in the world that phrase might mean or that it was either possible or plausible.

Elizabeth Grant had a shipload of spirit and a plentiful personality. No one who ever knew her even moderately well could forget her. She gave unique meaning to the description "live wire." She could light up a room, send an electric charge through any individual or group, and spark animated conversations or controversies with the most taciturn of humanoids. Whatever she thought she said, and she thought a lot about a lot.

She had a natural gift for seeing beauty in nature and character in people. She was very perceptive of visual stimuli. In two seconds, she could look at someone's face and peer into the very depths of that person. She loved faces, especially black faces—and even more especially the faces of little black children. She would go to The Children's Center and take photographs of the children at play and then paint them. She had a painting which still hangs in the First Presbyterian Church of Hilton Head Island called *The Great Escape*. It shows several little kids, black and white, crawling over the fence around the playground of what I always assumed was meant to depict the First Presbyterian Day School or, alternately, the Children's Center. I doubt that *The Great Escape* ever factually occurred, but it certainly did in Elizabeth's creative and fertile mind. Or at least she being she, she would think it should have. Children need to be free fully to express themselves, and how can they do that if they can't get over the fences life places around their youthful existence? No doubt Elizabeth was a little girl who was always "getting into it," so shouldn't every other child also get into it, whatever "it" might turn out to be?

She was commissioned to do a series of watercolors which featured the Heritage Golf Tournament at the Harbour Town Golf Links on Hilton Head Island. She painted some famous golfers from way back then, along with some island residents. Some were very recognizable by many, and others were recognizable by only a few. She would snap photographs as she strolled around the course and then work from the photos. Many years ago, she gave me a watercolor of two men eating hamburgers. Presumably, they are watching some PGA players go by on a Harbour Town fairway, but no golfers are actually shown. She gave me the painting because I am the man in the foreground. She told me she didn't remember who the other man was. I have always thought he was Lew Laderer, another member of First Presbyterian Church who died at least a quarter of a century ago. But I'll never know for certain.

Lois and I also have another Eliz Grant watercolor. It is of a little black girl who looks to be about four or five years old. It is a close-up of her face. She has several braids that emerge from her head like arcing strands of electric current. Her eyes are very bright, and her face reflects many different shades as the light passes over her pensive visage. But she is not looking at us. She is obviously far away. What is she thinking? She is somewhere else, but not here. Nevertheless, the "her" that *is* here displays the vitality of the young child, the promise of an unlimited future, and the prospects of a much better world because *she* is in it.

Elizabeth loved flowers, and she also loved to arrange them in the best manner to proclaim their radiant glory. One time, she went on the annual church retreat to Montreat, a Presbyterian center in the mountains of North Carolina. For decades, many individuals (many of them clergy and their spouses) have owned homes in Montreat. One morning, Elizabeth took a walk among these interesting, much-loved domiciles. She came upon a lovely garden, filled with many species of her favorite flowers. An inner voice apparently instructed her that she needed to pick some of them to make an arrangement for the large room in which our group had most of their meetings.

The lady who owned the house saw Elizabeth just as she was cutting the last flowers to give perfection to her bouquet. In an understandable huff, the lady asked in a not-too-friendly voice just what this interloper thought she was doing. "I'm with some church people on retreat," Elizabeth calmly and patiently explained to her, "and I wanted to brighten up our meeting room." The mistress of the manor was not pleased, not at all pleased. Her posies had already been plucked, so she thought it pointless to demand them back. She did, however, note in no uncertain terms that Elizabeth was not to engage in a similar theft ever again.

Only a genuinely free spirit would feel free enough to confiscate one person's flowers in order to bring visual pleasure and subconscious joy to a group of sixty other people. To Elizabeth, it was a perfectly ethical tradeoff. The utilitarian happiness of sixty greatly overshadowed the purloined posies of just one disgruntled homeowner. Besides, she said, when she told this tale to a few of the astonished and not a little aghast Presbyterian saints of coastal Carolina, there were so many flowers in the garden the lady would never have missed them if she had not happened along just as they were being purloined.

I suspect Elizabeth was not quite as live a wire or as liberated a spirit when she married Ben Grant as she was later in life. But the spark was always there, no doubt, and that may be why the much more staid magazine editor was drawn to the much more artistic and unconventional painter. She provided something he, the Presbyterian elder, could never provide in their marriage.

Ben Grant died while our family was on vacation in Nantucket Island, Massachusetts. When I received the call, we made arrangements to come home early so that I could officiate at his memorial service. Elizabeth had known for some time that Ben was dying, and when his death came, she was neither surprised nor overwhelmed. Because she was Elizabeth, she was naturally hurt but not hysterical; sad but not shattered. Lengthy mourning would not become this Electra. She never wore widow's weeds or their equivalent, nor did she visibly or orally bemoan her loss. She went on painting in a studio in a new house she had built for herself in another section of the island, and that was that.

Elizabeth had accompanied her husband to church for so many years that, despite her anti-institutional proclivities and her incipient agnosticism regarding many of the purported fundamentals of faith, she kept coming to church as regularly as she had before Ben died. I was happy about that because I was by no means certain that would be the case.

To go forward in her story a few years, one morning at 4 AM, I got a call from another man who, like Ben Grant, had previously served on the session of the church. Bob Little told me that his wife, Dottie, was dying. I had visited Dottie several times in her illness, and I said to Bob that if her condition was grave and he did not want to send her to the hospital again as he had already done several times, he should phone me at any time, day or night. And I would come to stay with him until she died. He called; I went, and within two or three hours, Dottie was gone.

A year or so later, Elizabeth Grant told me that she and Bob Little were, in the vernacular, seeing one another. I was somewhat surprised to hear this, but also pleased. I liked both of them very much. And while Ben Grant and Bob Little were two very different types of men, they also both were fine Christian gentlemen as far as I was concerned. So I wished Bob and Elizabeth the best, whatever that might be, however their relationship progressed.

Within a few months of their informing me of their budding friendship, Bob and Elizabeth informed me they planned to be married. I told them that was great news, and so we arranged for some premarital meetings to discuss the kinds of issues which inevitably accompany second marriages after long and very happy first marriages.

I noted to them that Ben and Bob were not alike. To be more specific, they were much more unalike than alike. The same was true for Elizabeth and Dottie. Ben was a journalist who rose to the top in his profession. Bob was a PhD chemist who worked behind the scenes at the Hercules Corporation of Wilmington, Delaware. Ben was affable and outgoing; Bob was more reserved and quiet. Ben was conservative in his politics and liberal in his thinking; Bob was traditional about nearly everything. Bob was by no means a stick-in-the-mud, but he wasn't a social butterfly either. I don't know whether Elizabeth foresaw these differences as impediments. Because I knew both men quite well, I did not anticipate there would be problems for Elizabeth and Bob after they were married. The differences between Dottie and Elizabeth were less pronounced, so I did not foresee that being a problem.

There were problems, however. Almost from the beginning there were. I did not know it for some time, and had it been up to Bob to tell me, I'm sure I never would have heard. But reluctantly, Elizabeth told me. I think she was depressed and not a little disgusted with both herself and Bob, but most of all, she was sad. She did not anticipate there would be troubles, but there were. And she didn't know how to deal with them. After several sessions with them, I did not know what to suggest either. Clearly, they were at an impasse, and they seemed incapable of going forward or backward. They decided to stick it out, no matter what might happen.

Thus did two very fine people endure a few more years of an increasingly unhappy marriage. They never separated, but they eventually came to endure very desperate lives in Elizabeth's—by now—not-so-new home. Each of them perceived their new spouse to be so different from their long-time first spouse that they could never fully adjust to their newly altered circumstances.

The marriage ended with Elizabeth's death. She had re-written her will in such a way that were she to be the first to die, the house was to be sold and the proceeds from the sale and everything else was to go to her children. That meant that Bob had to move out. That was both hard for him and hard on him. He died a relatively short time later.

It is immeasurably sad for me to recollect as I write this how unfortunate it was that Elizabeth Grant and Bob Little entered into a marriage in their final years which they both thought would bring them happiness and contentment during those years, but it did not. Sometimes, even with the greatest of effort, personal relationships can never seem to gel. Such was the case for two people, both of whom I loved and admired very much.

Over five decades, many parishioners have told me what their favorite hymns were. When my declining gray matter is able to recall that information, I often think of these folks when we sing "their" hymn in worship, and I can reconnect with them, even if, as Lois says, they "are on the other side of the Jordan."

Elizabeth Grant's favorite hymn was *Be still, my soul.*

> "Be still, my soul: the Lord is on thy side;
> Bear patiently the cross of grief or pain;
> Leave to thy God to order and provide;
> In every change He faithful will remain.
> Be still my soul: thy best, thy heavenly Friend
> Through thorny ways leads to a joyful end."

In nearly every imaginable way, Elizabeth Grant was both unconventional and unorthodox. But she always spoke glowingly of that magnificent and indescribably comforting hymn. Assuming I shall encounter her again on the far bank of the Jordan, I believe she will tell me that *Be still, my soul* inspired her through a long and very happy marriage, and it comforted her through a much shorter and sadly unhappy marriage. In all the circumstances of our lives, it is ultimately affirming to know that indeed, the Lord is on our side, on the side of all of us. And thus, are we all *saints*.

St. Tom Israel

Tom Israel was one among the most lively people I have had the privilege of knowing. He lived every day to the fullest. "Life" oozed from his every pore. He was physically, mentally, and spiritually active for his entire life.

Considering the life expectancy in the male line of his family, it was surprising Tom lived as long as he did. Almost all the men in his gene pool suffered from heart disease, and most of them had died in their forties or fifties. But Tom lived to be eighty-five. He was Exhibit A for many of the miracles of modern medicine.

Eighteen years before Tom died, he had a quadruple heart bypass. He lived in basically good health from that time until a month before he died, when it was discovered that three of his stents were 100 percent blocked, and the fourth was 60 percent blocked. He had more bypass surgery, and for several days, everything looked fine—until it looked anything but fine. And then, he was gone.

With the exception of the second post-operative episode, Tom was always the epitome of effervescence, energy, and ebullience. He always had a ruddy complexion, and his red cheeks gave him the appearance of one of Santa's elves or of a fisherman from the Shetland or Orkney Islands. Tom Israel looked incredibly *lively*.

Tom grew up in Washington DC, and attended the George Washington University law school in Washington. His wife, Joan, entered GWU at age fifteen. A regular child prodigy she was. A regular cradle robber of sorts he was, at eight years her senior. However, they waited to marry until Joan emerged from George Washington University with her bachelor's degree at the ripe old age of eighteen. By that time, Tom had decided the law was not going to be his vocational cup of tea. He went on to earn a master's degree in public administration.

With the surname, "Israel," one might deduce that Tom must have been ethnically Jewish. However, he came from a long line of Methodist pastors, and if someone was Jewish way back there, he was unaware of it.

Joan, on the other hand, was born into a Viennese Jewish family. They emigrated to the United States when she was a young child. At the time Tom and Joan were married, her grandfather insisted that Tom must have had some Jewish forebears to be named *Israel*. If so, Tom quietly declared, it was a mystery to him. Tom was not opposed to having Jewish roots if it were true; he just couldn't certify it one way or the other. The grandfather was mollified by his answer, and he told Joan, "Even if he isn't Jewish, he's a nice boy." And the nuptials were grand-paternally approved.

For most of his career, Tom was employed by the federal government in various capacities. But in addition to his employment, he also served the public in several other positions, most of them as a volunteer. He served twice on the Montgomery County Board of Education in the suburbs of the federal district, and for two of those stints he was the president of the board. He also served on the County Board of Appeals and the board of the Mental Health Association. He was an inexhaustible servant of humanity.

He and Joan also were inexhaustible square-dancers. They didn't just doe-see-doe a little bit; they seriously doe-see-doed with other very serious square-dancers. And they were always properly attired for their frenetic moves around the dance floor.

After the Israels moved to Hilton Head in retirement in the late `80s (Joan had been a school principal), Tom became a member of the Board of Appeals of the Town of Hilton Head Island, which is usually a thankless task for which one receives many brickbats and virtually no warm kudos. He also was on the property owners' association board for his residential development, and he was the president of the local Democratic Club. This was at a time when Democrats were almost illegal in South Carolina, and particularly on Hilton Head Island. Now they are merely an endangered species. But Tom Israel believed in doing whatever he could to improve the lives of his fellow citizens, and both in suburban Washington and on Hilton Head Island he did that with distinction and dedication. He was irrepressible in his devotion to public service.

As lively as Tom was in everything else, he also was a lively churchman. Despite that lengthy Methodist pedigree, the Israels became Presbyterians on Hilton Head Island, and both served as elders on the church session.

Once, when an issue was being energetically debated in a session meeting, Tom and Joan remembered that I as moderator of the session had said to Tom, one of the most energetic of the debaters, after he had gone on for some time about the issue, "Tom, you're full of prunes!" I don't recall having said that. The older I get, the less I can recall having said anything. But if they said I said it, I'm sure I said it.

A pastor should never tell a parishioner, especially in a meeting with twenty-five or so other people in attendance, that he is internally replete with shriveled plums. It definitely is not good form.

However, Tom Israel was the sort of person to whom one could say that sort of thing. Apparently, Joan hooted when Tom told her about this pastoral indiscretion, as did he in the telling of it. But as I said, one could declare such unseemly observations to Tom Israel without fear of piercing thin skin. Anyone who dealt with the public as long as he did inevitably had to develop the hide of an elephant, if he did not possess a hardened epidermis before.

St. Thomas Israel was the very essence of *joie de vivre*. To all who knew him, his every-ready grin or laugh, his ruddy complexion, his twinkling eyes, and his ever-evident love of the human race decreed as much every day that he lived. And he lived every day to its fullest.

St. Charles Edward Taylor

Charles Taylor was the most committed and conscientious Christian steward it has been my great privilege to know. Before coming to Hilton Head Island, I had known many other church members who perceived the stewardship of time and financial resources to be *a* major if not *the* major focus of their lives as Christians. Nevertheless, Charles and Ellen Taylor gave an entirely new meaning to the very notion of stewardship.

The Taylors moved from Ohio to the island in the early 80s, along with the great influx of people who arrived in those years. They had owned a small appliance business in Ohio, but it had dried up due to Big Box competition and other factors. Having owned an ocean-front condominium on Hilton Head for a few years, they decided to come to the island and rent their villa as the initial property in a new vacation rental business venture. (On Hilton Head, condos are called "villas." What can I say?) They would introduce themselves to other owners in their own building complex on South Beach, plus as many other Hilton Head owners as they could contact. Then, they would serve as the rental agents for people who wanted to come to the island on vacation and rent a unit of varying sizes for a week or two, or a month, or an entire season.

The three Taylor children were all adults by the time Charles and Ellen moved to Hilton Head. Eventually, all three also came to the island, and two became employed in their vacation-rental business after it had taken off. Charles' mother also became an islander, and eventually there were four generations of Hilton Head Taylors. Grannie died many years ago, but some of the Taylor grandchildren are old enough to marry and begin a new four-generation coterie of island Taylors, with Ellen as the matriarch.

When Ellen and Charles arrived on Hilton Head to start their new venture, they hardly had the proverbial two nickels to rub together. But they were people of faith. They believed strongly in God, in themselves, and in their ability to create a new and thriving business. And that they did.

Shortly after arriving on Hilton Head Island, Charles and Ellen went to a local branch of a large Southeastern regional bank for a loan of several thousand dollars to help get them started in their rental company. They were turned down, so they approached another bank and were accepted for the loan. That initial sum of money was the major financial startup for the Shoreline Rental Company.

Several years later, after Shoreline Rentals had begun to prosper, Charles asked Ellen to come with him for a car ride. They pulled up in front of the large commercial building where they had first applied for a bank loan. The building was then vacant as a result of one of the many bank mergers occurring throughout the country, but especially on Hilton Head Island, where banks are almost as prevalent as restaurants. Charlie told Ellen he thought they should buy the building for their new offices, which is what they did. People often say that when one door closes, another one opens. For Charles and Ellen Taylor, that took on an entirely new and unique meaning.

What is truly astonishing about their stewardship is that they made their annual pledge to the church on the basis of what they anticipated their income would be in the coming year and not for what it was in the previous year. However, both of them were absolutely convinced that God blesses those who bless others and God's kingdom by their contributions to God's work. Trusting that their new business would succeed, their stewardship reflected that trust even before the dream became a reality. Would that all of us had faith like that!

In several years, Charles and Ellen were so trustworthy in their business enterprise that they had many hundreds of owners who entrusted their condominiums to the Shoreline Rentals Company to be listed on the vacation rentals market. The company prospered, as did its owner-proprietors.

The Taylors had been active in their community in Ohio, and they freely gave of themselves to activities in their new community. In the church, they both sang in the choir, they served in various committees and organizations, and Charles became one of the leading elders on the session. He was one of the many church officers who gave much time and effort to church activities and congregational growth. In those days, an aphorism arose which declared that people needed not only "to talk the talk but also to walk the walk." Charles Taylor was certainly one of those people. But because he was the strong and fairly silent type, he was much more of a walker than a talker.

A group of volunteer local instrumentalists banded together to form a community orchestra. As time went on, they began to outgrow the Lutheran church where their performances were held for the first few years. This was at the same time that First Presbyterian Church had outgrown its sanctuary. The Presbyterians voted to expand the sanctuary and construct a large chancel area which could accommodate a full-size symphony orchestra, although some members voted reluctantly with respect to the first matter and very reluctantly with respect to the second.

The Taylors were major supporters of the Hilton Head Orchestra. Charles was elected to its board of directors, and eventually became the president of the board. Under his leadership the orchestra eventually became an all-professional ensemble. The orchestra board paid for several physical improvements in the sanctuary that enhanced the sound quality and the lighting during performances. In addition, each performance was attended by nearly a thousand people, which is extraordinary for a community of forty thousand residents. At every program, Charles made some introductory remarks as the orchestra board president, and his winsome manner and always-evident modesty did much to build community support among islanders for their orchestra. Furthermore, as he was such a committed steward for the church, so also was he committed to the financial growth of the orchestra.

At the time, discussions were going on regarding expansion of the church buildings, Charles was a major voice in supporting the proposal. There was opposition to the idea, which came from two directions. Some folks believed that if a new Presbyterian congregation on the south end of the island were established, enough of our own members would go there as charter members, and we would not need to expand. Others simply opposed the concept of our church getting any bigger. They thought it was already too big. As it was, within two years, the Providence Presbyterian Church was chartered, and nearly two hundred fifty First Presbyterian members became the numerical core of the new church. But by then, we had received more than two hundred fifty members in the intervening two years, so the expansion proved necessary anyway.

When the actual congregational vote on the building program was taken, 61 percent were in favor, and 39 percent were opposed. At a subsequent session meeting, the elders strongly felt that everyone who was opposed turned out to vote, while many of those who favored the expansion did not bother to attend the congregational meeting at which the vote was taken, supposing that it would pass by a landslide. A major landslide it wasn't, and probably the ballot was a true indication of sentiment for the project.

Nonetheless, a committee was formed to oversee the various aspects of what proved to be the largest building program in the history of the congregation, which, as it turned out, has specialized in building programs from its earliest days. Charles Taylor was one of the primary leaders in the effort. And when it came time to request three-year building-fund pledges from the congregation to pay for the project, Charles and Ellen made the heftiest pledge by far. And this was before their vacation rental company had really taken off. Once more they displayed faith in God and in themselves in their Christian stewardship. Considering the fact that they had almost nothing to give when they made their three-year commitment, it represented an enormous leap of faith.

On the Sunday the building fund pledges were presented, Charles and Ellen had not made a final decision about what they would contribute to the building fund. As they were walking into the sanctuary to sing with the choir, Charles told Ellen that it was time to decide. As usual, she said that whatever he wanted to do was fine. After the service, she asked what figure he had written on the pledge card, and he told her. In typical fashion, she smiled and said that was all right with her. And it proved to be a major impetus for the success of the building program. They had prayed that their new business venture would be successful, and that therefore they would be enabled to fulfill their pledge. So it was, and so they did.

After Lois and I returned to the island following the six-year period in which I was away doing interim pastorates, we would see Ellen and Charles socially on occasion. Then, three years after we came back, Charles was diagnosed with prostate cancer. Normally, that is not a serious situation, and various treatments can either cure the malignancy or render it a chronic illness which can be held at bay for many years.

However, it turned out that Charles had a fairly rare but very aggressive form of prostate cancer. At first, he responded well to his treatments; but over time, it was becoming evident that he was losing the battle. Ellen asked me to come to see Charlie, which I did several times. He and I always had good conversations, but neither of us tried to kid the other as to what was coming.

In the initial stages, he retained much of his strength; but as the months rolled on, it was clear that things were not going well. He had always been a large, stocky man; but at a glance, one could observe that he was losing weight all too quickly. Initially, Charlie may have believed he was going to defeat his cancer. Then, gradually, as it happens with many other cancer patients in similar situations, he came to realize that victory over cancer was not to be his, even if he was certain that victory over death had been promised to him. Almost at the end his voice, which had always been mellow and robust, was a reedy whisper. At the very end, he was nearly unable to speak.

His doctor had told him that he would not survive his illness. Charles had previously concluded that himself. But out of that physician-patient conversation came a question which was so Charles Taylorian: "What can I do to help other men who have this disease?" That was the genesis of a foundation which the Taylors set up to provide screening for any men in the surrounding area to receive prostate cancer testing without cost. Even at the end, Charlie was giving away his resources to assist other soldiers in the battle he himself was waging.

The day before Charles died, he told Ellen he thought the time had come. They had jointly decided to gather a group of people together to plan his memorial service. Ellen quickly phoned everyone to come to their home the next day.

When we arrived, Charles spoke briefly with each of us as we came into the room. Then he appeared to drift off to sleep in the hospital bed in the large kitchen where he had been ensconced for several weeks. The pastor of the First Presbyterian Church had retired, and the new interim minister was there. The others in the group consisted of the Taylors' son, Matthew, Matthew's secretary, the choir director and his wife, a long-time friend from the choir who also was the development director for the orchestra, the funeral director (not because he was the funeral director but because he too was a long-time friend), their accountant who also was a close friend, Ellen, and me.

As Charlie apparently lay sleeping, we all began by sharing "Charles stories," some very funny, others very poignant and touching. From time to time glancing over at Charles in the bed, it did not appear to me that he was hearing any of this, but I could see him breathing rhythmically. He and Ellen had wanted this meeting to occur, so we quietly went on with the plans for the service. What music would be played and what hymns would be sung were the first order of business, which, considering it was for Charles, was only proper. Then, we discussed what scripture passages either Ellen or Charles had chosen. Finally, we talked about who would speak, and when.

Just as we were wrapping up the plans, Ellen walked over beside Charles. After a few seconds of standing beside him, but with no histrionics or dramatics, she quietly announced, "He's gone."

On a very few privileged occasions, I have been in the room when someone died. The first time was in Bayfield, Wisconsin, when I was summoned to come quickly to the home of an elderly retired minister, who had served that congregation as pastor fifty years earlier. The next to last time this happened was in the kitchen-turned-sick-room of Charles Taylor.

It has always seemed almost biblical that there we were, getting ready for a memorial service we all knew would soon transpire. I have chosen to believe that Charlie could hear us talking, and that he decided, "Well, plans are being made that are out of my hands. I trust these people, but far more so, I trust God, and I shall now make my exit." And he did, silently and unobtrusively, as only Charles Taylor would do it.

I began this brief summary of some of the highlights in Charlie's life as a churchman by declaring that he was the most committed and conscientious Christian steward I have known over my long lifetime. I will end by saying that it was quintessentially Charles for him to ask when the doctor told him he was not going to be living much longer, "What can I do to help others with this?" Even in death, he continued his stewardship by means of the foundation regarding prostate cancer which he and Ellen instituted just before he died.

I am the first to admit that the Christian stewardship of both talent and treasure has been a major pastoral concern of mine over all these years. I am convinced that those who contribute the biblically suggested tithe live happier and more productive lives than those who do not. (Since you are the one reading this, I hope you are paying close attention!)

A high level of generosity among church members is one of the primary factors which enable churches to grow and prosper in mission and ministry to the community and the larger world. Those denominations and congregations that continuously encourage tithing are the ones which tend to grow the fastest: the Mormons, the Jehovah's Witnesses, the historic and the newer evangelical churches, and those individual Mainline Protestant congregations where there is a tradition of tithing.

Charles Taylor believed that God had called him to be an outstanding steward, and that he certainly was. The First Presbyterian Church of Hilton Head Island, South Carolina, is what it is today in an indeterminable but nevertheless real status because Charles was there in some of its most crucial formative years. Without ever trumpeting what he did, what he did was to serve as a leader in building up a congregation he loved and which loved him in return.

There is a hymn which personifies the life of Charles Taylor:

"Take my life, and let it be
Consecrated, Lord, to Thee.
Take my moments and my days,
Let them flow in ceaseless praise,
Let them flow in ceaseless praise."

Charlie's life expressed ceaseless praise to the God who made him and the God who blessed him. In gratitude to God, Charles Taylor lived and died as a steward of all he had, blessing countless others in the process, for Charles fully realized as do few others that everything he had came from God.

SAINTS OF FOUR INTERIM PASTORATES AND THE CHAPEL WITHOUT WALLS

MY FIRST WIFE, Nancy, and I separated in the summer of 1996, shortly after I resigned from the pastorate of the First Presbyterian Church in Hilton Head Island. My second wife, Lois, and I were married at the end of 1997.

I resigned from the Hilton Head church because I knew the circumstances leading up to the divorce could badly damage the congregation were I try to remain as pastor and ride out the storm. In rueful retrospect, I have been convinced many times my decision was correct. But also in retrospect, it would have been far less disruptive for everyone involved, including Nancy, had we separated from one another soon after our son went off to college.

However, for a year, I was stymied in attempting to secure a call to another Presbyterian congregation, either as a pastor or as an interim pastor. Finally, in mid-1997, I was asked to become the interim pastor at the First Presbyterian Church of Lynchburg, Virginia. That lasted until mid-1998, when Lois and I went to St. Paul, Minnesota, where I was the interim pastor of the House of Hope Presbyterian Church. In late 1999, we moved to Cleveland Heights, Ohio, where I was the interim pastor of the Fairmount Presbyterian Church. Following that, I was the interim at the Second Christian Church of Warren, Ohio, east of Cleveland, until late 2001.

All told, those four congregations collectively had over four thousand members. In the brevity of an interim pastorate, it is not possible to get to know that many people to any great extent. However, there are three men from those churches I want to highlight—both because they were key members of their congregations

227

and because they were important factors for Lois and me during our sojourns in their congregations.

St. Homer Venters

St. Homer Venters Sr. was an outstanding pediatrician and medical school professor. He and his wife, Maurine, were members of the House of Hope Presbyterian Church in St. Paul, Minnesota. Previously, I have mentioned that on every pastoral search committee with which I was associated I happened to have a particular individual who decided to become my unsolicited and unrecruited champion on the committee. Maurine Venters was the person who assumed that particular burden in St. Paul.

Though Maurine Venters was a native of the Twin Cities, Homer was not. He was born in Tampa, Florida. He graduated in a high school class of seven hundred fifty students academically as the first in his class. He was barely sixteen years old. Immediately, Homer went on to college, but he was socially immature for his age. What sixteen-year-old college student wouldn't be, among classmates who are a year or two older? He left to join the Navy in the last year of World War II. He came back, and like millions of other servicemen, courtesy of the GI Bill, he finished college and then went on to Emory Medical School in Atlanta. He became a partner in a pediatric clinic in Chattanooga, Tennessee, where he became involved in a congregation of one of the most conservative evangelical denominations in the USA, having not had a very active church background previously. He became very active in Bible study in the Chattanooga church and taught Sunday school to a group of rambunctious adolescent boys. There, Homer also met and married a woman who became the mother of his first three children. While in Chattanooga, Homer discovered that his pediatric partners were members of the Ku Klux Klan, and very soon thereafter, he and his family moved to Minnesota, where, if there are any Klansmen, they are as rare as ivory-billed woodpeckers.

In Minnesota, Homer became chief of pediatrics at a large city-county hospital and also a professor at the University of Minnesota

Medical School. It was in St. Paul where Homer's wife subsequently died, leaving him with three young children. A couple of years later he married Maurine, who, I suspect, was as different from his first wife as St. Paul is from St. Petersburg (either the Floridian or the Russian one). Maurine had been a hospital floor nurse, and then a psychiatric nurse, and then she earned a PhD in public health, and then she received a law degree. No academic grass was ever allowed to grow under Homer's new wife's feet.

Though he may have started out life socially shy, Homer Venters became a paragon of personal flexibility. Being married to a lady who plunged into all that graduate school academia after they took the matrimonial plunge was quite a plunge indeed. Within a couple of years, Homer and Maurine had two of their own children; so there were five youngsters in their household, which required an indefinable but undeniable element of flexibility on everyone's part.

Because Homer saw many children in his pediatric practice whom he suspected had been abused by their parents or other people, he organized a group of citizens who enabled legislation to be passed in the Minnesota legislature to provide legal protection to teachers who reported they believed that some of their students were being abused. Medical practice was not just a matter of seeing patients in an office for Homer; it also involved thinking outside the bounds of normal medicine to act on behalf of children all over the state who needed to be protected from predators or others who sought to take advantage of them.

Several years after they were married, Homer and Maurine joined the House of Hope Presbyterian Church. Both attended worship regularly, and both were involved in various activities. I got to know Homer best through a men's group who met for breakfast and study on a weekly basis. His years of Bible study during his evangelical years served him very well in that context. He remembered scriptural episodes and quotations that I and most of the rest of us had long since forgotten, if in fact we ever knew them.

It had long been Homer Venters's hope to go to Israel before he died. Lois and I happened to be leading a tour group to Israel during the time we spent at the House of Hope Church, so Homer and

Maurine happily signed on. Homer had not been feeling well before the pilgrimage, but he was determined to go anyway. It soon became evident he was not well enough to walk, so we got a wheelchair for him. With great inner resolve, he was painfully pushed in the wheelchair over the rough streets and paths where Jesus walked, and no one seemed to derive more inner spiritual inspiration from the whole experience than Homer. He especially enjoyed talking biblical history and Middle Eastern geography and politics with our tour guide, an American-born former rabbi who had emigrated to Israel many years before.

While on the tour, Homer told Maurine that he had become convinced as we traveled around the Holy Land that he would live only a short time after the tour group flew back to St. Paul. The Sunday following our return to the Twin Cities, the Cherub Choir happened to be singing in the service of worship at the House of Hope. The Venters' granddaughter was one of the members of the choir. They sang the old children's classic known to so many of us, "Jesus wants me for a sunbeam." At the conclusion of the service, Homer quietly and somberly announced to Maurine that Jesus wanted *him* for a sunbeam, and very soon.

Through the years, I have known a substantial number of parishioners who were physicians. A few of them died while I was the pastor of their church.

More than many other kinds of people, doctors usually seem to understand how best to die. They will do everything possible to keep their patients going, but when they conclude—as we say—that "their time has come," in general, they appear to be better prepared for the inevitable than the rest of us. Perhaps it is because they must professionally become very objective to the reality of death since, depending on their specialization, many physicians see many of their patients die.

Homer Venters was definitely in the category of a man who faced his own demise with remarkable and admirable objectivity. He went into the hospital early in the week after his granddaughter had indirectly bid him to become a sunbeam, and soon it was discovered that he was afflicted with pancreatic cancer. The doctors told him that he would not live more than nine months. It was more like nine days. For all I know, Homer decided to hasten the process by dint of will.

Because Maurine and Homer had always been so supportive of Lois and me, and because we had the always-coalescing experience of the pilgrimage to Israel with them and the others in the group, I felt very close to Homer at the end of his life. I visited him daily in the hospital as his pancreatic cancer quickly took its inevitable and terminal course. He seemed unusually appreciative of those visits.

Homer Venters was a doctor who knew by professional experience, personal knowledge, and intuition that he would die very soon. Physicians in general practice or in specializations where life-threatening conditions are fairly frequently encountered usually realize that their own demise is not a threat to the natural order but in fact is an inevitable factor in the human life cycle, as it is in the life cycle of every other living being. That being the case, Homer was able to speak calmly and rationally about his impending death. It was almost as though he were outside himself looking at himself slip away. But like countless other Christians through the ages, he voiced the conviction that he would transcend death into a new and indescribably glorious life. It was not made possible by anything he had done, he insisted, but purely by the grace of God. Both his fundamentalist and his Presbyterian theology convinced him of that.

When he died more than a week after entering the hospital, he simply stopped breathing. He was conscious almost to the very end. Maurine and several others from the family were there when he passed from this world into an existence of which he was certain but about which he could have no ultimate certainty.

Maurine asked me to officiate at his memorial service, which I felt very honored to do. In the service, his son, Dr. Homer Venters Jr., also a very gifted physician, spoke of his father's many virtues. The head of the pediatrics department in the hospital where Homer served and the dean of the University of Minnesota Medical School also glowingly eulogized their colleague.

I knew Homer Venters for less than a year. But in that relatively brief time, I discovered him to be a quietly radiant Christian gentleman who used his talents for the benefit of children and youth who had medical needs. Beyond his medical practice, he also was an excellent example of what it means to put one's Christian faith into everyday practice as a caring human being and as a practitioner of medical science and art. He lived by his faith, and he also died by it. Some do one very well, but perhaps not the other. Homer did both, and both very well.

St. John Davis Jr.

John Davis was born in northeastern Massachusetts, near the border with New Hampshire. To his dying day, he sounded like a man who had just come from "pahking his caah in the Hahvud Yaad." You can take the boy out of Massachusetts, but you can't take Massachusetts out of the boy.

John grew up in a very large family. He was one of the older children, but not the oldest. He went on to earn a Doctor of Education degree, which he utilized to ascend high into the ranks of public school administration, ultimately becoming the superintendent of schools in Minneapolis.

From there, John was enticed to become the president of Macalester College in St. Paul. Considering the state the school was in, it took great enticements, the least of which was monetary, which was a factor never high on John Davis's list of professional perquisites. Macalester was a liberal arts college which had rightfully earned a reputation that deliberately promoted an international student body. Kofi Annan, a former Secretary General of the United Nations, graduated from Macalester. So, for that matter, did Walter (Fritz) Mondale, U.S. Vice President and presidential candidate, his wife, Joan Mondale, whose father was chaplain of the college, Scott McCallum, former governor of Wisconsin, and Sharon Sayles Belton, former mayor of Minneapolis. Hubert H. Humphrey, U.S. Senator and also a presidential candidate, taught there. You might deduce from that list of names it was not the epitome of rock-ribbed conservatism, and it wasn't. Nor was John Davis.

But when John was coaxed into becoming Macalester's president, things were looking dark indeed for the Presbyterian institution which had been well regarded throughout the Midwest for decades. The college's finances were in rocky condition, the faculty was unhappy, and the students were also anything but thrilled with the current state of their alma mater. If things didn't turn around—and soon—Macalester might go under. After several years of Herculean effort, John Davis did re-transform "Mac" (as it is known locally) into the institution it once had been. For that, and a host of other civic activities, including his service on the Minneapolis Federal Reserve Board, he was named Minnesotan of the Year by the leading newspaper in the Twin Cities.

John had a host of winsome qualities that destined him to greatness. He had endless curiosity about almost everything, he was perpetually optimistic, he put genuine "hum" into humility, he had a delightfully sardonic sense of humor, he was traditional but also very innovative, he *never* uttered a mean word or engaged in a nasty deed, he was a constant promoter—for his wife, Joy, his family members, Macalester College, the Twin Cities, and Minnesota—and he always deliberately understated his own abilities. He made everyone he met feel important, and to him, they truly all were important. He could enable people who were not individually unified to make unified group decisions. He was extraordinarily thrifty. John Davis could squeeze a dime or a dollar bill and make them squeal like a pig which was caught trying to escape a Norwegian bachelor farmer's tight grasp. He had opinions on almost everything, but he didn't force them on anyone. That is a rare, almost impossible, talent for all opinionated people.

John and his wife, Joy, were married after John's first wife died. Joy was a college professor of English literature. They made an excellent two-person team in their marriage. Joy had two sons, and John became like a genetic second father to them and a genetic grandfather to their children. John owned a farm in western Wisconsin, just across the border with Minnesota. It wasn't really a *farm* farm; it was a former farm out in the countryside. The Davises often invited their assembled offspring and various grandchildren, and other friends and relatives were often invited to the farm. When they arrived, they were issued work gloves in the hope (for the guests) and the expectation (for the family) that they would want to participate in a character-building effort to make the green acres even greener, or at least more tidy and less weed-choked.

Education was John Davis's primary professional passion. For that reason, his doctorate was an EdD not a PhD It is very unusual, nonetheless, for a college president to have an EdD rather than a PhD. But John was a very unusual man. All the abilities which served him so well when he was a teacher and administrator in public school systems also served him well as a college president. In retirement, the "John Davis Personal Package" also greatly benefitted Mankato State University in Minnesota, where for a time, he was the interim president, guiding them out of the hole in which, unhappily, they found themselves. To John, education was a lifelong, challenging, difficult, and demanding pursuit, and he inspired others to catch and absorb his educational vision. He was the quintessential team player as opposed to the solo miracle worker. For a man with a truly great breadth of talent, he also had a truly small amount of visible ego.

Up until the last year or two of his life, John Davis retained his membership in his home church back in Massachusetts. What can I say? He was a traditionalist, and he was not about to sever himself from his New England roots without careful forethought and consideration. Before he died, however, he concluded it was high time that he joined the House of Hope Presbyterian Church. It surprised nearly everyone, including his wife and pastor, that he had not been a member since he arrived in the Twin Cities many years before. He had always been an active member in everything but name, and for reasons known only to himself, he finally decided to add his name to the official roll of the House of Hope Church.

John Davis died several years after we moved from St. Paul. In what seems to me to be a typically Davisian singular stroke of gritty determination to mark the milestone, he managed to hang on to make his exit from this world until the very date of his twenty-fifth wedding anniversary with Joy. His memorial service at the House of Hope Church was the second largest in the church's history, sur-

234

passed only by that of Hubert Humphrey many years before. It lasted for two hours, with many participants adding their wistful encomiums to John. Joy played a recording of the service for Lois and me, and in it, there was frequent laughter and applause. John's son, John III, noted that his father eschewed "vitriolic diatribes that pass for public discourse." How true that was! He encouraged spirited, but never spiteful, debate.

It is not surprising that Robert Frost was John's favorite poet. He even looked a little bit like Robert Frost, with the bushy eyebrows and the same shock of white, slightly unruly hair. Unlike most of us, John Davis very intentionally and consciously took the road less travelled, and in his life and the lives of everyone around him, that has made all the difference.

John was not what anyone, no doubt including God, would call an orthodox Christian. He had certain inalienable doubts, and he was far more accepting of religious and personal diversity than many Christians would suppose any proper believer should be. But as Chaucer said of one of the Canterbury pilgrims, "Gladly did he learn, and gladly teach." In his Christianity, as in all other facets of his life, John Davis was perhaps a seeker much more than a finder, a man who discovered more comfort in being found by God than in finding God.

St. Karl Bruch

Karl Bruch was a man who could pillory a pill of a person in such a way that the one who had thus been pilloried might assume he had just received the highest of compliments. Karl always refrained from effusive and inauthentic praise, but he might skillfully damn with extraordinarily faint praise. In other words, he told it like he saw it, but he did so with a deft touch and a gentle manner.

Despite all pronunciations, German or otherwise, you might give to his surname, it was pronounced "Brew," not "Bruccchhh." I don't know why. I being I, no doubt I asked, but I don't remember his answer.

Karl was a lifelong member of the Fairmount Presbyterian Church in Cleveland Heights, Ohio. He grew up two or three blocks down Fairmount Avenue from the church. Fairmount Avenue is a beautiful boulevard which wends its way through the first-ring Cleveland suburb of Cleveland Heights. As with the homes along Summit Avenue in St. Paul, where the House of Hope Presbyterian Church was located, with its manse next to it, the homes along Fairmount Avenue were spacious, elegant, and solid domiciles, built mainly in the 1920s—not long before The Crash. And as in St. Paul, the Fairmount manse was also next door to the church. Both manses had large ballrooms on the third floor. That tells you something of the nature of those times and of those neighborhoods. In my entire career as a Presbyterian parson, I lived in four manses. Two of them had ballrooms, and two did not. I do not believe that represents a statistically accurate reflection of all Presbyterian parsonages throughout the country, however, and you should keep that in mind.

It may sound as though I digress, but I do so for a reason. Karl Bruch grew up in a privileged neighborhood in a privileged household. His parents were upper-middle class people. His extended family, most of whom also lived in the Cleveland area, also were upper-middle class. Many folks within the city itself, back when Karl was a boy or when I knew him as an elderly elder at Fairmount, might consider him upper class. However, sociologists would not do so, I think, nor urban economists. But Karl was definitely what once was called "well off," in a kinder, gentler time.

Karl loved adventure, both in his personal and his professional life. He told me that when he was boy in high school, he used to practice the track-and-field sport of the javelin by flinging his javelin from one side of Fairmount Boulevard to the other. One might suppose that was a simple feat for even a less-proficient-than-average javelin chucker, except that where Karl lived, the street is perhaps two hundred feet from one curb to the other. So it would require a prodigious toss to get your average javelin to make it safely across the divide without clanking off the pavement or smiting a passing Chevie in the side. But Karl loved a challenge, and I imagine his beleaguered parents could never dissuade their offspring from using

Fairmount Avenue as his preferred javelin field. Karl was not really a wild child; he was, instead, just determined.

He also loved the adventure of captaining sailboats. For most of his life he sailed, mainly on Lake Erie, but also all along the Eastern Seaboard of the United States and out as far as Bermuda, Triangle and all. He would regale anyone who would listen with tales of sails hither and yon, and of storms which tested his mettle and that of everyone else on board. His wife, Ginny, always listened with a combination of affirmation of the facts being reported and utter disbelief that she or anyone else had ever been willing to subject themselves to such damp dangers. Eventually, Ginny stopped going out with Captain Courageous altogether, and Karl had to rely on equally daring male companions to crew for him on his voyages.

The eastern suburbs of Cleveland have several excellent private schools, and Karl went to the University School, one of the best of them. Then, he went on to college, and then into business, where he excelled—in ability, dedication, and enthusiasm.

I cannot imagine that anyone who knew Karl Bruch disliked him, unless he and that person happened to locked horns on particular issues over which the other disputant was utterly unbending. Karl did not remain silent when he felt strongly about something, but he did not make a perfect nuisance (or even an imperfect nuisance) of himself. It was never his intention to be a nuisance at all. Rather, he always wanted to debate issues openly and honestly, without personal rancor or discord. It was not in his nature to seek discord, but he did not dodge it either.

I had known Karl for a number of years before we came to the Fairmount Church. Indirectly, that came about because I knew both of the previous pastors of Fairmount Church—the more recent one as a seminary classmate in Chicago and the previous one as a minister in Chicago Presbytery when I was at Fourth Church. The older one, Hank Andersen, formed a group of like-minded Presbyterian ministers from around the country who gathered for a few days twice a year in the city or town where one of us was located. Usually, we focused our meeting on a unique factor in the ministry of that particular church or something in the area which might be of interest to us.

When we gathered the first time in Cleveland Heights (which is where I first met Karl Bruch), we discussed advances in medicine, listening to some highly able doctors and administrators from the Cleveland Clinic. They led us through some fascinating and difficult scenarios regarding medical ethics. In each church where one of us was the pastor, several elders would help in the organization of the meeting, and Karl was instrumental in making the Cleveland Heights clambakes productive and happy events the two times we met there when I was a member of the group. In addition, some of the elders came with their pastors to other places, and Karl travelled with Hank Anderson or Kent Organ a few times. Thus, I felt I was well acquainted with Karl before I came to the Fairmount Church as the interim pastor after Kent Organ left.

The Fairmount Presbyterian Church had a checkered record with its pastors for much of its history, but I was not aware of that when we went there. In fact, I did not know it until we had been in residence for seven months or so as the history was slowly unveiled for me. Karl Bruch was one of the primary unveilers.

Of the five pastors and four interim pastors who had been at Fairmount prior to my arriving there as the interim, only one had not left under some sort of duress. The stormy conditions were almost always caused by members of the church, not by the clergy themselves, at least according to Karl. The minister he most admired had been there in the `60s, when the membership of the congregation was over three thousand people. But the `60s were even more disruptive in Cleveland than in many other cities. Almost two years before Martin Luther King was assassinated, there were riots in the Hough section of Cleveland. Hough was a predominantly black neighborhood about three or four miles from the church. Four blacks were killed, and over thirty people were critically injured. Fires were widespread. The rioting continued for six days before it was brought under control. Cleveland was never the same after that.

The pastor of the Fairmount Church at that time refused to ignore the problems and injustices he felt were inherent in the larger Cleveland community. He voiced his concerns in sermons, and for that, he became increasingly unpopular among some of the leaders of the upper-middle class congregation. Despite the church having remarkable growth under his leadership, he was forced out.

Karl Bruch strongly agreed with that pastor regarding what the two of them believed was the ill-treatment the poor and disenfranchised were receiving at the hands of the greater Cleveland community. For that reason, Karl was particularly dismayed when the minister was unceremoniously edged out. Only when it became evident to me—and also to Karl—that I was likely to experience what eight out of the nine previous heads-of-staff had encountered did Karl feel free to reveal his side of the past half-century of Fairmount history.

He didn't present his case to me with bitterness or anger. He did it more out of dismay and sorrow. How could a church act as his church had acted, the only church he to which he had ever belonged? He didn't ask the question Rodney King had asked after having been severely beaten by some Los Angeles policemen, but he might have: "Can't we just get along?" I was starting to ask that myself with respect to a small number of key leaders of the Fairmount Church, "Can't we just get along?"

I will go into very few details of what happened when my annual contract as interim pastor was not renewed. I will only say that Karl Bruch went out of his way to be especially supportive, as did many other parishioners. It was probably less than ten people who eagerly wanted me to be gone, but they were ten people in key positions.

Dear reader, if I were you and I was reading this, I would ask myself, "Why is he telling us this? Is he trying to absolve himself of whatever it was he did wrong?" Well, that may be true. The only thing I ever said from the pulpit which apparently upset some people had to do with the commendable desire on the part of many leaders to see the congregation more racially integrated than was currently the case. I strongly supported that goal myself. Furthermore, Fairmount was by far the most integrated Presbyterian church with which I had ever been personally involved.

However, I opined homiletically that Fairmount was a UMC church. I explained that did not mean "United Methodist Church" because obviously they were not Methodists. UMC stood for Upper-Middle Class, I said. Low income people, whether black, brown, or white, were unlikely to join the Fairmount Church. That was not because Fairmount people would not welcome them because definitely they would. Instead, it would be evident at a mere glance to lower-income visitors that their social class and that of the Fairmount social class and status were worlds apart. The nature of the neighborhood in which the church was located and the kind of people who came to it from many of the eastern Cleveland suburbs represented a different slice of the demographic pie than the slice represented by the folks the open-hearted people of Fairmount wanted to attract. That is a sad reality faced by thousands of liberal-minded congregations throughout America.

Protestants, especially Mainline Protestants, are not very effective at crossing economic and class lines in their churches. Roman Catholics and evangelicals manage to do that on a broad basis, but not Mainline Protestants. So, said the outside-agitator-interim-preacher, the way to make the Fairmount Church grow is to seek the same sort of people who had been attending Fairmount since its inception three-quarters of a century earlier. They were UMC folks. Invite them, whatever their color, to come in. Their hope for growth lay in the UMC.

That seemed readily apparent to me in terms of Ecclesiastical Sociology 101. But for some members, that notion was a red cape waved before a powerfully peeved bull. I did not intend to provoke controversy; understanding and dialogue was what I sought by that sermon. I believe it would be safe to say I did not get it.

Several people expressed gratitude that I said what I said, and no one directly challenged it, if I recall correctly, which I might not, by sublimating the painful results of that sermon. It definitely got under a few key collars, and for me, The End was near.

Karl Bruch was particularly complimentary for what he described as my courage in that sermon. I told him it wasn't courageous at all; it was merely a statement of what would seem obvious to someone who had been in that congregation for only a few months.

One might wonder why someone of Karl's theological and ecclesiastical leanings would remain for over eighty years with a congregation which frequently nearly drove him to despairing distraction.

Why did he subject himself to the almost continuous pain which his allegiance heaped upon him?

Ah, but precisely there was one of the most crucial factors in the laudable character of Karl Bruch! It was *their* church, the church of some of the people with whom he so strongly disagreed, but it also was *his* church. He refused to allow anyone to snatch it away from him. No matter what others might do, no matter how short-sighted or pig-headed they were in his opinion, he would stick with the ship, leaky hull, torn sails, and all. Karl reminds me so powerfully of the sentiments the prophet Hosea expressed on behalf of God in Chapter 11. God felt devastated by so much of what Israel had said and done, but He declared He could never abandon them. God cried out, "How can I give you up, O Ephraim? How can I hand you over, O Israel? ... My heart recoils within me, my compassion grows warm and tender. I will not execute my fierce anger, ... for I am God and not man, ... and I will not come to destroy" (Hos. 11:8–9).

Karl was a saintly, salty, long-suffering Christian and church member. Though some of the people in his church enormously exasperated him, he stuck with it and them through all the days of his long and wisdom-graced life. Nobody was ever more loyal to a congregation which severely tested loyalty than Karl Bruch. When I think back over the whole host of saints I have known in all the churches with which I have been associated for nearly eight decades, Karl stands out as one of the wisest and finest. It is people such as he who enable the Church of Jesus Christ to weather the inevitable storms which have assaulted the Church through the twenty centuries of its existence. Were it not for the Karl Bruchs of the ecclesiastical realm, the Church might have silently slipped beneath the turbulent surface of the ocean ages ago.

The Chapel Without Walls

After my contract was not renewed as the interim pastor of the Fairmount Church, Lois and I began attending the Euclid Avenue Christian Church in Cleveland Heights. I had come to know their pastor, Houston Bowers, through the Cleveland Heights Ministerial

Association, and I was strongly drawn to him and his outstanding preaching. Through Houston's assistance, I received a call to become the interim pastor of the Second Christian Church of Warren, Ohio, an old industrial small city forty miles east of Cleveland. I very much enjoyed my association with the Disciples of Christ denomination. It convinced me, not that I needed much convincing, that people other than Presbyterians also know how to "do church."

When the Warren interim ended, I was completely unable to arrange another ministerial call anywhere, either as an interim or as a called pastor. I was over sixty-two years of age, and I deduce that any congregations looking for a minister figured I was then three-quarters as old as God, which they assumed was too old. I had no fiscal choice other than take early retirement. By so doing, I lost 20 percent of both my pension and my social security. There simply was not enough income to sustain us.

Lois and I became substitute teachers, and we were called occasionally to fill in at area schools. We also worked part-time for a member of Fairmount Church who ran a search firm for attorneys. It quickly became obvious, however, that there still was insufficient income to keep us going indefinitely.

Therefore, we decided to return to Hilton Head Island to launch a new interdenominational congregation. We both knew several hundred potential prospects for such a church, and it seemed the best possibility of getting onto firmer fiscal ground for the future. Starting a new church because the pastor needs the money is not the most ideal or idealistic reason for establishing a new congregation, but the sober bottom line is that was what motivated us to return to the community in which we both had lived for almost twenty years.

The first service of The Chapel Without Walls was also the largest attendance of any service in the by-now fourteen years of the existence of The Chapel Without Walls. Likely, many people wanted to give their support for the new ecclesiastical start-up in its initial worship experience, while others may have wanted to know what the pastoral prodigal son would have to say his first time back in his familiar home territory.

Now The Chapel has two geezer parsons who provide pastoral leadership to a dedicated group of lay people who also are primarily geezers. John Melin, a relative child compared to me, is our associate pastor. He is a minister of the Evangelical Lutheran Church who spent his entire career in overseas congregations, including Jerusalem, Moscow, and Amsterdam. From its inception, The Chapel has consisted of fairly liberal, mainly Mainline Protestant-type Christians, some of whom are skeptical seekers after truth. We are an odd bunch, but we are content in our peculiarity.

For most of the years The Chapel Without Walls has been in existence, we held our services in Congregation Beth Yam, the local Reform synagogue on Hilton Head Island. That is the most evident reason why we don't have walls; we met within the confines of Beth Yam's walls. In the summer of 2016 we moved into a local retirement home, where we now hold our services. It seems reasonable, since most of us are retired. But the primary reason we are known as The Chapel Without Walls is that we do not try to wall anyone into a restricted set of doctrines or beliefs nor to wall out anyone who might disagree with us on any matters of faith. We certainly do not claim to have all the answers to everything in life, but we do attempt to pose important questions, even if the answers are not easily forthcoming.

What follows are brief biographies of five people who were associated with The Chapel Without Wall as members of the Church Militant who are now part of The Church Triumphant, whatever that means and wherever it is.

St. Richard Greene

Richard Greene became part of The Chapel family by means of Beth Whitney, the lady who, late in life, became his wife. Beth and her first husband attended First Presbyterian Church on the island when I was its pastor. By the time we returned to Hilton Head, he had died. Eventually, Beth found her way to The Chapel.

Then, a while after that, Dick Greene started coming to church with Beth. They had met when Dick, a professional physicist, was teaching a course on elementary physics in a continuing education program which has operated on the island for many years. The course may have been elementary to Dick, but it was utterly incomprehensible to Beth. She did not understand a single concept he was attempting to explain. Nevertheless, she thought he was a very interesting man, and she made it her business to get to know him better. One thing led to another, and suddenly, there also was Dick Greene in the house of the Lord, which in this case was Congregation Beth Yam and the interlopers in their midst, namely, us, who had no walls of our own, but we met within their walls.

Over the next several years, I came to know Dick Greene very well. He was born Jewish, though he had never regularly attended any synagogue anywhere. However, Beth convinced him he should try to discover and recover his religious roots, so they began attending Beth Yam as well as The Chapel together. And together, they took a Hebrew class which the rabbi taught. In due time, they were married by the rabbi. For the first years of their marriage, they were the enthusiastic ecumenical duo who were involved in both congregations. Only when neither of them was able to see well enough to drive to the Friday night services did they cease going regularly to Beth Yam. (They were in their eighties when they married.)

Dick and Beth usually came to the discussion forum following our Sunday morning service. There, and in other classes that I taught, Dick explained his background to us. He was born in Brooklyn to parents who were secular Jews. That is, ethnically they identified themselves as Jews, but not as religious Jews.

When it came time to go to high school, he was enrolled at Erasmus Hall School, a public school which had been founded by the Dutch Reformed Church just after the American Revolution. It provided a classical education, meaning that the students learned a great deal of Greek and Latin. The faculty and student body must have been extremely gifted academically because Dick would lead us through arcane and sometimes convoluted explanations of the root meanings of words with Greek or Latin origin. It was evident that he had absorbed all that knowledge of classics like a thirsty sponge absorbs a pail that is half full of water.

Besides having a Dutch origin (Desiderius Erasmus was a Renaissance Dutch humanist), Erasmus Hall also had a decidedly Christian orientation, despite being a public school. So there was Richard Greene, secular Jew, absorbing Christian hymns like he absorbed variations of various Greek and Latin verbs and nouns. His mind was a walking Wikipedia long before Wiki had invented his pedia. He was rapidly becoming the intellectual giant he turned out to be.

When he was still a teenager, his Erasmus Hall physics teacher was so impressed with his research ideas that he decided he should go to Los Alamos to see whether he might assist in whatever was going on out there in New Mexico. The teacher knew something was going on, but he did not know specifically what it was, except that it had something to do with science and physics. Dick was soon dispatched to the secret enclave in the desert, but apparently the leaders of the scientific enclave decided they did not need a boy in their midst, no matter how bright he might be. Who knows what might have happened if they had allowed him to stay?

Dick attended Lehigh University in Bethlehem, Pennsylvania, where he had an evening job shoveling coal into the open, fiery maw of a Bethlehem Steel blast furnace. After that, he would go back to his room to study the math and physics required for his engineering degree. Following his graduation from Lehigh, he went to the University of Pennsylvania, where he earned a PhD in physics. His thesis advisor noted that Dick was writing something in his thesis which was related to something Albert Einstein had written about in his Second Law of Thermodynamics, but which Einstein never bothered to explain. The advisor sent a letter to Einstein about it, and the greatest scientist of the twentieth century sent a letter back to Dick, commending him on his insight, apparently admitting that he, Einstein, had not thought of that himself. Dick being the absent-minded-professor-type he was, he misplaced the letter somewhere along the line, but I have no doubt the story unfolded exactly as he told it because he remembered everything that ever happened in his life. He was a fascinating raconteur regarding matters about which the average humanoid knows nothing but which are absolutely fascinating to hear about, all those deficiencies notwithstanding.

Somewhere along the way, Dick got married. He and his wife adopted two children. Unfortunately, the marriage last only fifteen years or so.

In the meantime, after he finished his doctorate in physics, he went to work for the U.S. Navy Research Laboratory in Maryland. There, he helped develop weapons systems and other intricate gizmos. Because much of his work was classified, he would not have told you about it. And if it were not classified, he would probably be unable clearly to explain it to you unless you are a physicist, which, if you are reading this book, you probably are not. I was intrigued by what intrigued him, but I almost never had a clue what he was talking about when he launched into the field of physics. I was also quite limited when he declined Greek and Latin verbs.

Dick and Beth Greene had a natural affinity for one another because both were still quietly and carefully searching for a Significant Other and because they both had an intense intellectual curiosity, which each admired in the other. For example, Dick took up bridge at age eighty-three. He would have been an excellent bridge player, except that he couldn't remember very well the cards which had previously been played. When Lois and I played bridge with Beth and Dick, he was always very pleased with himself when he remembered to play the cards properly. I think it gave him pleasure and pride to know that he still had it for recollections of recent matters, even if it didn't matter much. But the memory section of his prodigious gray matter for recent events was the first part of his brain to go. However, the rest of his intellect remained intact up to the very end.

The Greenes were frequent participants in the Sunday forums and in weekday classes I taught. By this point in your perusal of this small tome, it will come as no surprise to you that I tend to be toward the left side of the spectrum in matters theological as well as political. It is also true that most of the people who attend The Chapel Without Walls are also skewed to that side of the continuum. But I suppose it is understandable. Who would put up with me other than folks at least somewhat like me?

Dick Greene, on the other hand, was a convinced and very voluble conservative, at least in his politics. He was fairly liberal in his religion and theology, or else he could not stomach that to which he was subjected weekly from the pulpit. But when politics entered our debates in the forums or in the classes, as frequently it did and does, Dick would stand his ground like Barry Goldwater in the Election of 1964 or Ted Cruz in the Republican Presidential Primary of 2013–16. Regardless of how many wishy-washy liberals would pile on, he expounded his views with undiminished gusto. "Damn the torpedoes; full speed ahead!" said he. I always admired his undaunted courage in the face of The Enemy Within.

Somewhere along the line late in his life, Dick got the idea that he was being called, possibly even by the Almighty One of Israel, to provide fresh water to the Negev Desert in the southern part of Israel. He talked about the desalinization of salt water from the Mediterranean, then piping it underground to the Negev. He was sure it could be done at a reasonable cost. But he was distressed that he had stumbled upon this notion so belatedly. The idea stuck with him until he died, and while he was unable to do anything to bring it to fruition, it kept his intellectual juices constantly bubbling in the posterior chambers of his mind.

It would be entirely misleading to think that Richard Greene rather swiftly became either an orthodox Jew or an orthodox Christian in the final years of his earthly existence. Most assuredly, he did not. He was too bright to accept the traditional teachings of either religion on face value, and he was too much a scientist to affirm preachments which relied too much on faith and too little on reason, at least to his way of thinking.

There were times when I thought to my astonishment that Dick might have consciously climbed onto the biblical buckboard, but then, he would say something which convinced me he was still himself, and that he was not about to swallow what to him seemed like the flaccidly flawed fallacies of faith. Dick was an eminently reasonable man, and faith was intellectually probably too much of an insurmountable challenge to him.

For a few years before he died, Dick Greene was afflicted with a pair of kidneys which operated at the minimum level of efficiency necessary to sustain human life. It was as though the inner workings of his kidneys were made of Swiss cheese, and miniature mice had gotten in and had gnawed them into mere wisps of their former selves. He legs, arms, and fingers would swell up, and he had difficulty walking. He also endured considerable pain.

Nevertheless, the new lease on life which had happily overtaken him when he married Beth kept him percolating as best he could. Only in the last few weeks of his life was it necessary for him to be in a nursing home, where he was given oxygen and medications that could not be administered at home.

I visited Dick almost daily in his final days. I wanted to be of whatever spiritual assistance I could provide to a man who whose brain was far more expansive than mine in the Big Picture of life on our planet. Dick reveled in the concept of The Big Bang. He had pretty well resolved for himself how it had happened, but both he and I were at a loss to declare beyond any doubt why it had occurred. I concluded that Dick was more of a How Man, and I was more of a Why Man.

There was no doubt that Richard Greene wanted to be a believer, and in many respects, he was. But by no means was he anything close to being an orthodox believer. The physicist in him simply would not allow that to happen. He was almost certainly not an atheist, but he would likely insist it would be incorrect to describe him as anything other than an agnostic.

He knew that he was about to die, and he seemed to have accepted that inevitability. Thinking I knew what his answer would be, I asked him if he was afraid to die. He said he was. I was very surprised. I would have guessed he would say he was ready to go, even if it meant leaving Beth.

What that indicated to me is that as stellar a human being as he was, with an extraordinarily gifted and expansive intellect, Dick was still a human being, like the rest of us, with the same kinds of uncertainties and insecurities that we all have. He died a few days after that conversation. He was not terrified by any means, but he was not really at peace either. He did not go quietly into the night, nor did he rail against the fates. He went as an agnostic, good, true, and without invincible knowledge.

Dick Greene was an intellectually superior, socially somewhat limited, spiritually determinedly searching sort of a man. He brought an element into my life I had never observed up so close and so personally. He was marvelous man, a scintillating scientist, and a faithful friend. He was almost always complimentary of my sermons, even the ones with which I knew he would have insurmountable philosophical differences. To his great credit, he never seemed to hold my lunacies against me.

To alter the words of the apostle Paul a bit, when Dick Greene was a child, he was a physicist child. He spoke like a physicist child, he thought like a physicist child, he reasoned like a physicist child. When he became a man, he did not give up physicist ways. His mind gravitated toward the immense and the infinite as well as toward the indescribably tiny and minute. It was no more possible for him to become an ordinary card-carrying Christian than for a flaming fundamentalist with a sixth-grade education to become a committed aficionado of Paul Tillich or Karl Rahner. But no one ever sought God more fervently than Richard Greene, and no one ever found God to be more enigmatic, mysterious, and ultimately indescribable than Dick Greene.

His memorial service was unlike any other in which I was a participant. I have co-officiated with rabbis several times at weddings, but only once did I co-officiate with a rabbi in a memorial service. And that was for Dick. Rabbi Brad Blum of Congregation Beth Yam and I together led his service on a Sunday morning at 11 AM in the sanctuary of Congregation Beth Yam, after we had finished our own service. Brad led the Jewish part and I led the Christian part, but Dick Greene was larger than both parts put together. Neither of us could pin him down into our own tradition, nor did we try. He had a foot in both camps, but he stood outside each tradition as well. He was, in the best Yiddish tradition, a true *Mensch*.

St. Rita Litz

Rita Litz was a tall, statuesque, warm, friendly, and talkative lady. When she first came to The Chapel Without Walls, she was in her early eighties, and she was the solo passenger who was killed in a car accident in her mid-eighties. She was never nimble of foot as long as I knew her, but the nimbleness of her mind never eluded her for an instant until the day of her death.

Rita had lived most of her life in the Chicago area. She had been a fashion model and a principal in a successful business venture, and then, she was the host (or in those days, probably "hostess") on her own local television show. It was the kind of program women would watch. She focused on all matter of matters feminine. Rita was nothing if not quintessentially feminine. However, she was the type of woman who did not depend on feminine wiles, whatever those mysterious and indefinable realities may be, to get her through life. She called spades *spades* and hearts *hearts*, but she was not taken in by diamonds, nor would she resort to clubs to use against anyone— female or male. But in all things, a lady she was.

While in Chicago, she became a very accomplished golfer, and she had many trophies in her home. Several times, she invited Lois and me to her condominium, and she loved to display her Christmas and Easter and Fourth of July seasonal trinkets. She was always dressed to the nines, with never a hair out of place. I suspect that even when she did her housework (which she must have done frequently; her home was always immaculate), she probably looked like a latter-day June Cleaver.

By the time I first met Rita, she was no longer swift or agile. She suffered from fibromyalgia, a nerve disease which impedes normal movement and eventually may result in quite severe pain. Sadly, pain inflicted itself on Rita through most of her final years. Nevertheless, she still got through each day with a smile which would light up a whole room, if she were indoors, or the entire visible landscape, if she were outdoors. She was a marvelous fake who always looked like she had not a care in the world even if she were hurting so much she wanted to scream.

At some point in her life, a group of friends interested her in Christian Science. Perhaps that is why she acted so unimpaired by her frequent neurological assaults. Other friends invited her to go with them to the Unity Fellowship. For whatever reason, Rita was attracted to unusual forms of religious expression. That may be why she happened into The Chapel Without Walls one particular Sunday. Nobody collared her to come along; she probably saw our ad in the local newspaper and decided she might like to try us. We looked like her type of untraditional traditional church. Apparently, she liked what she saw, for she became a Chapel regular. I gather that Rita had never been an orthodox Christian in any recognizable form during her entire life, and she concluded that coming to The Chapel Without Walls would keep her life's trend intact.

Rita was a unique, larger-than-life member of The Chapel during the first few years of our existence as a congregation. She exuded genuine warmth, and she had an abiding interest in the life of everyone she met. She loved to chat with people during the coffee hour after the service, which, if it were up to Rita, would truly last for at least an hour—which it never did or does. In the forum, in our discussion about the sermon topic or anything else anyone wanted to talk about and almost always did, Rita added her own Litzian slant to whatever was being said, which was usually not what anyone was saying or even thinking. She wasn't ditzy, really, but with regularity she was either incapable of or unwilling to follow the line of thinking which was being expressed by other forum folks. Her comments always exhibited fresh nuances of thought or inquiry. Her ever-active mind operated in grooves most of us had never discovered, nor were we likely to do so.

When I was a young minister, and much more committed to proper doctrines and predictable patterns of theological inquiry, a Rita Litz would have made me very nervous. In my old age, I enjoyed her unusual personality and her offbeat observations. If variety is the spice of life, Rita brought a level of spiciness into our lives that no one else could provide in precisely the same way. She was a lovely lady in every sense and also a rare one, and every Sunday, we encountered new levels of meaning for what that meant.

Many people would probably call Rita's death a tragedy. She was riding in the front passenger seat with a woman who apparently was not a sufficiently careful driver. The driver turned left without paying heed to a line of rapidly oncoming traffic, and a car hit them full-force in the front right door beside which Rita was riding. She did not die instantaneously, but she lived for only a few minutes, never regaining consciousness. The driver, fortunately and providentially, was not seriously injured.

My guess is that Rita would have approved of her method of demise. She would not have been thrilled by the exact circumstances, probably, but she would be grateful that death came so swiftly, and without a moment of lasting pain. She had endured far more than her share of pain because of her fibromyalgia, and she was liberated from experiencing any more debilitation or distress because of her continuing, permanent illness. She even might have found some unique humor in the fact that a life which was all-too-slowly playing itself out by pain-wracked bits and pieces was over in one giant nanosecond collision of a motorcar and mortality.

It may be correct to say that there have always been more characters than people who chose to affiliate themselves with The Chapel Without Walls. The "Without Walls" part may explain why the "characters" characterization is so true. Rita Litz was one of those characters. She definitely was a person—and a very special one at that. But to me, she will always live in my memory as one of our unique Cast of Characters. No one could ever accuse her of being an orthodox believer, but she was without question a most committed unorthodox believer. I shall never forget her sweet disposition and her sunny smile. Of such people does my ever-bulging memorial file of beloved parishioners continue to grow.

St. Donald Havlish

Don Havlish was one of several parishioners with whom I was associated in both the First Presbyterian Church and The Chapel Without Walls of Hilton Head Island. Don and his wife, Alma, were at First Presbyterian when our family moved to the island in 1979. He con-

252

tinued to worship regularly at both First Presbyterian and The Chapel once The Chapel was instituted in 2004, and he kept attending both congregations almost until the time of his death in early 2015.

Don received a degree in engineering from the Carnegie Institute of Technology, which later became Carnegie-Mellon University. His entire business career was spent with a national manufacturing company. He rose through the ranks to become their national sales manager.

Don Havlish was the proverbial born salesman. He was able to converse with even the most taciturn of individuals, and he knew how to make them talk—even when they were convinced it violated their very nature to do so. Don never met a stranger, and everyone he did meet soon became an acquaintance known personally by name, if not also as a long-time fast friend. He had a genuine warmth that was not learned or forced. "Warmth" and "Friendliness" were Don's middle names. These qualities came as naturally to him as breathing.

Don was sufficiently successful in his vocation as super-sales-man that he and Alma were able to construct a home on the ocean on Hilton Head Island, moving there a few years before the normal retirement age. However, Don did not retire to have fun by play-ing golf or tennis or walking on the beach. He had been very active in his church in suburban Pittsburgh and in the greater Pittsburgh community, and he was even more active as practically a fulltime volunteer on the island. He became a leader in the Rotary Club and several other service organizations.

But it was in Don's service to the First Presbyterian Church where I became the best acquainted with his outstanding skills. He was the sort of person who could always be counted on to do what he said he would do. He was a tireless elder of the church, a mainstay in the Men of the Church group, and a permanent presence in other church organizations. Probably his most lasting contribution to the life of the congregation was to be the spearhead in the planning and construction of the church's columbarium, which eventually will be the final resting place for the ashes of over a thousand parishioners. It is a testimony to the demographics of the membership of First

Presbyterian Church and of Hilton Head Island that by now, perhaps two-thirds or more of those niches are filled.

Toward the end of my pastorate at First Church, Alma Havlish was afflicted with cancer. Over the past two years of her life, it was evident that she was rather quickly declining. Eventually, Alma was unable to walk. Nevertheless, every Sunday, Don would bring Alma into the sanctuary in a wheelchair after the opening hymn had begun. He would push her up beside the front pew where she could better see what was going on. Then, during the singing of the closing hymn, he would take her out to avoid creating a traffic jam in the movement toward the exits. It was so typical of Don Havlish to see that his wife was able to continue attending church, but he did not want to deter anyone from beating a hasty retreat to the rear doors when the organ postlude began.

A few years before Alma died, the Havlishes moved into one of the three large retirement homes on the island. Don wanted to be sure they would be in the best possible environment should either of them encounter a serious illness or debilitation. There, the Havlishes made and nurtured many new friendships. After Alma died, Don stayed in their home. In time, he became close to a widow whose husband had died about the same time as Alma. Don and Joan spent many happy hours of most days together. Many of us wondered whether they would get married. Don used to grin at people who could summon up courage to ask whether he had finally popped the question, telling them, "I'm very willing, but she won't have me!" I suspect Joan decided not to marry at such an advanced age because she feared it would complicate her family's finances, which I think were likely quite complex. But Joan's reluctance did not prevent them from having a close and loving relationship in the last years of her life.

As happens with many nonagenarians, Joan's mental acuity began to decline. Her memory started to deteriorate to such a degree that her children decided she needed to go into the assisted care facility of the retirement home. Almost every day, Don would go to see her, and he would often take her in a wheelchair to the community dining room at the clubhouse. He was as solicitous to Joan as he had been to Alma, which always struck me as an indicator for what an outstanding man he was. No doubt the following is a sexist statement, but it seems to me that in general men are not as good as caregivers as women. I don't know if that is a cultural or a genetic phenomenon, but I think it is true.

However, Don Havlish was a wonderful caregiver to Alma, his wife of more than fifty years, and to his very close friend, Joan, for several years. No one could fault him for the extraordinary devotion he displayed to these two women, and in fact, he deserved much praise for his solicitous assistance.

Don was in his upper nineties when he died. He had always been an unusually handsome man. He dressed well, and he always came to church with a coat and tie. It would never have occurred to him not to do that. On cold winter days (which are not very cold or wintery in southern South Carolina), he would wear a high-quality overcoat he had probably owned for years; and in it, he looked like an ad for Brooks Brothers.

For the last several months of his life, he had given up driving. An employee from the retirement home would drive him to The Chapel. I have had the habit of greeting people at the front door of the synagogue as they arrive. Don would slowly extricate himself from the front seat of the car, invariably with a giant, economy-sized grin on his face. He looked like as stately and regal as the Prince of Wales, not the current one but the 1930s chap who gave up the throne for the woman he loved.

No one who was old enough to grasp the enormity of what happened on September 11, 2001 will ever forget the horrific events of that day. And no one who knew Don Havlish could ever forget how 9/11 was forever chiseled into Don's life. His son, Donald Havlish Jr. was in one of the World Trade Towers when it collapsed into that incomprehensible heap on that never-to-be-forgotten morning. He was one of the nearly three thousand victims of the attack who did not make it out alive.

We were living in Cleveland at the time of 9/11. I did not see Don personally until we moved back to Hilton Head in late 2004. When I did go to visit him, of course I asked how he was faring following his son's death. I was prepared to hear that it was the worst thing that had ever happened to him or that he had become an understandably bitter opponent of every actual or would-be Muslim terrorist in the world, but there was nothing of the kind. Naturally, he was still greatly grieved that the younger Donald Havlish had died in the attack, and that would never cease. But he visibly nurtured absolutely no animosity toward the men who had carried out the devastating plot, and he said there was nothing to do but to go on with life—as terrible as that day had been for him, the other members of his family, and for the countless thousands of people scattered all over the Northeast, the rest of the USA, and the entire world.

It was clear to me that the death of his son in a vicious and senseless strike of terrorism did not shake the faith which Don Havlish had maintained throughout his entire life. It must have shaken other things for him although he did not even hint at that. But it certainly was no threat to what Don believed about God, grace, or goodness.

Don Havlish was not a man who would painfully linger over terrible events that he could not change. What was done was done, and it was in his nature to press on from there, challenging as that might be. Even in the midst of the most memorable attack on United States soil since Pearl Harbor, Don refused to dwell on it. His cheerful and optimistic demeanor sustained him. Obviously it was not that he acted as though nothing had happened, because something horrendous had without question occurred. But he was not going to allow it virtually to end his life before it ended naturally. He lived for thirteen contented and productive years after 9/11. He was like the Scottish poet, William Ernest Henley, in *Invictus*: "My head is bloody, but unbowed."

Shortly before Don died, he and his surviving children decided it was time for him to move to the assisted living facility in the retirement home. This meant going from a beautiful, spacious single-family home to a single, small room. I visited him a couple of days after the move. I was concerned about how he would make the transition. I need not have been. As always, there he was with the big smile and the hearty hello, and it was as though he had been there for ten years living in the absolute lap of luxury.

Don Havlish was a man whose strong inner spirit could not be dented, let along broken. He always rolled with whatever punches were thrown at him, never acting as though nothing bad ever happened to him but also never acting as though slings and arrows could possibly ruin his cheerful and confident existence.

Sometimes, when I visited Don, he asked for a prayer, and sometimes, he did not. I offered whatever he requested. But we never talked at any length about what his deepest beliefs were.

I concluded that what he believed was illustrated by how he lived: with confidence, with conviction, and with assurance. If he were asked to give a religious testimony at a Men of the Church meeting or in a session meeting or before the entire congregation, my guess is that instantaneous heart palpitations might have sped him toward an early demise. But the man demonstrated who he was by what he did, and what he did was to live with the inner assurance of a person who trusted that God was with him whatever challenges or obstacles might cross his path. Because he believed that was so, he overcame every challenge and obstacle. Like the old codger Paul, who was a lot younger than Don Havlish when he said it, Don also could triumphantly declare, "I have fought the good fight, I have finished the race, I have kept the faith" (2 Tim. 4:7). And I'm sure that Don died with a smile on his face. I never knew Don Havlish not to smile.

St. LucieStrayer

Lucie Strayer was invited to attend The Chapel Without Walls early in our existence as a congregation, and she continued with a fair degree of regularity until her death a couple of years later. Lucie had been born in Holland, and she lived there throughout World War II.

As I did with anyone who started to come to The Chapel regularly, I went to visit Lucie. She was a little bit of a lady, scarcely five foot tall, as I remember. She was in her early nineties when she first attended, and she died within two years of becoming active.

There were several things about Lucie which immediately struck me as being unusual. She was born into an upper-class family in Rotterdam. Through the decades, I have known a few parishioners from Holland, but not many. The Dutch tend to join either the Reformed Church in America or the Christian Reformed Church, both of which are of Dutch origin. So Lucy was unusual in my experience simply because she was Dutch.

The factor which most astonished me about Lucie when we began our first in-depth conversation is that she had never attended church in her life before being invited to come to The Chapel Without Walls. She said she had attended weddings in churches, but never even a funeral until her third husband died. Further, she said that in more than ninety years, she had never actually attended a church service. Ever. That bowled me over. Why would a nonagenarian woman agree to go to church who had never done so in her previous ninety years? Was it necessary for the time to be "just right" for her? Apparently so.

But there is more to it than that. Lucie came to church for the first time *because she was invited.* Lyle Schaller was a widely-known church consultant who came to the First Presbyterian Church of Hilton Head Island in the mid-1980s to advise us on what steps we might take which would best prepare us for growth in a resort community. Although I remember very little specifically of what he told us, I distinctly remember him saying that the number one reason most people start going to any church anywhere for the first time is because someone invited them. Surely for Mainline Protestants, invitation evangelism is the primary factor for expanding the membership of any given church. Asking Mainline types if they are saved or if they have accepted Jesus Christ as their Lord and Savior and therefore they are probably worthy to affiliate with a particular evangelical congregation is also probably off-putting to a very high degree. But sometimes, if people who are not church-goers are invited, cold turkey, to go to church with friends, they will warily if not exactly eagerly comply. So it was with Lucie Strayer. A Chapel regular asked her to come with her to church, and lo, and surprisingly furthermore behold, she came.

Nevertheless, I was still amazed that someone who had avoided The Church, any church, for over ninety years seemed not only happy but committed to attend church with regularity after she first entered into our small conglomerate of somewhat unconventional believers. Lucie told me she had been virtually an atheist her whole life. Having lived as long as she had, she had more than sufficient rationale for continuing to be a determined unbeliever.

This is not to say that Lucie became a committed ordinary Christian once she began to go to church. I don't know whether she would consider herself a Christian at all although from my perspective, she seemed to subscribe at least minimally to some basic Christian understandings of God, Jesus Christ, and a life consciously lived in service to God and His kingdom. She didn't live long enough to develop whatever convictions she had into a well-founded Christian framework.

Nevertheless, for that two-year stretch, she came to church frequently. She liked the people, and the people liked her. She participated in discussions, and enjoyed sharing her experiences, or perhaps I should say some of them.

Lucie had had, by her own admission, an usually colorful life. When she was quite young, she agreed to enter into an arranged marriage with a wealthy widowed physician who was much older than she. He had grown children. When she found out he was a collaborator with the Nazis, in horror and disgust she left him.

Perhaps because of the revulsion she felt for his political leanings, she joined the Dutch Underground. She did not tell me many stories from those days, but I gathered she was involved in some very exciting, and also dangerous, operations. One did not need to speak with Lucie very long without concluding that she had been a very live wire as a young woman. Even as an old woman, she was still a live wire.

After the war, she went to Indonesia to live with her brother, whom she idolized. He was an officer in the Dutch Army. While in Indonesia, she became involved with another Dutch military officer. It was never clear to me whether she was officially divorced from her husband, the doctor, if she simply abandoned him, or if she actually exchanged marriage vows with the Dutch Army man. Lucie had a way of communicating certain things with crystal clarity while other things seemed intentionally allowed to wallow in the murky flats where unimpeachable reality is impossible to discern. She was a mysterious lady who loved being mysterious.

She left Indonesia to work for the Holland-America cruise-ship company. There, she met and married another Holland-America employee. When they retired from Holland-America, he bought a liquor store somewhere in New England. They had no children, nor did Lucie have any other children from any of her other marriages or long-or-short-term relationships. I don't know if she couldn't have children or she didn't want to have any, but I do know she said she had none of her own. However, she did have various step-children along the circuitous, colorful path of her long and inevitably unpredictable life.

It was through a step-son that ultimately Lucie moved to Hilton Head Island. After her Holland-America husband died, she fairly quickly married another man. Lucie was not shy about declaring that she felt she always needed what she called "a *mon*." Further, she admitted she did not want a man to have to take care of; rather she wanted a man who would have to take care of her. When her third (or was it her fourth—or fifth?) husband died, she resolved to move to Hilton Head Island, where his son lived. She did this, she boldly asserted, in the hopes that her step-son and his wife would take care of her in her rapidly advancing age. Lucie was not ashamed to state that Lucie watched out for Lucie, even if she did not express it in quite those terms. In the meantime, she established a relationship with another man, whom she met in a retirement home, but they did not marry. It may be that she invited him out of her life; that was one of those factors about which I could not derive any clarity.

I can easily imagine that Lucie would have been a handful to live with. She was so lively and feisty and independent that being married to her would be a challenge for any man. Despite that, she was drawn to men, and men apparently also were drawn to her. And thus was her life cloaked in males and mystery and mystique.

It probably seems odd to you that I would include Lucie Strayer in a book about memorable parishioners, relatives, and friends called *The Communion of Saints*. She was a lady who clearly had a past, and likely, she was not proud of everything in her past. It is just that it is so singularly extraordinary that a woman in her early nineties who had never once attended church started attending at that lengthy age and did so with admirable frequency, especially considering her age, until she died at ninety-six.

"Ah," you might say, "she was merely cramming for her finals!" Perhaps. But I seriously doubt it. Lucie had too much personal integrity of a particular kind and she was too true to herself for her to suppose she could pull the wool over the eyes of the Almighty in the last two years of her life.

I have a minister friend who is of Dutch extraction. He always loved to tell us that he was *zuiver Hollands*. It is, I assume, a colloquialism which means "pure Dutch" or "totally Dutch." It was no "conversion experience" which coerced this little old Dutch lady into the House of the Lord, whether that would be perceived as Congregation Beth Yam or The Chapel Without Walls. From what I know of the Dutch, they are not emotionally swept into anything unfamiliar, including religion. Initially, Lucie came to church because she was invited, but she stayed because, even at a very advanced age, she somehow concluded there might possibly be something to religion after all. No one forced her to stay, least of all she herself. She *enjoyed* church; going to church brought her a *joy* she may not previously have known.

Does that mean she acquired a strong foundation of faith? Only God knows the answer to that, but I, as an experienced observer (I hope), would doubt it. She didn't have sufficient time. Having devoted virtually no thought to spiritual matters in her first ninety-four years, she did not have enough years left to build the necessary groundwork for a reasoned and reasonable working Christian faith. Besides, who in her nineties would ever conceive of trying to do such a thing?

A few months before she died, she started to decline physically rather quickly. She still came to church when she could, but she did not always feel up to the effort. For whatever it is worth, when I went to visit her in her home as she was dying, sometimes she asked me to pray for her before I left: and other times, she indicated she did not want a prayer. I never sensed she believed my prayers would guarantee her eternal salvation, whatever "eternal" and "salvation" may actually mean. But she did sometimes seem to find comfort in having a prayer verbalized on her behalf.

Was Lucie a saint? In my book she was. But would God consider her a saint? God alone can determine the certifiable sainthood of any individual at any point in human history, but in the very loosely-organized institution of The Chapel Without Walls, Lucie walked in during her last two years on earth. And she participated with everyone else in the loosely-instituted congregation of The Chapel Without Walls. For many Christians, especially evangelical ones, Lucie Strayer would not pass the test of sanctity for several reasons. I am not included among that group of Christians.

Furthermore, I remember a man on a cross saying to another man on a cross, "Today you will be with me in Paradise." If that was good enough for him, it's good enough for me too.

St. Tom Miller

Tom Miller was technically Thomas W. Miller Jr., but no one called him Thomas. He was "Tom" to everyone he knew, and he made it his business to know hundreds and hundreds of people for over nine decades. He died at age ninety-five, a widely loved and admired grinning jokester and raconteur. He was no relation to me, but I would have been very proud to have had him as a father or older brother.

Tom was raised in the small town of Hillsboro, Texas. He always went back to Texas whenever his high school class had a reunion. Through the years, they had many get-togethers. Surprisingly, he never graduated with his class, as you shall subsequently learn. One of the greatest disappointments of his life is that he was too sick to attend the last reunion of his class after it had been planned. It proved to be the last reunion they ever had. I guess they figured if Tom Miller couldn't make it, they might as well agree that the party would forever be over.

Tom was an only-child. His father owned a small, two-floor town department store. It was, Tom liked to recall, a thriving business, and Tom was a child of privilege. He and his parents were members of the Presbyterian church in Hillsboro.

There were four major disruptions which affected Tom as a boy, any of which would have been sufficient to place him on a psychoanalyst's couch. The first was the institutionalization of his mother when he was a very young teenager. She had suffered a mental collapse, and when it became evident she could no longer be a productive member of the family, she went to live in a mental hospital for the rest of her life. That left Tom and his father to fend for themselves as best they could. Needless to say, it could not have been easy.

Then, when Tom was starting his junior year of high school, he was suspected of having tuberculosis. He was sent by bus to Sanitorium, Texas, for six months or so. (Only in Texas would there be a place-name like that.) It was always believed he had had TB, but subsequent medical tests indicated he might not have. In either event, as in many such things, Tom chose not to dwell on it. He was not a dweller-on-bad-stuff.

That experience for most teenagers would have been utterly spirit-crushing. But with his sunny disposition and talkative nature, Tom knew all the patients and staff within a week of his arrival, and he became a friend to all of them, carrying on lengthy conversations with everyone. His indefatigable optimism couldn't be dented by a little half-year teenage stint in a tuberculosis hospital. When it was decided he was well enough, the staff was happy to send him home. But Tom himself did not feel unmitigated happiness. He told me he missed his inter-generational chums at the sanitarium although he very much looked forward to seeing his classmates once again at Hillsboro High School.

The Great Depression had enveloped the nation by that time. Eventually, it wrapped its tentacles around his father's retail business, and the store and his father went bankrupt. Early in his senior year of high school, Tom's father took him to Dallas, where his father got a menial job, and he put Tom in a boarding house until Tom graduated from a Dallas high school.

Tom's uncle, his mother's brother, had been the president and owner of a bank in Hillsboro. The uncle withdrew funds from the bank which Tom's father had set aside for Tom's college education. Therefore, Tom had to go to work as soon as he finished high school. As it turned out, circumstances prevented him from ever attending college. A short time later, his uncle committed suicide.

Tom found a job as an office boy in what was then known as United Press but eventually became UPI, United Press International. Within six months, Tom was a cub reporter, then a news manager; and eventually, he worked his way up through the ranks as a respected newsman in one of the two major international wire services. He remained with UPI for twenty years. Following that, he was recruited to work for the National Labor Relations Board, serving for many years as their information officer to the press.

In the meantime, he served in the Army Air Corps in World II as a navigation instructor, having graduated first in his navigation class of almost two hundred officers. Tom liked to remind people that he was injured in the war when he broke his little finger playing volleyball. He was called back to active duty during the Korean War, afterward serving in the Air Force Reserves for over twenty years, and retiring as a lieutenant colonel.

Tom was married in 1942. They had one daughter. It slowly became evident that his wife suffered from bi-polar illness. Her swings into depression became more serious and uncontrollable. In 1969, when their daughter was sixteen, Tom's wife committed suicide. It harkened back to a similar situation in Tom's own teenage years when his father and he were suddenly left to themselves. Now here, Tom Miller and his teenage daughter were also on their own.

Life for many people is sadly learned largely in the School of Hard Knocks. Tom Miller received a PhD from that universal and ubiquitous institution, although he was unable to pursue even a bachelor's degree from any other institution of higher, if not also harder, learning. Nevertheless, he never lost one iota of his outstanding optimism, his sense of humor, or his unquenchable zest for life. To his dying day, he remained always positive and upbeat.

One of the primary reasons that he continued to maintain his optimistic outlook is that three years after his first wife died, Tom married his second wife, Vivian Asplund. They met at the NLRB, where Vivian was an appellate court attorney.

For the final forty-one years of his earthly existence, Tom was blessed by Vivian's intelligence, supportive nature, and no-nonsense attitude. Vivian often refers to herself as "a gloomy Swede," but she brought only happiness and contentment into their marriage without a single glitch of gloom. If there were an organization called The American Atheist Association, and they had cards for their members, Vivian Miller would be a card-carrying member of the AAA. Nevertheless for their forty-one-year marriage, she accompanied him infrequently to his Presbyterian church in Alexandria, Virginia, regularly to the First Presbyterian Church of Hilton Head Island, South Carolina, and then later, weekly to The Chapel Without Walls of Hilton Head Island. In fact, Vivian was such a valued participant in The Chapel that she was elected to the board of trustees. The Chapel assiduously avoids walling anyone outside its small but dedicated community. Everyone, including atheists, is welcome.

In the late `80s the Millers moved to Hilton Head Island, where Tom could pursue one of his life's most passionate avocations: golf. He played the grand auld game during nine separate decades of his life, becoming very good although not to his own satisfaction sufficiently expert. Both he and Vivian clearly remembered that on their honeymoon at the Greenbrier Resort in West Virginia, he sank a thirty-foot putt on the eighteenth hole to break eighty. Vivian never had an interest in sports, but she supported Tom's fanatical devotion through their entire marriage. He was fiercely loyal to many college and professional teams in many sports.

Probably, Tom Miller's greatest gift to the human race, other than his relentlessly optimistic spirit, was his unique love for children, especially young children. At First Presbyterian Church, he became involved in a tutoring program sponsored by the church for middle school students. For a couple of years, he participated in that, but he decided he was better suited to teaching kindergartners how to read.

There were two lengthy feature articles in the Hilton Head local newspaper, one about Tom the golfer, and the other about Tom the tutor. The second one, called *Groovy grandpa*, quoted him as saying, "I volunteered for younger children because I don't think I'll every grow up." Without a hint of either irony or satire, Vivian Miller said of her husband that he was so good with children because he was one himself. When he was in his eighties, he would get down on the floor with his youthful charges, helping them to decipher the mysterious squiggles on a page which, he managed to convinced them, were actually words.

After Tom died, Vivian told me that one time, they were having lunch in a very fine restaurant. A young mother was there with her baby in a high chair. The baby was fussing, as every baby worth her salt is wont to do from time to time, and the poor mother was unable to eat her lunch. Having finished their meal, Tom went over to the woman and told her, in his friendly, earnest way, that he was a qualified grand-father and that he would be happy to try to quiet her child while she finished her lunch. She looked at him either like he should be someone whose picture should be hanging in the post office or else he was who he claimed to be, and she gratefully turned over her daughter to this strange man. Holding her, cooing to her, and strolling bouncily around the restaurant, Tom managed to quiet the child long enough to allow her mother to eat her theretofore un-munched lunch—at the end of which he handed the baby back to her mom. And all four of them went their separate ways. Unquestionably, Tom Miller had a way with little kids.

Tom was a very intelligent man, but he was also a very uncomplicated personality. He was not particularly inquisitive. I cannot recall him ever asking a single religious or theological question, even though in his last two years I visited him each week in an assisted living facility, and we had many long conversations. He may have made such inquiries, and I just don't recall them. But I think it was not part of his personal makeup to ask such questions. Nevertheless, he was a lifelong committed churchman, an elder, a head usher, and a very generous steward. For the first few years, he was our first usher and greeter at The Chapel Without Walls, until he could no longer stand by himself without support. Tom never met a stranger, and all strangers who showed up at The Chapel were strangers only for mere seconds.

For the first fifty years of his life, Tom Miller had some major setbacks, bordering on the tragic: his mother's mental illness and institutionalization, his diagnosis of tuberculosis and his many months in a sanitarium, the loss of his father's business and income, being uprooted in his senior year of high school to be placed in a boarding house in Dallas and to graduate with students he did not have enough time to know well, the theft of his college fund by his own uncle, and the loss of his first wife when, due to unresolved depression, she took her own life. How could anyone remain completely optimistic about human existence, given that mélange of misanthropic misfortune?

I am moved to assert that being a Presbyterian or at least a Presbyterian-type is not what made Tom Miller a lifelong optimist. That had nothing to do with it. Being a Christian, whether Presbyterian or otherwise, was not a factor either. Tom was a happy optimist because it was etched into the very deepest recesses of his DNA. After all, there are many Presbyterians, especially Calvinists, who are committed pessimists. In truth, Calvinism and optimism are such strange bedfellows that they scarcely, if ever, are located within miles of one another.

Just as Christianity cannot guarantee anyone a carefree life, so also it cannot render an inevitable joyful disposition. Genetics determines much of who each of us turns out to be. And in the case of Tom Miller, genetics dealt him an extraordinary hand, despite the mental problems in his mother and his first wife. He sailed through their complete collapses seemingly unscathed. However, in the face of those tragedies, Tom never feigned happiness; he was simply, always, and only happy.

Tom was a lovely man. He was a loving son, husband, father, and grandfather, a friend to everyone he knew, especially to very little people, and he and Vivian were extraordinarily generous to Lois and me at two or three particularly difficult times in our lives. I know very little of what Tom Miller actually believed, but I know a great deal about how he lived. And how he lived was exemplary in every respect. Of his particular kind there are, sadly, very few. What a unique saint of God he was!

CONCLUSION

IN PRAISE OF MAINLINE PROTESTANTS AND THEIR TAPESTRIES

NOBODY KNOWS WHO wrote the Letter to the Hebrews in the New Testament. Up until a century ago or so, it was widely assumed that the apostle Paul had written it; but now, biblical scholars almost universally dismiss that idea. Whoever wrote it, the main point of the epistle was apparently to try to convince first-century Jewish Christians that by his death and resurrection, Jesus had become the great high priest who himself was the sacrifice that made possible the salvation of those who believed in Jesus as the promised Messiah of God. In other words, the author claimed that Jewish history was leading inexorably to Jesus Christ. Subsequent history shows that most Jews did not believe that, and they rejected Jesus as the Messiah and as the destination to whom their faith was leading them.

The eleventh chapter of Hebrews begins with a famous verse, which is worth repeating as the beginning of this summary concerning sixty-eight saints I have known who have died and about whom I have written herein plus many other saints still living whom I have briefly mentioned in previous pages. The anonymous writer of the Letter to the Hebrews writes, "Now faith is the assurance of things hoped for, the conviction of things not seen" (11:1). That is a profound, thoughtful, and thought-provoking statement. Whatever else it may be, faith by its very nature must include the assurance of things hoped for and the conviction of things not seen. If we could see and touch and audibly hear that, or more precisely *Him* in whom we have faith, it would no longer be faith, but factual or intellectual or even scientific certainty. But faith is not like that, nor can it be. Faith is *faith*; it is not *fact*.

269

After his opening description of the nature of faith, the writer of Hebrews gives several examples of biblical people of faith. Among them are, in his order, Abel, Enoch, Noah, Abraham, Sarah, Isaac, Jacob, Joseph, Moses, and Rahab. (Some of those folks will no doubt be more familiar to you than others.)

Then, realizing that his readers might like to hear about more heroes and heroines of faith, the writer says, "And what more can I say? For time would fail me to tell of Gideon, Barak, Samson, Jephthah, of David and Samuel and the prophets—who through faith conquered kingdoms, enforced justice, stopped the mouths of lions, quenched raging fire, escaped the edge of the sword, won strength out of weakness, became mighty in war, put foreign armies to flight. Women received their dead by resurrection. Some were tortured, some refused to accept release, that they might rise again to a better life. Others suffered mocking and scourging, and even chains and imprisonment. They were stoned, they were sawn in two, they were killed by the sword" (Hebrews 11:32–37).

That is a genuine litany of lamentation and woe. And it's historically, or at least biblically, accurate, even if there is some literary license in the gruesome way it is described. The Hebrew Bible does include accounts of faithful Israelites who suffered all those types of tragedies and hardships.

I trust it is evident to you, the reader of this short tome, that none of the people of faith about whom I have written experienced any of these horrendous tests of faith. Such illustrations of immense adversity did not occur in the lives of any of these twentieth-century saints.

If we are honest with ourselves, we would have to admit that it is far easier to be a biblical believer now than it was during the historical period covered by the Bible, namely, from about the eighteenth century BCE to the early years of the second century CE. In those days, as in the early days of Christianity, many people did die for their faith. But when we come to the twentieth and twenty-first centuries CE, at least in the USA and in most other western nations, being a Christian or a Jew has not been so counter-cultural as to risk being mocked, scourged, sawn in two, or killed by the sword. In

Saudi Arabia, Somalia, Syria, or Iran that might happen to Christians on very rare occasions, but not in America or Canada or Switzerland or Singapore or Paraguay or Peru.

Further, if the truth is told, for most Americans in the twentieth and twenty-first centuries, the majority of our citizens would consider the USA to be a "Christian culture," even if they might not use that particular term to describe our society. The majority of Americans are Christians, and the majority of the majority up until recently were what are called by themselves and by others "Mainline Protestants."

Mainline Protestants are the kinds of church members who belong to the historic denominations which evolved out of the Protestant Reformation and the century or two which followed it: the Lutherans, the Episcopalians, the Presbyterians, the various Reformed Churches, the Congregationalists (now primarily the United Church of Christ), the Baptists (including, by historical extension, the Southern Baptists), and the Methodists. You may want to include other denominations, and that's okay—provided they were formed prior to the middle of the eighteenth century. But any denominations or churches that came into being after about 1750 cannot, by definition, be called Mainline Protestants. That's my definition anyhow, and I'm sticking with it.

All the individuals whose lives I have briefly chronicled were what I would classify as Mainline Protestants, and most of those were actually Presbyterians. Further, all these people were what I call "Mainline Protestant types."

It seems to me that certain personality types gravitate to certain types of denominations or churches. Very generally speaking, those who feel most comfortable in a rules-oriented atmosphere prefer fundamentalist or evangelical Protestantism or Roman Catholicism. Those who feel most comfortable in a more open or open-minded atmosphere may prefer Mainline Protestantism. To describe it in different terms, those who like a more authoritarian religion will likely be happier in Roman Catholicism or fundamentalist or evangelical Protestantism, whereas those who like a more democratic or collegial kind of religion may prefer Mainline Protestantism.

Having said that, it is important to note than Mainline Protestantism is a shrinking part of American Christian demography, and that it now represents well less than half of the American Christian population. When the American Revolution established the USA in the late eighteenth century, probably almost all of the Christian population would have been Mainline Protestants. Thus, the percentage of Lutherans, Presbyterians, Episcopalians, and so on is declining, the percentage of Roman Catholics is probably maintaining itself, and the percentage of evangelically oriented Christians is increasing. But by far, the fastest-growing segment of the American population are those who are described by sociologists and religious pollsters as Nones, those who claim no religious affiliation at all.

If particular kinds of *personality types* gravitate toward certain types of Protestant denominations, the same is true for particular kinds of *people*. Upper-class people tend to be Episcopalians. Upper-middle and middle-middle-class people tend to be Presbyterians, Lutherans, Methodists, and Southern Baptists. Lower-middle-class and lower class people tend to be Pentecostals, independent Baptists, Nazarenes, Seventh-day Adventists, Jehovah's Witnesses, or other kinds of Evangelicals. However, these are generalizations which are not at all clear cut and have many exceptions. You may strongly wish to take exception to my generalizations, and that is quite acceptable.

I am attempting to suggest that the brief portraits I have tried to paint here are exhibits of a large group of people and personality types and that there is a similarity among these folks which would not be evident, say, among most Roman Catholics or Assembly of God members or Church of God members or fundamentalist Baptists or those who have been derisively called Holy Rollers. Mainline Protestants have not been programmed to state what they believe, except when going through a confirmation or catechism or communicants class as teenagers. After that, most of them either deliberately suppress what they were taught or gradually allow it to seep into near oblivion. They come to believe what they choose to believe, and they resist having anyone, especially the clergy, dogmatically telling them what they must believe.

What are Mainline Protestant types, exactly? Let's begin by repeating what they are not. They aren't Roman Catholics, Eastern Orthodox, or "evangelicals." You know what Catholic and Orthodox Christians are, but what, in more detail, are "Evangelical" Christians— or if you prefer, "evangelicals"? Evangelicals are Christians who are more likely to be biblical literalists, but by no means is that true of all evangelicals. They are more rules-oriented than are Mainline Protestants. They tend to put their theological emphasis on Jesus Christ more than on God although some of them, the Pentecostals, may put more emphasis on the Holy Spirit than on either God the Father or God the Son. Most Evangelicals believe that only Christians, and perhaps only evangelical Christians, can be saved and thus will end up in heaven. To be sure, some Mainline Protestants are close to being biblical literalists, and they too put most of their emphasis on Jesus rather than God. And some of them also believe that only Christians can be saved.

However—and here is where I think the primary difference may be best understood—Mainline Protestants have an ecclesiastical culture which is different from the ecclesiastical culture of Evangelical Protestants or Roman Catholics or Eastern Orthodox. To use words which may or may not explain its culture very well, Mainline Protestantism is broader, deeper, perhaps culturally more refined and more tolerant, less judgmental, and more committed to ideas than to particular doctrines than are Evangelicals or other Christians. Mainline Protestants may also seem too tolerant and easygoing and diffuse for the others and perhaps also for themselves.

I realize all this may seem very nebulous or confusing or inchoate to you. And for that, I apologize. But I feel like Supreme Court Justice Potter Stewart who famously said of pornography that he couldn't define it, but he recognized it when he saw it. Well, I can't very accurately or completely define Mainline Protestants or Evangelical Protestants, but I recognize them when I see them or better, hear them. Mainline and Evangelical American Protestants use the same language, but they do not use it in the same way. They speak quite differently when referring to the same things.

Mainline Protestant types generally are quite serious about the contents of their faith and their religion, but they don't usually talk about it a lot, especially to strangers or people they don't know well. Because that is culturally true, many Evangelicals would accuse Mainliners of being wishy-washy. Many Mainliners would feel hard pressed to declare their faith in public or even in private to anyone. But many others simply feel very uncomfortable about sharing what they believe with others, even people with whom they are very well acquainted. They have deep-seated convictions, but they prefer to keep them deep-seated within themselves. That may seem peculiar, but in general, I think it is an accurate description of reality. Mainliners are much more private about their faith, while Roman Catholics and Evangelicals are more public about their faith.

However, there is another reason why Mainline Protestants are so closed-mouthed about their beliefs. In the culture in which they live, it is considered bad form to talk about faith. From their early childhood, Mainline Protestants—most of whom are middle class—are told there are two topics one must never address in public: politics and religion. And if they are pressed to talk about one or the other, most Mainliners would choose politics, not because they necessarily know more about that subject, but because they may feel more insecure or private about the other subject.

Mainline Protestant Christians, like Christians of every other variety, are acculturated into a particular understanding of Christianity. As much as we might like it otherwise, this acculturation is both inevitable and unavoidable. Over the course of a lifetime, many Mainliners, but by no means all of them, make their peace with acculturated Mainline Protestantism. Most of those who cannot abide the Mainline worldview eventually abandon it. The same is true for Evangelical, Catholic, and Orthodox Christians; if they strongly reject their acculturated form of Christianity, they leave it. All four types of Christians tend to bail out with roughly the same percentages, although Mainline Protestants and Roman Catholics are perhaps more likely to drop out altogether than are Evangelicals or Orthodox.

Of the sixty-eight saints whose stories I briefly recounted, inevitably some were more active in their church membership than were others. There were several hundreds of others I knew quite well about whom I might also have written, but I selected each of these people for particular reasons of my own. Many other people were more devoted to their church membership or were more involved in church life than some of the Saintly Sixty-Eight. However, I selected these particular people because I believe they represent a very broad spectrum of Mainline Protestants, who themselves represent perhaps the broadest spectrum of any denominational family within Christendom.

As I reviewed each chapter that I have written, it struck me that the very choices I made to describe these particular people may say as much or more about me than it does about them. Some of these people were far more dissimilar than similar to me, but most of them were more like me than unlike me—or so it seems to me. And I must leave it to you, the reader, to determine for yourself what that may mean.

You may have concluded some of these saints were not very saintly. In the common understanding of that word, some of them probably were not especially saintly at all. Nevertheless, to repeat something I said in the opening chapter, I am convinced that the first characteristic of a saint in the biblical sense is that a saint is a person who believes in God, and in the case of Christian saints, they also believe in Jesus Christ. In the case of all saints of every stripe, they believe it is important to see themselves as part of the people of God, whether that is called Israel or the Church or just the human race.

I believe there are three factors which determine genuine biblical sanctity. First, *the saints of God must have faith in God.* It need not be a very narrowly defined type of faith and, in fact, is usually *not* narrowly defined. Second, *saints ordinarily must have a commitment to God via the people of God in worship.* Circumstances may prevent certain saints from worshipping regularly, including alterations in the nature of personal faith over time. But to me, worship attendance is important in determining sainthood. Thirdly, *saints must contribute to the mission of the people of God* via their "time, talent, and treasure," in the age-old hackneyed expression. In other words, in my understanding, sanctity requires stewardship.

By those qualifications, I assume that every person I wrote about was a genuine saint. They all affiliated themselves with a Christian congregation, which to me implies that they possessed faith of some sort. It may not have been sufficiently well-informed for some observers or strong enough or clear enough, but for me, and I think for them, it was faith. And it sufficed for them and for me. They worshipped regularly, at least for long periods of time, and most of them for most of their lives. And they contributed their time and their financial resources to the churches of which they were members.

However, it is not primarily behavior which determines sainthood; it is faith. Initially, it isn't deeds; it is convictions in the face of temptations to believe otherwise. Only God can rightfully judge the acceptability of anybody's faith, but I trust He is more tolerant of our faith foibles than we are concerning the depth of one another's faith.

On the other hand, it is important to state that sainthood—or "sanctity" to use a synonym of necessity—must include good behavior. The root meaning of "saint" is "holy," and anyone whose behavior is generally unholy cannot be a saint. None of the Christians about whom I wrote was perfect because no one is or can be perfect, but they all essentially exhibited commendable behavior most of the time. Some people could never legitimately be called saints—people such as Rasputin, Hitler, Stalin, Mao, or Jim Jones. I am convinced that most genuine believers are saints, but perhaps not all of them. Ultimately, of course, it is God, not us, who determines who of His children are saints.

It is anthropologically certain that saints technically should either be classified as "saint-sinners" or as "sinner-saints." Every saint is also a sinner, but it does not automatically follow that every sinner is also a saint. All saints are sinners, but not all sinners are saints. Some sinners are anything but saints, and without a change of both convictions and behavioral conventions, some people shall likely never qualify as saints. For my purposes in writing this book, however, I stand by my own conclusion that everyone contained herein was a saint of God, and their sanctity had a ripple effect to everyone around them.

I did not have lengthy conversations for many hours at a time over many weeks or months with any of the folks in this sanctified litany regarding the essence of Christian faith. For fifty years, almost every week I inflicted my beliefs, convictions, and opinions upon parishioners from the pulpit; but only in classes, discussion groups, and hospital rooms have others had the opportunity to tell me in detail what they believed and to dispute what I may said. Why are Mainliners so diffident? It is simply because most Mainline Protestants don't openly or frequently debate matters of faith. They just don't. They do not express their deepest beliefs in a public setting, and probably not often in a private one either. Maybe they should do that, but they don't.

Now, of course, it is possible these particular parishioners and countless others like them did not give testimony to their faith because I did not insist on it or encourage them to do so. I must plead guilty to that accusation, should anyone choose to accuse me. But who am I to *demand* that anyone give testimony to what she or he believes? Furthermore, for better or worse, religion for most Mainline Protestants is a very private matter, and they very strongly want to keep it that way. Again, that is fundamentally a cultural phenomenon, not a religious one. It is not that Mainliners do not have faith values; rather it is that usually they choose to keep those values to themselves. Whether they realize it or not, they *live* what they believe every day, but they may not ever *declare* what they believe. They are convinced that their faith is between them and God. That may be inimical to evangelical Christianity and to Mainline Protestant evangelism, but it is where many Mainline Protestants live their lives nonetheless.

There are two other factors I feel compelled to address as I come to my conclusion. The first is that in reading over everything I have written to edit it, I feel like I have inserted myself too much as a part of these saints' stories. I can easily understand how someone else might also conclude that. There are probably too many "I's" and not enough "he's" or she's. In retrospect, it almost seems like this is an indirect and circuitous pastoral autobiography rather than a series of short biographical snapshots of several dozen parishioners and others.

As I draw to the end of this scribal exercise, I have pondered that impression long and hard. Ultimately, I decided there may have been no other way to tell these short stories. I knew most of these people as either their pastor or their pastoral colleague, and they were the ones I chose to write about. But if I had not had that particular relationship with them, I could not have known the particular circumstances in which we became acquainted with one another. Therefore, I have deduced that there may have no other way to present this pastoral pot-pourri of saints without presuming it to be a work of fiction, which it is not.

And that brings up the second factor I feel compelled to explain. Previously, I said that there is very little dialogue in any of these sainted glimpses. I could have created dialogues I might have had with these people, but that is what such conversations would be: literary creations. My memory, never good, seems to evaporate by the thimbleful every day of my aging process. While I did not spend scores of hours interacting with these saints, I did speak to all of them at some length on several occasions apiece. But I just don't remember much of what was said by either them or me.

If Lois had been a pastor (which she seriously considered at one point in her life), she would remember conversations she might have had with every one of these folks or others like them. She has a memory like a steel trap; alas, I have a memory like a steel sieve, or in a more appropriate analogy, like a colander with huge holes in it to disperse all the liquid that the colander is intended to eliminate.

Before I began to write these brief biographies, I consciously decided it would not be honest for me to construct conversations which may not actually have taken place, but whose general essence would be an accurate portrayal of these people. In the rare occasions where I did include dialogue, it reflected specific things which were said, even if they may not have been verbatim reports of what was said.

Perhaps it is not only unnecessary but unwise to bring up these issues I have with myself, and why I wrote as I did. Nonetheless, in my peculiarities and quirks, I wanted to get these journalistic ethical concerns off my chest. I have done it at the end rather than the beginning, and that in itself may be another such peculiarity; I leave that for you to decide.

Had I been born when I was born in a rural village in India or in a city in Saudi Arabia or on a kibbutz in Palestine or in Soviet Moscow, almost certainly I would never have become a Christian. Instead, I was born to Christian parents in the United States of America in 1939, and thus, from my infancy onward, I was raised in a Christian household.

But more than being simply a "Christian" home, it was a Mainline Protestant home. Thus, our family could be distinguished from other Christian families of other types of Christians: Roman Catholics; Pentecostals; Independent Baptists; Russian, Greek, or Serbian Orthodox; Seventh Day Adventists; Jehovah's Witnesses; or Mormons. Once again, to borrow from and slightly to alter the words of the apostle Paul, we spoke like Mainline Protestants, we thought like Mainline Protestants, we reasoned like Mainline Protestants. However, unlike Paul, when we all grew up, we did not give up Mainline Protestant ways—none of us. Well, one brother did fall off the wagon, more or less; but the rest of us, including our parents, stuck with our Mainline Protestantism to the end of our days. (This statement assumes I will remain a Mainliner to the end, which I firmly do assume. It probably won't be as a Presbyterian, but rather as a Chapel Without Wallsian although that cannot be guaranteed beyond dispute either. But I will be a Mainline Protestant till I die not because I think it is the only proper way to be a Christian, but because it has been a lifelong status—for the first twenty years, by circumstance of birth, and for the last almost sixty-plus years, by choice.)

If I had it to do over again, would I still go into the ministry, knowing everything I know now? I have no doubt that I would. To be absolutely candid, on occasion, being a parson can be a genuine trial, but it also is a privilege of exquisite and surpassing value. A couple of decades ago, I wondered whether I might have preferred politics. The past decade has forever cured me of that fantasy, however. I also have pondered whether the law or working for the United States State Department might have had some appeal. In all these daydreams, I concluded that every vocation, including the pastorate, has its infrequent rough patches. All things considered, though, I would much rather live with the minor aggravations of the ministry and its multitude of visible and invisible blessings than with the considerable advantages of any other vocation, profession, or occupation.

Being a pastor to anyone is a privilege, but to make an admittedly subjective statement, being a pastor to Mainline Protestant types is a special privilege. Mainliners are stereotypical community movers and shakers. They are better educated than average. They tend, with many notable exceptions, to get down to church business when church business is the business which it is required to get down to. They have big ideas because they are big thinkers. Of all the people from all the various Christian "families," Mainliners are the ones more likely to be in charge of business, government, educational, military, or interdenominational religious agencies. It is both an honor and an additional responsibility to be a preacher to the people who either make the decisions or lead the process which results in decisions being made which affect society at large.

It is evident, however, that Mainline Protestants do not have the influence on American life they had half a century ago. Then, a majority of big business and small business CEOs, Members of Congress, U.S. Presidents, heads of universities, two-, three- and four-star military officers, and leaders of major charitable organizations were Mainliners. Mainline Protestants still serve in those capacities far in excess of their actual numbers in our society, but they represent a smaller percentage of overall leaders than they did fifty years ago. Now, people of other Christian groups or non-Christian religious groups or no religion at all have risen to positions of influence throughout America, and that is all to the good. But the Mainliners are still there and will likely be there for the foreseeable future, despite the grim predictions of some ecclesiastical sociologists that they are slowly disappearing into oblivion.

However, as pleasant and fulfilling as it may be to minister to bright, well-educated, and unusually able people in the Mainline Protestant churches, that is not the primary reason why being a pastor to Mainliners is so rewarding. It is because, for the most part, Mainliners are truly good folks. The great majority of them aren't frauds or deceivers or ne'er-do-wells, at least not generally. Oh, some of them have greater-than-average deficiencies than the population at large, but a very sizable percentage are willing, able, and gifted members of the ecumenical Christian community. They pony up; they pitch in. It may take some deft coaxing to get them to do things in the church because they always have many other things to do, but those who are dedicated church members, which is most of them, will rise to the occasion when the occasion needs to be risen to.

Because of my remarkable good fortune in having been associated with the particular congregations I served, there was always an unusually intelligent cadre of people who were leaders in those congregations. It is not necessarily easy to work with very bright people. But it is a joy to do so, for they enhance a parson's life in countless ways. Smart Mainliners have been my happy métier for fifty years. What member of the clergy could be more blessed than that?

Ultimately, however, Mainline Protestants are not the most important people in Christ's Church. It is *all* Christian people, grouped together in their countless varieties and permutations, who comprise the Church's most important people. *Everyone* is crucial to the successful mission of the Church. God refuses to overlook any of His people.

And that's where the saints come in. It is the saints who construct the Church—the theologians, biblical scholars, planners, ecclesiastical organizers, church officers, architects, engineers, general contractors, artists, and musicians. Included are also the stone masons, bricklayers, glazers, janitors, housekeeping staff, ushers, choir members, leaders of organizations, Sunday school teachers, youth leaders, Scoutmasters, A. A. volunteers, and lay people who are hospital and home callers. Further, the Church of Jesus Christ needs a wide variety of Christians to function at peak efficiency: Roman Catholics, Eastern Orthodox, traditional or Mainline Protestants, Evangelicals, Pentecostals, newer denominations which the older denominations consider odd or off-beat, and individual congregations which perceive themselves as being disconnected from any other Christians anywhere but who in fact are connected to all Christians everywhere.

Tapestries

Shakespeare's play, *Cymbeline,* is rarely performed. It was written in the last period of the Bard's life, and apparently, there are textual problems which render the drama suspect to certain scholars. The plot revolves around an ancient king in England, named Cymbeline, who ruled at the time of the Roman occupation of Great Britain.

However, in the fourth act, just after their father has died, Cymbeline's two sons sing a song over the monarch's body. When I was in the Trinity College Choir in Glasgow, William Barclay chose this song as one of the pieces we sang in our concerts. It was a way for Guiderius and Arviragus to try to resolve the ambivalent feelings they had toward their father and to attempt to give themselves closure to the profound uneasiness they experienced because of his death. It was also a way for future minister graduates of Trinity College, almost all of them Scottish, to express the thoughts of one of the greatest artists in immortal words regarding one of the greatest mysteries the clergy must face on a regular basis in their vocation, namely, the sober reality and mystery of death.

> Fear no more the heat o' the sun,
> Nor the furious winter's rages;
> Thou thy worldly task hast done,
> Home art gone, and ta'en thy wages:
> Golden lads and girls all must

As chimney sweepers, come to dust.

Fear no more the frown o' the great;
Thou art past the tyrant's stroke;
Care no more to clothe and eat;
To thee the reed is as the oak:
The scepter, learning, physic, must
All follow this, and come to dust.

Fear no more the lightning-flash,
Nor the all-dreaded thunderstone;
Fear not slander, censure rash;
Thou hast finished joy and moan:
All lovers young, all lovers must
Consign to thee, and come to dust.

No exorciser harm thee!
Nor no witchcraft charm thee!
Ghost unlaid forbear thee!
Nothing ill come near thee!
Quiet consummation have;
And renowned be thy grave!

Shakespeare had a uniquely powerful talent for addressing terribly stark realities in beautifully comforting cadences. The king's sons remind us that all of us shall die, but there shall be something that transcends the grave. The end is not the end; it is, in some unknown and unknowable fashion, a beginning.

No man is an island,
Entire of itself,
Every man is a piece of the continent,
A part of the main.

If a clod be washed away by the sea,
Europe is the less
As if a promontory were.
As well as if a manor of thy friend's
Or of thine own were:
Any man's death diminishes me,
Because I am involved in mankind,
And therefore never send to ask for whom
the bell tolls;
It tolls for thee.

John Donne, who wrote that poem, was an English Anglican priest and poet. He clearly heard and fully appreciated, as few of us do, "the still, sad music of humanity" as another great English poet, William Wordsworth, described it.

Every saint I have briefly described herein has been a piece of the continent of the human race, and they now have disappeared from our sight. The funeral bell has tolled for all of them. But in tolling for them, it has tolled also for us because we all are involved in mankind. As they were lost to us, so also we were lost to them. Or so it would appear at first glance.

But it is only the first glance which creates that false appearance. Though those in the Church Triumphant are no longer seen by us, it does not mean they are no longer seen at all. If the Christian Gospel is correct in one of its central proclamations, they see one another in a new light and a new life, and they are seen by and see God.

Therefore, as John Donne also said,

Death, be not proud, though some have called thee
Mighty and dreadful, for thou art not so:
For those whom thou think'st thou dost overthrow
Die not, poor Death; nor yet canst thou kill me.
From Rest and Sleep, which but thy picture be,
Much pleasure, then from thee much more must flow;
And soonest our best men with thee do go –
Rest of their bones and souls' delivery!
Thou'rt slave to fate, chance, kings, and desperate men,

And dost with poison, war, and sickness dwell;
And poppy or charms can make us sleep as well
And better than thy stroke. Why swell'st thou then?
One short sleep past, we wake eternally,
And Death shall be no more: Death, thou shalt die!

"The Church Militant" refers to the earthly ecclesiastical community. Sadly, our Christian militarism often divides us within the Church, and it certainly divides us from people outside the Church in other religions and from those who have no religion. On this side of death, we tussle and wrestle and resist those with whom we have theological or sociological or cultural differences, vainly supposing our battles serve the interests of the kingdom of God.

In "the Church Triumphant," however, there are no disputes, no controversies, and no ongoing disagreements. Further, I trust it is not really "the Church Triumphant" at all; it is rather "the Eternal Community Triumphant." There shall be no Christians or Jews or Muslims, no Hindus or Buddhists or Zoroastrians, no animists or atheists or agnostics.

Death shall render all our theological and philosophical controversies meaningless. One short sleep past, we wake eternally, and Death shall be no more. As Hamlet plaintively observed, 'tis a consummation devoutly to be wished.

Each of us is a large and complex tapestry. There are countless strands of thread in each of our tapestries. All the people we have ever known have woven themselves into the pattern of who we are. It is ultimately impossible to determine the origin of every thread in our own tapestry because many of these people died long before we lived, yet their lives touched our lives by what they said or did or wrote or who their children were. William Shakespeare is in the tapestry of every English-speaking person born since the seventeenth century and in many non-English speakers as well. So also with Socrates, Aristotle, Plato, St. Augustine, Thomas Aquinas, Luther, Calvin, and others like them. We all have thousands of spiritual ancestors over hundreds of human generations who inevitably have had an influence on us, but it is possible to know only a small number of who those people actually were.

Who am I? I have many strands of Warren Miller and Margaret Hutt Miller in me. There are Bob Miller threads, Ray Miller threads, and Al Miller threads. I am who they are. There are many Nancy Christensen threads and Lois Seifried Landis threads. There are Knight strands, George and Nancy; Kalkbrenner strands, Al and Ruth; and Davies strands, Elam and Grace. There are Christ Presbyterian strands from Madison, Wisconsin, and Bayfield Presbyterian and Fourth Presbyterian and Morristown Presbyterian and First Presbyterian and Chapel Without Walls–Hilton Head Island strands. For virtually every pastor and for many congregants, the communion of saints is experienced mainly through congregations of Christian believers.

Who are we? We are, in a sense, all of us. The so-called six degrees of separation unites all of us into one inexpressibly huge tapestry, which consists of billions of smaller tapestries. Nobody is truly disconnected from anyone else. Even the most misanthropic of individuals or the people who deliberately and carefully live by themselves in small huts in the woods are related by blood to certain other people and, by being members of the human race, to every other person who ever lived. We cannot escape the communion of saints, even if we try our hardest.

Penultimately, we end with the text of an English children's hymn composed by a lady named Lesbia Scott. Mrs. Scott wrote several hymns for her own young children, and then, she published them in a small collection of hymns in 1929.

The hymn originally appeared in an Anglican hymnbook, but strangely, it never became popular in England. Many years ago, the American Episcopalians inserted into one of their previous hymnals; and from there, it spread to the hymnbooks of other American denominations. The Presbyterians first published it in their 1990 *Presbyterian Hymnal*. (That hymnal has already been replaced by an even newer one. Hymnals don't last the way they used to, and in some respects, that is both a musical and a financial shame. But then, hymn writers have to make a living too.)

Every single time I sing this hymn, it brings tears to my eyes. I don't know why; I'm just very unpredictably sentimental, I guess. I suppose it reminds me that I wish I could recover the admirable innocence implied in these words, but I know that it is gone forever. The text is very simple, here and there syrupy, and a bit too Christocentric for my theological tastes, yet it also is strikingly profound. *I sing a song of the saints of God* is an ideal penultimate capstone for a book called *The Communion of Saints.*

> I sing a song of the saints of God,
> Patient and brave and true,
> Who toiled and fought and lived and died,
> For the Lord they loved and knew,
> And one was a doctor, and one was a queen,
> And one was a shepherdess on the green:
> They were all of them saints of God, and I mean,
> God helping, to be one too.
>
> They loved their Lord, so dear, so dear,
> And God's love made them strong;
> And they followed the right, for Jesus' sake,
> The whole of their good lives long.
> And one was a soldier, and one was priest,
> And one was slain by a fierce wild beast:
> And there's not any reason, no, not the least,
> Why I shouldn't be one too.
>
> They lived not only in ages past,
> There are hundreds of thousands still;
> The world is bright with the joyous saints
> Who love to do Jesus' will.
> You can meet them in school, on the street, in
>   the store,
> In church, by the sea, in the house next door;
> They are saints of God, whether rich or poor,
> And I mean to be one too.

And now, ultimately, we come to the last of our closing "saint hymns," one that is sung regularly in Mainline Protestant and other Churches throughout the year, but especially on November 1, All Saints Day. And that was the day for which the hymn's author especially wrote his hymn. Nothing else seems as fitting to me as the final benediction, the concluding "good word" as *For all the saints who from their labors rest*. The hymn was written by Anglican Bishop William Walsingham How, who lived in England in the late nineteenth century.

Bishop How wrote over sixty hymn texts, of which twenty-five still appear in various hymnals. Four of them are still frequently sung: *We give Thee but Thine own*, a hymn which was sung every Sunday in the First Presbyterian Church of Fort Scott, Kansas, in the late 1940s as the offering was brought forward; *O Word of God incarnate*, which explains and extols the nature of the Bible; *O Jesus, Thou art standing*, a wonderfully and warmly evangelical text based on Revelation 3:20—which reminds us that Jesus stands outside the door of our hearts, knocking, waiting for us to open the door and to welcome him into our lives; and finally, what I presume is the best-known of all of Bishop How's hymns, *For all the saints who from their labors rest*.

There are two tunes to which the hymn is normally sung. Ralph Vaughan Williams, the great English composer of the first half of the twentieth century, wrote the more popular of the two tunes. It is called *Sine Nomine*, "Without Name," and why he named it "Without Name" I do not know because *Without Name* is its name. It is pitched quite high, and Williams directed that it was to be sung in unison, requiring everyone to sing the soprano line. By the end of the traditionally six stanzas (Bishop How actually wrote eight stanzas), all altos and basses find their vocal cords have been stretched to the very physical limit but to immense spiritual benefit. The combined effect of both text and tune makes it worth the major vocal workout every All Saints Day or on ordinary Sundays or in the funerals or memorial services, where the hymn is requested by the family or chosen by the clergy because it seems particularly appropriate, considering the nature of the life of the deceased. Therefore, here, at book's end, is the hymn text, which also often evokes my tears:

"For all the saints who from their labors rest,
Who Thee by faith before the world confessed,
Thy name, O Jesus, be forever blest.
Alleluia! Alleluia!

Thou wast their Rock, their Fortress, and their Might;
Thou, Lord, their Captain in the well-fought fight;
Thou, in the darkness drear, their one true Light.
Alleluia! Alleluia!

O may Thy soldiers, faithful, true, and bold,
Fight as the saints who nobly fought of old,
And win with them the victor's crown of gold.
Alleluia! Alleluia!

O blest communion, fellowship divine!
We feebly struggle, they in glory shine;
Yet all are one in Thee, for all are Thine.
Alleluia! Alleluia!

And when the fight is fierce, the warfare long,
Steals on the ear the distant triumph song,
And hearts are brave again, and arms are strong.
Alleluia! Alleluia!

From earth's wide bounds, from ocean's farthest coast,
Through gates of pearl streams in the countless host,
Singing to Father, Son, and Holy Ghost,
Alleluia! Alleluia!"

I believe in the communion of saints. I truly do.

ABOUT THE AUTHOR

JOHN M. MILLER was ordained as a Presbyterian minister in late 1964. He has served as pastor of PCUSA congregations in Bayfield, Wisconsin, Chicago, Illinois, Morristown, New Jersey, and Hilton Head Island, South Carolina. Following the Hilton Head Island pastorate, he was the interim pastor of four congregations in Virginia, Minnesota, and Ohio. In early 2004, he and his wife Lois returned to Hilton Head Island, where he established an interdenominational congregation called The Chapel Without Walls. Now, more than fifty years after being ordained, he is still preaching most Sundays of the year in his new pastoral venture. He has previously written six other books. John and Lois live in The Seabrook, a retirement community on Hilton Head Island. There, they happily declare with Robert Browning, "Grow old along with me. The best is yet to be!"

CPSIA information can be obtained
at www.ICGtesting.com
Printed in the USA
FFOW05n0856220217

9 781635 259063